AF699842

SOCIAL PARENTHOOD IN COMPARATIVE PERSPECTIVE

FAMILIES, LAW, AND SOCIETY SERIES

General Editors: Nancy E. Dowd and Robin A. Lenhardt

Justice for Kids: Keeping Kids Out of the Juvenile Justice System
Edited by Nancy E. Dowd

Masculinities and the Law: A Multidimensional Approach
Edited by Frank Rudy Cooper and Ann C. McGinley

The New Kinship: Constructing Donor-Conceived Families
Naomi Cahn

What Is Parenthood? Contemporary Debates about the Family
Edited by Linda C. McClain and Daniel Cere

In Our Hands: The Struggle for U.S. Child Care Policy
Elizabeth Palley and Corey S. Shdaimah

The Marriage Buyout: The Troubled Trajectory of U.S. Alimony Law
Cynthia Lee Starnes

Children, Sexuality, and the Law
Edited by Sacha Coupet and Ellen Marrus

A New Juvenile Justice System: Total Reform for a Broken System
Edited by Nancy E. Dowd

Divorced from Reality: Rethinking Family Dispute Resolution
Jane C. Murphy and Jana B. Singer

The Poverty Industry: The Exploitation of America's Most Vulnerable Citizens
Daniel L. Hatcher

Ending Zero Tolerance: The Crisis of Absolute School Discipline
Derek W. Black

Blaming Mothers: American Law and the Risks to Children's Health
Linda C. Fentiman

The Ecology of Childhood: How Our Changing World Threatens Children's Rights
Barbara Bennett Woodhouse

The Politicization of Safety : Critical Perspectives on Domestic Violence Responses
Edited by Jane K. Stoever

Living Apart Together: Legal Protections for a New Form of Family
Cynthia Grant Bowman

Social Parenthood in Comparative Perspective
Edited by Clare Huntington, Courtney G. Joslin, and Christiane von Bary

Social Parenthood in Comparative Perspective

Edited by

Clare Huntington, Courtney G. Joslin, *and*
Christiane von Bary

NEW YORK UNIVERSITY PRESS
New York

NEW YORK UNIVERSITY PRESS
New York
www.nyupress.org

© 2023 by New York University
All rights reserved

Please contact the Library of Congress for Cataloging-in-Publication data.
ISBN: 9781479814114 (hardback)
ISBN: 9781479814138 (library ebook)
ISBN: 9781479814121 (consumer ebook)

New York University Press books are printed on acid-free paper, and their binding materials are chosen for strength and durability. We strive to use environmentally responsible suppliers and materials to the greatest extent possible in publishing our books.

Manufactured in the United States of America

10 9 8 7 6 5 4 3 2 1

Also available as an ebook

CH: For Nestor, Zoe & Sam

CGJ: For Carolyn and Niko

CvB: Meiner Familie

CONTENTS

Introduction

CLARE HUNTINGTON, COURTNEY G. JOSLIN,
AND CHRISTIANE VON BARY

What makes a person a parent? Traditionally, the law answered this question by looking at childbirth, marriage, and adoption. If a woman gave birth, she was the mother. If a man was married to the woman who gave birth, he was presumed to be the father. And if a couple adopted a child, they were the parents. But these legal rules establishing parenthood—which are still in force, largely unmodified, in several countries—do not sit easily with modern family life. In countries around the world, families are changing. Same-sex couples are raising children together. Parents are divorcing or separating and finding new partners, creating blended families. And children are living with grandparents, family friends, and other primary caregivers, often because of economic and social stressors on families. In each of these contexts, there is often an adult who *acts* like a parent but who is unconnected to the child through childbirth, marriage, or adoption. In many countries, this person is called a social parent. Psychologically, and especially from a child's point of view, a social parent *is* a parent. But the legal status of a social parent is hotly debated.

To explore options for legal recognition of social parents, this book asks how the law does—and how it should—recognize social parenthood.

To answer this question, we begin with a psychological account of social parenthood, from the perspective of both the child and the social parent. Abundant research demonstrates the importance of a relationship between a child and a social parent as well as the harms that can befall both if the relationship is not protected. Without legal protection, the social parent may have no right to see the child over the objection of a legal parent. This can result in severing or attenuating the relationship, which threatens to compromise the child's development and cause significant distress for the child and the social parent. A starting assumption of this book, then, is that developing legal rules for the recognition of social parents is important for the well-being of children and their families.

To better understand social parenthood, this book turns to social scientists to identify and explore some of the circumstances when a child may have a social parent. In lieu of overly simplified descriptions of social parenthood, we lean into specific examples to illustrate broader trends. An anthropologist thus examines same-sex parenting in Italy, showing how rules that fail to provide clear protection to these families inflict emotional harm on the family members and inhibit the ability of the social parents to care for their children. The chapter includes, for example, interviews with social parents explaining that they are unable to consent to medical treatment for their children in the absence of written authorization from the legal parent. In another chapter, two social scientists look at stepparents around the world and especially in Canada. The authors document the frequency of stepparenting; in one city, for example, 30 percent of children have lived with a stepparent by age seventeen. The chapter also explains the importance of these relationships in the lives of children. And, in a third chapter, a sociologist explores nonparental primary caregivers—grandparents, family friends, and similar persons—in a rural community in Appalachia, in the southeastern United States. This study describes the impact of the opioid epidemic on families, showing that a large percentage of children are living with neither parent and instead are growing up with friends and relatives.

With these psychological and sociological accounts in mind, we turn to the law, examining the legal response to social parenthood in nine countries across North America and Europe. Authors from each country describe the existing laws governing social parents, critique their efficacy, and offer new insights regarding social parenthood. To facilitate comparison of the countries' approaches, each legal chapter addresses three common contexts of social parenthood: same-sex parents, stepparents, and nonparental primary caregivers. The discussion of same-sex couples includes both married and unmarried couples, although typically unmarried same-sex couples face more challenges with parental recognition. The category of stepparents includes both the married and unmarried new partners of legal parents. With regard to the third common context, this book uses the term "nonparental primary caregiver" to refer to a broad category of individuals who are caring for children but who are not, and were not, in an intimate relationship with someone who is a legal parent to the child. This category includes family friends, extended family members, and fictive kin who care for children informally or through formal foster care arrangements. These adults function and act like a parent to the child but are not legally recognized as a parent under the traditional rules establishing parenthood. Using the term "nonparental" might suggest that these people are not parents to the child, but our intention is to describe the *legal* connection with the child, not to negate the social and psychological ties. Indeed, those ties are the reason we include this diverse and therefore difficult-to-describe category of individuals in this book.

Our survey of legal approaches identifies several trends. First, most countries recognize social parents in some manner, although the nature and extent of the recognition vary widely. To evaluate the approaches, a reader needs to understand three broad categories of legal protection for parental or parent-like relationships. The details differ by jurisdiction, as explained in the respective chapters, but all countries recognize legal parenthood—a status that can be changed only through legal proceedings. Many countries also recognize parental responsibility. This is a more fluid form of recognition. It is not as comprehensive as legal parenthood, but the holder of parental responsibility has the right to be involved with decisions regarding the child, and this person has obligations to the child. Additionally, many countries recognize a right of contact. This is a more limited form of protection that allows for personal interaction between the adult and child but does not include decision-making authority.

Applying these categories to social parenthood, the book demonstrates that countries take different approaches. In some parts of the United States and Canada, for example, the legal system treats a broad range of social parents as legal parents, with full rights and duties. The same is true for same-sex parents in some other countries, such as the Netherlands. But in many countries, the recognition of social parents is more limited, often protecting an ongoing relationship between a child and social parent and, in some countries, according some legal rights but not granting a full legal relationship. In England and Wales, for example, social parents can acquire comprehensive parental responsibility, meaning that although they are not legal parents they still have considerable influence over the day-to-day care of a child. In Germany, a more limited form of parental responsibility is used to grant certain rights to social parents in a few situations, but a separate contact right exists to supplement this protection. And in other countries, such as Greece and Russia, legal protection is embryonic and still uncertain, with the possibility only just starting through recent legislation or court rulings.

Second, legal recognition depends on the type of social parent. For same-sex couples, there is a close connection between the legal recognition of the same-sex partnership and the legal recognition of social parents in same-sex families: the more legal recognition a country extends to same-sex adult relationships, the more likely the country is to value and protect social parents in same-sex families. Protection for stepparents, a common form of social parenthood, is more complicated, and legal recognition varies widely. Some countries provide robust protections for married stepparents, but most do not. There is even less protection for an unmarried partner of a legal parent. Nonparental primary caregivers are the least likely to be recognized, even though from the child's perspective they may be just as important as other social parents.

Third, in most jurisdictions, the decision of whether to accord a social parent some rights and responsibilities generally turns on a functional inquiry into the nature of the relationship between the social parent and the child. This fact-specific inquiry takes account of the reality of social parenthood and seeks to protect it in some fashion. The functional approach recognizes that social parenthood takes many forms and at least implicitly acknowledges that a more rigid, one-size-fits-all legal rule may well be over- and underinclusive.

Finally, the social parenthood rules in some countries acknowledge the reality that a child may have more than two parents and allow for all of them to be recognized in some form. This is the most nascent trend, but a few jurisdictions are moving in this direction, with varying degrees of legal recognition for the third person. Some provinces in Canada and some U.S. states recognize more than two adults as full legal parents. But in most countries that allow the possibility of protecting three adults, the recognition is more limited. The Netherlands and England and Wales, for example, allow a third person to exercise parental responsibility—which gives a protected right for a day-to-day relationship—although they do not recognize the third person as a legal parent.

In addition to these emerging trends, the book demonstrates that social parenthood raises difficult issues for a legal system. From the psychological perspective of both the social parent and the child, it is critical to protect the established parent-child relationship. Yet if legal rules too readily grant legal rights to adults who are not acting as parents, this can compromise and undermine the legal rights of existing parents, which also poses risks to the child. Thus, one of the central challenges for developing legal rules that recognize social parents is distinguishing between a person who is playing a full parental role in a child's life and a person who may be important to the child but is not acting as a parent.

Further, the interests of the child and those of the social parent often align, but this is not always the case. If the question is whether the social parent is legally obligated to support the child, for example, the child has a strong interest in receiving the support; some social parents may welcome this obligation, but others may resist it. This book thus considers the issues raised by social parenthood from the perspective of both the child and the social parent. Given the focus on the relationship between children and social parents, the book does not consider issues such as the child's relationships with siblings, half siblings, stepsiblings, and other adults who have a close relationship with the child that does not rise to the level of social parenthood.

Promoting equality among families is another challenge for legal systems. Many—but not all—countries are seeking to place same-sex parents on the same legal footing as different-sex parents. Legal recognition of social parents plays a foundational role in this equality effort because families with same-sex parents typically include at least one nongenetic parent. Thus, parentage rules that place weight on function as a means of establishing parentage, or at least more limited parental rights and obligations, can help accord equality to such families. Another aspect of equality is addressing the needs of low-income and other marginalized families. As the chapter on Appalachia describes, families facing multiple challenges often turn to nonparental caregivers for help with raising their children. Clarifying the legal rights and obligations of everyone involved helps these families provide for the needs of children.

Choice of Countries

We made a deliberate decision to focus on jurisdictions in North America and Europe. Countries around the world are grappling with the reality of social parenthood, but it is not feasible to address the legal response of all jurisdictions. The selected countries have relatively similar legal systems and yet diverse legal responses to social parenthood, making a comparison both possible and worthwhile. With the collection of countries included in the volume, the book identifies different approaches to social parenthood. Some parts of Canada and the United States are expanding the understanding of a family by recognizing more than two legal parents, and the Netherlands is committed to ensuring equal rights for same-sex parents and is seeking to provide legal recognition for intentional multiparent families. By contrast, Russia does not recognize same-sex parents and Greece places heavy emphasis on families headed by married, different-sex couples. Thus, although the book does not canvass every possible jurisdiction and approach to social parenthood, it does provide readers with a range of responses within a collection of jurisdictions that share similarities as well as differences.

Our hope is that by highlighting and evaluating diverse legal approaches to social parenthood, this collected volume will help policy makers, legislators, judges, and academics understand, assess, and imagine potential legal rules for recognizing social parents. An appreciation of the underlying structural questions will, in turn, broaden and deepen our understanding of the rules in each jurisdiction and provide a blueprint for different approaches.

Challenges of a Comparative Approach

There are challenges in any comparative project. Legal systems and social contexts vary, sometimes widely. There are limitations to language and terminology, different starting points, and different legal cultures. And legal rules often use specific terminology to explain certain concepts, but if these concepts do not exist in another legal system, it is hard to compare rules.

In addition to these common complexities, there are challenges specific to comparing social parenthood. This area of the law is particularly dynamic, and social parenthood is a relatively new legal concept. Indeed, social parenthood is not a ubiquitous legal term, and the terminology and rules continue to be in flux even within each country, with legal regulation still emerging. This made even the descriptive parts of the book challenging. This book uses the term "social parenthood" to describe the psychological relationship between a child and an adult who acts like a parent but lacks a traditional legal tie to the child. And yet legal systems use different terms or do not have a fixed terminology to describe such a person. For example, some U.S. states refer to such people as "psychological parents," but others use the terms "functional parents" and "de facto parents." In other countries, "social parent" is the common term.

Finally, parenthood is a concept that touches many areas of the law that contribute to or have an impact on the question of recognition. This includes child custody and support, adoption, foster care, marriage, social benefits law, probate law, and citizenship law, to name a few. Although not all of these areas are explicitly addressed in this book, any analysis of the recognition of parenthood requires either previous knowledge of several of those topics or an extensive explanation reaching outside of the core question of comparison. The authors struck a careful balance between addressing relevant areas of the law and focusing on legal recognition of social parents. Additionally, the delineation between these areas of the law and forms of recognition vary among countries. This affects the perception and the understanding of which areas are relevant to the discussion of social parents. For example, some countries—such as the United States—consider foster care solely a question of the public child welfare system and see the connection between a foster parent and child as contractual, not giving rise to any parental rights or responsibilities. Other countries, in contrast, view foster care through a broader lens that includes the care by relatives without involvement of the state, which can lead to some legal recognition.

A final challenge is an absence of data about family forms in general and social parenthood in particular. Some countries have robust data, but others do not. Some countries, for example, do not collect data on the number of families with same-sex parents, and many countries, especially in Europe, do not track the race of family members. When a country does collect data, rapidly changing social circumstances may mean the factors that are tracked do not reflect the lived experience of all families. For all these reasons, it is not possible to provide a uniform set of statistical data as a basis at the beginning of each chapter. Rather than omitting all country-specific demographics, however, we decided it was preferable to work with the available data, acknowledging their limitation and impact on our understanding of a country's treatment of social parenthood.

Despite these obstacles, this comparative project is worthwhile and important as countries around the world explore options for protecting the relationship between a child and a social parent.

* * *

Families have always come in many forms, but the law has rarely reflected this reality. This mismatch between family life and family law is growing even more pronounced with rapidly changing social norms and advances in reproductive technology. For social parents and their children, this mismatch poses a serious threat. There are numerous ways to address this problem, as a comparative approach illustrates. We hope that readers will learn as much as we did in compiling and editing this book.

I

Psychological and Sociological Contexts

1

A Psychological Perspective on the Significance of Legal Recognition of Diverse Social Parent Relationships for Children

ABBIE E. GOLDBERG

This book addresses the issue of legal protection for social parental relationships. The current chapter situates that legal analysis by providing a psychological perspective regarding the importance of diverse social parent relationships to children. It further addresses how children are impacted when these relationships are disrupted, and/or not legitimized either socially or legally.

Specifically, this chapter addresses the significance of attachment (i.e., lasting psychological connectedness; a strong and enduring bond) as it relates to children and their caregivers, addressing factors that enhance or impede attachment, and the consequences of disrupted attachments for children's socioemotional development and outcomes, including risk for delinquency, adult intimate relationships, and mental health. This chapter draws from research on divorce, stepparenting, foster care, and other areas to highlight the significance of disrupted attachment bonds, and various factors and dynamics (e.g., timing of the disruption; role of other caregivers in amplifying or mitigating the disruption) that impact the extent and consequences of the disruption for both children and caregivers (e.g., divorced fathers). It focuses in particular on the specific case of two-mother families in which one mother is biogenetically related to the child and the other is not, underscores the importance of facilitating attachment between nonbiological (nongestational) mothers and children—for example, via relational, symbolic, and especially legal mechanisms—and highlights the consequences of fragmented or compromised attachments in this context for all family members. The chapter also briefly considers the case of attachment or bonds between children and genetically related adults who are not legally recognized as parents, such as known sperm donors,[1] and how, when, and why such relationships may be significant and warrant protection.

Attachment

Attachment is generally defined as a lasting psychological connectedness between human beings. Some people refer to it simply as a "bond" or a "strong bond"; or they refer specifically to the parent-child/caregiver-child bond. Attachment theory is influential in many psychologists' understanding of children's early social development and is one of the most broadly accepted and well-known theories in the area of child development. According to psychologist John Bowlby, widely regarded as one of the original attachment theorists, infants and young children seek closeness with their primary attachment figures (caregivers) and will experience considerable distress if these individuals are not consistently available, physically and emotionally, to meet their needs.[2] Relationships with primary caregivers promote a sense of safety in young children, facilitating their ability to gradually adapt to others. Preferences for particular people develop over time, and these preferences (or attachments) are shaped by how adults respond to them and the type of relationships that they form with these adults.[3] On the whole, infants become attached to adults who are sensitive and responsive in social interactions with the infant and who remain consistent caregivers for some time; such adults may include fathers, mothers, siblings, and other caregivers.[4] Although attachment theory has historically accepted the primacy of the mother as the main caregiver, there is nothing in the theory to suggest that fathers are not equally likely to become principal attachment figures if they provide most or all of the child care.[5] Research on children's attachment to male and female caregivers suggests that more important than parent gender in determining the strength of the attachment relationship are other factors, such as children's temperament and caregiver behaviors.[6] Further, although fathers may have a different type of bond with their children (e.g., they may be more likely to stimulate their children and encourage them to overcome their limits), the strength of the bond is not necessarily different (i.e., weaker than) the bond between mother and child.[7] Further of note is that although Bowlby emphasized the significance of one primary caregiving relationship in his early work, his later work reflects an awareness of the importance of multiple, or even a network of, caregivers (e.g., mothers, fathers, grandparents, day care providers, stepparents)—a perspective that is generally held by contemporary attachment researchers.[8]

Thus, children can and do bond with multiple caregivers, and having multiple stable caregivers during one's early life and beyond is clearly beneficial for children. Specifically, Bowlby proposed that children who enjoy secure attachments early on will demonstrate positive socioemotional and developmental outcomes. Empirical data suggest that children who are securely attached to their caregivers tend to do better in life, showing greater resilience and overall competence—most notably, with respect to relationships[9] as well as mental health.[10] On the flipside, Bowlby proposed that children who do not develop secure attachments to at least one caregiver are vulnerable to a variety of negative outcomes, such as delinquency and criminal behavior,[11] an assertion that has been demonstrated empirically in numerous studies.[12] In addition, individuals who lack secure attachments are more likely to demonstrate poor mental health[13] and physical health[14] outcomes in adulthood.

Disruptions in Attachment

Early disruptions in attachment due to the temporary or permanent loss of a caregiver can have long-term effects, especially if these disruptions occur during the first few years of life.[15] During children's first year in particular, they develop a cognitive model (also called an internal working model) of what they can expect from caregivers in times of need, based on prior, repeated experiences of security or insecurity.[16] Disrupted attachment can create attachment insecurity, or the feeling that one cannot count on a caregiver to "be there," which can foster fear and clinginess, or the opposite—aloofness and detachment—in interpersonal relationships. For example, research on children who have been in foster care—which may involve multiple caregiving transitions and therefore repeated attachment disruptions, often at an early age—indicates that these youth often face impairments in their ability to attach to subsequent caregivers.[17] Additionally, these youth tend to face worse mental health outcomes, especially if they entered foster care at an early age, were mistreated while they were in care, and/or had many temporary placements.[18] Such repeated attachment disruptions can create intense stress and uncertainty, which—especially when combined with prolonged separation from their original primary caregivers (e.g., birth parents)—can have implications for future relationships.[19]

Insomuch as ruptures in the caregiver-child relationship are associated with loss and attachment challenges, emphasis should be placed on minimizing the number of caregiver transitions that children experience and maintaining relationships with those caregivers (e.g., birth parents, foster parents) with whom the child has strong and established relationships.[20] Children in foster care, for example, show the capacity to form and maintain simultaneous attachments to both their foster parents and birth parents.[21] Further, while in care, they often benefit from ongoing contact with their birth parents, especially in the context of a collaborative, mutually respectful, and nonconflictual relationship between foster parents and birth parents.[22] However, under certain circumstances (e.g., history of abuse by the birth parents, lack of desire on the part of the child to see the birth parents, high levels of tension between foster parents and birth parents), ongoing contact with birth parents may be linked to negative outcomes for children, including escalating emotional/behavioral challenges.[23]

Likewise, children who have experienced their parents' divorce, especially at an early age, may experience prolonged effects of this disruption, reporting insecure relationships with at least one parent in adulthood for example.[24] Divorce's impact on attachment may be particularly profound when one parent relocates and/or rarely sees the child.[25] When young children and their nonresident caregivers (typically fathers) have little contact early on, this tends to predict an ongoing lack of contact and weakening bond over time,[26] which is unfortunate since closer relationships with nonresident fathers have been linked to better emotional/behavioral outcomes in children.[27] By contrast, joint physical custody has been linked to more enduring relationships between the child and the nonresident parent, at least in the context of low interparental conflict.[28] Longitudinal research indicates that children who have moderate contact with their nonresident fathers postdivorce, and whose parents have low levels of conflict over time, tend to have particularly positive outcomes—for example, high academic outcomes and few emotional/behavioral problems.[29]

Notably, in the case of divorce, the primary custodial or residential parent's behavior can make a difference in terms of securing the bond between the child and noncustodial or nonresidential parent. In other words, primary custodial parents can help to ensure that the noncustodial parent-child relationship is not damaged and that the separation does not result in detachment and potential alienation.[30] When custodial parents praise the noncustodial parent, for example, this enhances the likelihood of the child continuing to feel a close attachment to them despite the parents' separation. The child will know that it is "allowed" to feel loved and cared for by both parents and to reciprocate that love in return. Lack of contact, in combination with the negative commentary by the custodial parent about the noncustodial parent, can result in alienation.[31] Notably, when the custodial parent (e.g., mother) undermines the relationship between the child and noncustodial parent, this can also cause damage to their own relationship to the child: indeed, the child may experience the custodial parent's actions as controlling or destructive, and this may create relational friction or distance.[32]

Thus, attachment ruptures may arise from disruptions in caregiving situations—but such ruptures can be minimized when the number of transitions is minimized, relationships between adult caregivers (residential and nonresidential parents in the case of divorce, foster and birth parents in the case of foster care placement) are positive, and children's best interests are maintained.

The Power and Significance of Social Parenthood

Society—and U.S. culture in particular—has tended to equate biology with "naturalness" in constructions of family, to assume greater closeness in biological relationships than in nonbiological parent (i.e., social) relationships, and to presuppose that biological and genetic connections are fundamental to the parent-child bond. But biogenetic connections alone are not sufficient to ensure attachment, and, likewise, children can develop attachments to people who are not biogenetically related to them. For example, egg and sperm donors do not generally think of themselves as the parents of offspring; and, interestingly, egg donors may be even less likely than sperm donors to think of themselves as "parents," perhaps because women especially recognize the significant disconnect between supplying biological material and parenting/mothering.[33] This is not to say that children do not deserve to know their genetic heritage: they do. But genetic connections are not the central basis for attachment, and, by extension, children can and do develop attachments to non–genetically related caregivers. We should not confuse parental legitimacy and biological relatedness, as doing so would actually reinforce patriarchal assumptions and ideas about family and undermine the development and creation of new family forms.[34]

Families formed using reproductive technologies, in which a couple has relied on a sperm and/or egg donor to become parents, represent one context to study parent-child attachment in the context of unequal biogenetic ties (i.e., only one parent is biogenetically related to the child). Significantly, heterosexual parent families that have used egg donation, donor insemination, and/or surrogacy show few differences in terms of parents' mental health or stress[35] or child psychological adjustment and self-esteem.[36] Although there are few differences in parent-child relationships across family types, longitudinal research suggests that the absence of a genetic link between mothers and children (i.e., in egg donation families) is associated with somewhat less positive mother-child relationships, as compared to mother-child relationships in natural conception families, surrogacy families (wherein there is a genetic but not a gestational link between mother and child), and donor insemination families.[37] However, the differences in relationship quality are not large and need to be further substantiated by future work.[38]

Although not entirely comparable, insomuch as adopted children often have histories of trauma and separation that impede their ability to attach, research on adoptive (i.e., non–genetically related) families also shows the strong potential for parent-child, and often child-parent, attachment. Many adoptive parents do develop strong attachments to their children (which serve to promote caregiving behavior), which in turn facilitates children's attachment security—although such attachments are more difficult to establish when children demonstrate challenging behaviors (e.g., due to a history of trauma, neglect, and/or abuse—features of relationships that impact their ability to engage appropriately with and bond to subsequent caregivers).[39] Some adoptive parents lack a sense of entitlement to be parents—due to both guilt associated with the birth mother's inability to parent as well as society's emphasis on biogenetic ties as central to the parent-child bond—and this too can interfere with parent-child attachment.[40] Regarding children's attachment to parents, children who experience early neglect, abuse, or institutionalization show notable recovery in the quality of their attachments after being placed with their adoptive families.[41] However, children's experiences of preadoptive adversity can also have long-lasting consequences for their attachments, development, and overall well-being.[42] Stronger child-to-parent attachment in adoptive families is predicted by an earlier age at placement, fewer preadoptive placements, and more positive feelings held by the parent toward the child.[43] Significantly, research on early-placed adopted children (typically defined as children placed in infancy) suggests that they tend to demonstrate relatively low levels of attachment problems.[44] Further, early-placed adopted children in gay father, lesbian mother, and heterosexual parent households tend to demonstrate similar levels of attachment security across family types, with children of gay fathers in fact showing the highest incidence of secure attachment.[45]

Research on stepfamily relationships also provides insight into the potential importance of other caregiver or parent relationships—and the reality that these relationships need not necessarily compete with or replace legal/biological parent-child relationships, such as the nonresidential parent-child tie. King found that close relationships with both stepfathers and nonresident fathers were associated with better adolescent outcomes (e.g., emotional and behavioral well-being), although interestingly ties to stepfathers were somewhat more influential than ties to nonresident fathers.[46] This finding dovetails with other work showing that length of shared residence is often better than biological ties per se in predicting the quality and closeness of individuals' relationships with their parents (including stepparents and nonresidential biological parents) in adulthood.[47] Stepparents' degree of involvement in caretaking is also of importance when considering child-stepparent relationships and closeness: in one study of over three hundred residential parents and stepparents, in just 18 percent of cases was the stepparent described as a primary caretaking parent together with the residential parent.[48] Thus, stepparents vary widely in the degree to which they take on a significant role in caretaking, which in turn informs the strength of the (step)parent-child relationship.

Children's relationships with stepparents vary widely, as do their level of distress if the relationship between their parent and stepparent dissolves.[49] However, children who consider their stepparents—and step-grandparents, in fact—"kin" (i.e., members of the family) tend to be profoundly upset by the loss of these ties if their parents' remarriage dissolves.[50] Children who maintain relationships with former stepparents and step-grandparents may benefit from receiving additional, valued sources of love and support.[51]

Social Legitimacy of Social Parents: The Role of Parenting and Symbolic Recognition

Despite clear evidence that parents who are not genetically related to their children can and do develop attachments to their children and, further, that children can develop attachments to non–genetically related parents, non–genetically related parents face a lack of social and sometimes legal legitimacy in society. Lack of legal and/or social recognition as a parent can powerfully undermine confidence and self-efficacy as a parent, which impacts attachment by interfering with parent behaviors. In the same-sex couple context, nongestational parents (i.e., gestational parents' partners) may lack legal and societal recognition, which can undermine their sense of security in the parental role. In the absence of a strong sense of legitimacy and equivalency, these individuals may not feel entitled to parent and may not see themselves as "full" parents. Even when these parents are legally recognized as their children's other parent, they still must overcome the prevailing assumption that biology equals real parenthood and they are "second rate."[52] In the female same-sex couple context, the distinction between biological (or gestational) parent and nonbiological (or nongestational) parent is often significant to outsiders, including friends and family. There is a tendency for people to view the biological mother as the "real" mother, echoing heteronormative notions of parenthood, which in part involve the idea that there can only ever be "one mother"—which, of note, is also problematic for adoptive parents, who may have open adoptions and maintain relationships with their children's birth mothers.[53] Family members of the biological mother, in turn, may be more likely to embrace the child as one of their own, whereas family members of the nonbiological mother may be slower to "get on board" and to see themselves as grandparents (or aunts or uncles).[54]

Aware of the primacy often placed on genetics and biology, female couples in which one partner carried and gave birth and is also genetically related to the child[55] may endeavor to ensure that the nonbiological mother contributes equally to caregiving, especially early on—which can be challenging amid the demands of chestfeeding,[56] which is usually undertaken by the parent who gave birth. Nonbiological mothers may engage a number of strategies to enhance feelings of confidence and competence, which in turn promotes the parent-child bond. These strategies are often behavioral (e.g., spending equivalent time engaged in child care, taking on special roles such as that of the bedtime or bathtime parent) but also symbolic (e.g., being called mama or mommy, having the child take their last name).[57] In addition to encouraging outsiders to view them as parents, engaging in caregiving behaviors fosters parenting skill and confidence; as time goes by, nonbiological parents tend to report feeling more competent and legitimate in the role of parent.[58] Further, longitudinal research with female same-sex couples who are parents indicates that although some parents perceived their children as showing a preference for their biological mothers early on (e.g., due to breastfeeding and greater time spent with her), most perceived little stability in children's preferences across early childhood, such that children preferred both mothers equally, highlighting the power of "social motherhood" in fostering maternal connections that transcend biological relatedness over time.[59]

Significantly, the biological parent plays an important role in encouraging others to perceive the nonbiological parent as occupying an equal and valid parental role. The biological parent also plays a key role in facilitating—or undermining—their partner's self-confidence and competence. Some biological parents may "gatekeep"—that is, assert control or ownership over certain tasks and responsibilities of parenthood—which can undermine the other parent's confidence and skill. Research on same-sex couples who are parents indicates that parents who feel more conflicted or ambivalent about their relationships, perceive themselves as highly skilled in parenting, and/or perceive their partners as less skilled in parenting tend to engage in more gatekeeping in relation to child care tasks.[60] Over time, gatekeeping can discourage a parent's participation in child care and lead to an unequal division of labor as well as interparental tension.[61]

Social Legitimacy of Social Parents: The Role of Legal (Non)Recognition

Beyond caregiving behaviors and symbolic recognition, legal recognition is a means of addressing and to some degree undermining societal perceptions that one parent is more important than the other(s). Being legally recognized as a parent can be a powerful way of legitimizing nonbiological parents' parental role and status and may enhance their sense of entitlement and deservingness.[62] Legal recognition promotes parental confidence and in turn benefits parent-child relationships: for example, Gartrell et al. found that nonbiological lesbian mothers who had adopted their children felt greater legitimacy as parents.[63]

Legal recognition also serves an important role in the event of divorce or relationship dissolution, which can threaten the presumed significance and therefore stability of the nonbiological parent-child relationship. In a longitudinal study of lesbian mothers who dissolved their relationships, Gartrell et al. documented that 71 percent of separated mothers were sharing custody.[64] Women were likely to share custody if the nonbiological mother had legally adopted the child(ren), highlighting the importance of legal protections in ensuring nonbiological mothers' rights after parental relationship dissolution. Further, the percentage of adolescents who reported closeness to both mothers was significantly higher in families with coparent adoption. Qualitative research by Goldberg and Allen further suggests that when nonbiological mothers' rights are not protected and parents split up, this can cause a relational rift between children and nonbiological parents, especially when the split is acrimonious or biological mothers act as gatekeepers or limit contact.[65] Indeed, some of the young adults who were interviewed for this study suggested that they missed out on important emotional support and practical resources as a function of losing the tie to their nongestational mothers. Likewise, research on postdivorce heterosexual couples suggests that when residential parents prevent children from maintaining relationships with their nonresidential parents, this can cause harm to those relationships and can negatively impact children's sense of safety and well-being.[66]

Also significant here is research on second-parent adoption, which allows a second parent to adopt (i.e., become a legally recognized parent) a child without the "first parent" losing any parental rights. Namely, in studying what happened when the gay adoption ban was lifted in Florida, Goldberg and Allen found that lesbian, gay, bisexual, and queer parents described appreciable differences in their sense of security surrounding parent-child relationships when they were able to finally adopt their own children (e.g., children who they were previously fostering but could not adopt and children whom their partners gave birth to but for whom they could not previously complete a second-parent adoption).[67] Other research, too, has pointed to the importance of second-parent adoptions in alleviating nonbiological parents' sense of fear and worry regarding the preservation of parent-child relationships in the event of biological parent death or divorce.[68] Interviews with lesbian mothers, for example, reveal that second-parent adoptions are regarded as crucial for their families, such that if parents divorce or one parent dies, legal parenthood has already been established and cannot be challenged in court.[69] Interviews with eight young adults who had been raised by lesbian couples but were born prior to the legal recognition of same-sex parenthood highlighted how the lack of legal parenthood was devastating or problematic in the event of divorce or death.[70]

In sum, the parental legitimacy of nonbiologically related parents is often questioned and undermined because society does not grant them equal social recognition. If such lack of social recognition is accompanied (and amplified) by a lack of legal recognition, their relationship to the child may be vulnerable, as in the event of parental divorce or death. Likewise, children whose relationships with nonbiological parents are legally protected may benefit materially and psychologically through the preservation and reinforcement of these bonds.

The Importance of Allowing for More Than Two Parents

In some cases, lesbian, gay, bisexual, and queer individuals—as well as an increasing number of heterosexual individuals—choose to parent in ways that defy and transcend the "two parent model" that so many societies regard as normative and typical. However, such parents ultimately face the reality that neither their own interests nor the well-being of their children is adequately protected in law.[71] Lesbians and gay men in collaborative coparenting families, for example, wherein a lesbian couple or individual raises children with a gay couple or individual (one of whom may be the sperm donor), are often unable to ensure that all parents' parenting rights are legally protected. In such cases, there is a clear disconnect between parents' desires and preferences and the allowances and limits of the law.[72] Likewise, parents in consensually non-monogamous (e.g., polyamorous) relationships may share parenting responsibilities with multiple partners, but these partners' parent-child relationships are rarely formally, much less legally, recognized and in fact carry a fair amount of stigma.[73] It is possible that highly stigmatized or invisible parent-child relationships in particular may especially benefit from legal protections, given their vulnerability to social censure.

In some cases, known sperm donors play a role in children's lives that is parental in nature and express a desire for legal recognition of that role. Yet even if a female couple wanted their sperm donor to have legal rights to the child, which many do not,[74] enabling this reality is tricky. Indeed, most known donors abdicate their legal/parental rights so that the non-biological mother can be the "other" legal parent. This requirement of two legal parents is optimal and desirable for many families, but not all.[75]

Known sperm donors can play a meaningful role in the lives of their donor-conceived offspring and in some cases may even function much like another parent—for example, in the context of intentional coparenting arrangements.[76] However, there is notable variability in how men conceptualize and view their relationships with these children. In a study of known sperm donors, Hertz et al. found that almost half of respondents considered their donor-conceived offspring to be like a family member but were also cognizant of the need to respect the boundaries and integrity of the family in which the offspring were raised.[77] Other studies suggest a multiplicity of donor-child relationships within lesbian-mother families,[78] with many known donors playing a nonparent but kin-type role (e.g., uncle) and occasionally a third-parent role. In their study of lesbian-mother families with ten-year-old children, Gartrell et al. found that,[79] among the twenty-seven children with known donors, thirteen (about half) considered and referred to them as "Dad";[80] and, by adulthood, ten (about one-third) of them considered their known donor to be a father.[81]

Considering the Three Common Contexts for Legal Recognition of Social Parents

Speaking about legislation in California that allows courts to recognize more than two legal parents for a child if it is found that not doing so would otherwise be harmful to the child, and writing specifically about the context of lesbian/gay stepfamilies, Acosta noted that such legislation could be "a positive expansion of parental policy if implemented with the intent of preserving stepparent–child relationships irrespective of a parent's sex, gender, or gender identity. Such a policy could be particularly beneficial in hostile states that explicitly prohibit same-sex couples from adopting children . . . and greatly minimize the legal vulnerability of stepparent–child relationships in gay, lesbian, and heterosexual stepfamilies."[82] Acosta further noted, however, that legislation to recognize more than two legal parents for a child must be carefully developed "so it cannot be used against the best interests of a child. For example, donors whose gametes are used to conceive children using assisted reproductive technology and are strangers to the child cannot currently enforce legal parental rights. This need not change with policy legally recognizing three parents. Furthermore, a legal avenue granting stepparents . . . a legal relationship to the children they are raising does not mean that this legal avenue would be appropriate for all families."[83] In sum, decisions about if and when to award parenting rights to nongestational parents, sperm donors, stepparents, and others should always be determined on the basis of the caregiver's relationship with the child, the child's relationship (e.g., attachment) to the caregiver, the stability or instability of the family system (e.g., whether other ties have been severed, through relationship dissolution or death), the legal parents' wishes, and children's own preferences and desires, when developmentally appropriate. Resolution of such legal vulnerability will benefit parents and children and in turn families, insomuch as children benefit from having multiple stable relationships with caregivers and/or legal parents and genetic ties are not fundamental to or required of parent-child relationships.

Thus, from the perspective of the child, let us consider the three common contexts where legal recognition of social parents is most relevant and where the question of whether children can have more than two parents is raised.

Families Headed by Same-Sex Couples

Female same-sex couples who become parents often do so using assisted reproductive technologies, whereby they conceive a child using a gamete from an anonymous or known sperm donor. In this scenario, only one member of the couple typically has a genetic tie to the child, raising a question: *What is the legal position of the person without the genetic tie?* The nongenetic parent in this case should for all intents and purposes be considered a legal parent. They are presumably committed to parenthood, engaged in parenting behaviors, and residing together with the child. From the perspective of the child, they have two parents who care for them, to whom they are attached. Establishing legal parenthood for their nongenetic parent will alleviate stress and uncertainty associated with having a parent whose parenting status lacks legal recognition and protect their relationship with that parent[84]—and the social, emotional, and financial resources to which they are entitled—in the event of death or relationship dissolution.[85]

What about a situation where a same-sex couple has a child with sperm from a known donor and that donor plays an active parenting role in the child's life? *What is the legal position of that donor?* Here, the central concern is the couple's desires, and whether they wish to grant a third parent legal recognition. To the extent that the couple perceives legal recognition as benefiting the child, either now (e.g., by legitimizing the donor's parental role) or in the future,[86] this may be desirable. Depending on the child's developmental level, they also may be consulted.

Families That Include Stepparents, Both Marital and Nonmarital

Consider a scenario where two parents end their relationship—through either divorce or separation—and one parent enters a relationship with another person. The new partner assumes full parental responsibility for the child and, when speaking with others, refers to themselves as the parent of the child. *What is the legal position of the new partner during the partnership and, if the partnership ends, afterward? Are they a parent?* From the perspective of the child, receiving resources (including love, support, and money) from multiple—even three—parental figures can be beneficial.[87] And, under certain circumstances, maintaining a relationship with a stepparent after the dissolution of the parent-stepparent relationship can be very positive for the child: for example, if this relationship is supported by the primary/residential parent and assuming that the stepparent-child relationship was positive and relatively well-established prior to relationship dissolution. And yet the utility and benefits of awarding legal recognition to a third-party caregiver depend mightily on whether to do so is acceptable to the legal parent(s) and whether this action has the potential to undermine the child's relationships with their other legal parents or caregivers. Studies on stepparents / nonresidential parents, foster parents / birth parents, and lesbian parents / donors all highlight the potential for friction between legal and nonlegal caregivers as well as the importance of centering the child's well-being at all times.[88]

Situations in Which the Child Has a Nonmarital Primary Caregiver (Informal Care by a Relative, Formal Foster Care Situations)

Consider a situation where both parents are unable to care for a child and the child is living with another adult (a relative or unrelated adult), but not through formal foster care. Assuming this person acts, and is viewed, as a parent by the child, a central question is this: *What is the legal position of the primary caregiver during the arrangement and afterward if the child returns to the legal parents after a significant amount of time with the primary caregiver?* Legal recognition of a caregiver can benefit children insomuch as it provides social legitimacy and legal protection. The importance of such legal recognition is amplified if children themselves view caregivers as parents and are strongly attached to them. However, again, the relationship between the temporary and original caregiver(s) is important to consider when evaluating the costs and benefits of awarding the caregiver legal recognition: when tensions are high between foster parents and birth parents—particularly in kinship arrangements—children may suffer.[89] Length of time with the temporary caregiver is also relevant, as the length of the coresidential arrangement is associated with the strength and durability of attachment post-residential transition.[90]

Now, let us consider a different situation, where a child is placed in formal foster care. The foster parent hopes to adopt the child, but after a year in care, the child returns to the care of the legal parents. *What is the legal position of the former foster parent?* From the child's perspective, it can be useful to maintain contact with a former foster parent and/or caregiver. Whether or not this relationship needs to be legally recognized is questionable, but legal parents should be aware that relationships with temporary foster parents can be maintained with benefit to the children. Youth can indeed benefit from maintaining relationships with former stepparents and former caregivers, including former foster parents. Particularly in the latter case, continuity of important social relationships can be profoundly impactful for children with a history of disrupted relationships and attachments.

NOTES

1 A known sperm donor is typically a friend or acquaintance who provides their sperm to help an individual or couple (e.g., a lesbian couple) become pregnant. In contrast, an anonymous sperm donor is someone who is not known to the recipient but who provides their sperm to a sperm bank. The recipient then purchases the sperm from the sperm bank.

2 J. Bowlby, "Maternal Care and Mental Health," *Bulletin of the World Health Organization* 3 (1951): 355–533.

3 J. Bowlby, "The Nature of the Child's Tie to His Mother," *International Journal of Psychoanalysis* 39 (1958): 350–373.

4 M. D. Ainsworth, "Object Relations, Dependency, and Attachment: A Theoretical Review of the Infant-Mother Relationship," *Child Development* 40, no. 4 (1969): 969–1025.

5 R. Coles, "Single-Father Families: A Review of the Literature," *Journal of Family Theory & Review* 7 (2015): 144–166; L. F. Lowenstein, "Attachment Theory and Parental Alienation," *Journal of Divorce & Remarriage* 51, no. 3 (2010): 157–168.

6 M. van Polanen, C. Colonnesi, L. Tavecchio, S. Blokhuis, and R. Fukkink, "Men and Women in Childcare: A Study of Caregiver-Child Interactions," *European Early Childhood Education Research Journal* 25 (2017): 414–424 (e.g., responsiveness to the child, time spent with the child).

7 C. Dumont and D. Paquette, "What about the Child's Tie to the Father? A New Insight into Fathering, Father–Child Attachment, Children's Socio-emotional Development and the Activation Relationship Theory," *Early Child Development and Care* 183 (2013): 430–446; D. Paquette, "Theorizing the Father-Child Relationship: Mechanisms and Developmental Outcomes," *Human Development* 47 (2004): 193–219.

8 R. Duschinsky, *Cornerstones of Attachment Research* (Oxford: Oxford University Press, 2020).

9 P. D. Rasmussen, O. J. Storebø, T. Løkkeholt, L. G. Voss, Y. Shmueli-Goetz, A. B. Bojesen, E. Simonsen, and N. Bilenberg, "Attachment as a Core Feature of Resil-

ience: A Systematic Review and Meta-Analysis," *Psychological Reports* 122, no. 4 (2019): 1259 (e.g., developing secure relationships as adults, wherein they trust and get along with others).

10 L. A. Sroufe, "Attachment and Development: A Prospective, Longitudinal Study from Birth to Adulthood," *Attachment & Human Development* 7 (2005): 349–367.

11 J. Bowlby, "Forty-Four Juvenile Thieves: Their Characters and Home-Life," *International Journal of Psychoanalysis* 25 (1944): 19–53.

12 M. Hoeve, G. J. Stams, C. E. van der Put, J. S. Dubas, P. H. van der Laan, and J. R. Gerris, "A Meta-Analysis of Attachment to Parents and Delinquency," *Journal of Abnormal Psychology* 31 (2012): 127–142.

13 Y. U. Girme, R. E. Jones, C. Fleck, J. A. Simpson, and N. C. Overall, "Infants' Attachment Insecurity Predicts Attachment-Relevant Emotion Regulation Strategies in Adulthood," *Emotion* 21 (2021): 260–272.

14 A. Marks, K. Horrocks, and N. Schutte, "Emotional Intelligence Mediates the Relationship between Insecure Attachment and Subjective Health Outcomes," *Personality & Individual Differences* 68 (2016): 188–192.

15 D. Hyman, "Young Children, Attachment Security, and Parenting Schedules," *Family Court Review* 50 (2012): 471–480; A. Nickerson, R. Bryant, I. Aderka, D. Hinton, and S. Hofmann, "The Impacts of Parental Loss and Adverse Parenting on Mental Health: Findings from the National Comorbidity Survey-Replication," *Psychological Trauma* 5 (2013): 119–127.

16 I. Bretherton, "Updating the 'Internal Working Model' Construct: Some Reflections," *Attachment & Human Development* 1 (1999): 343–357.

17 Y. Gauthier, G. Fortin, and G. Jéliu, "Clinical Application of Attachment Theory in Permanency Planning for Children in Foster Care: The Importance of Continuity of Care," *Infant Mental Health Journal* 25 (2004): 379–396; R. M. Penzerro and L. Lein, "Burning Their Bridges: Disordered Attachment and Foster Care Discharge," *Child Welfare* 74 (1995): 351–366.

18 S. Villegas and P. Pecora, "Mental Health Outcomes for Adults in Family Foster Care as Children: An Analysis by Ethnicity," *Children and Youth Services Review* 34 (2012): 1448–1458.

19 Penzerro and Lein, "Burning Their Bridges."

20 Gauthier, Fortin, and Jéliu, "Clinical Application of Attachment Theory."

21 A. M. Maaskant, F. B. van Rooij, H. M. W. Bos, and J. M. A. Hermanns, "The Well-being of Foster Children and Their Relationship with Foster Parents and Biological Parents: A Child's Perspective," *Journal of Social Work Practice* 30 (2016): 379–395.

22 C. Boyle, "What Is the Impact of Birth Family Contact on Children in Adoption and Long-Term Foster Care? A Systematic Review," *Child & Family Social Work* 22 (2017): 22–33.

23 Boyle, "What Is the Impact of Birth Family Contact?"; D. Chateauneuf, D. Turcotte, and S. Drapeau, "The Relationship between Foster Families and Birth Families in a Child Welfare Context: The Determining Factors," *Child & Family Social Work* 23 (2018): 71–79; D. Chateauneuf, G. Page, and B. Decaluwe, "Issues

Surrounding Post-adoption Contact in Foster Adoption: The Perspective of Foster-to-Adopt Families and Child Welfare Workers," *Journal of Public Child Welfare* 12 (2018): 436–460. Of note is that contact between birth parents and adopted children (which is increasingly common in the context of open adoptions) is generally associated with benefits for children, including greater levels of satisfaction with their adoptions, higher self-esteem, and more positive feelings toward birth parents, although, again, these benefits may be mitigated amid high levels of tension between adoptive parents and birth parents. Boyle, "What Is the Impact of Birth Family Contact?"; A. E. Goldberg, *Open Adoption and Diverse Families: Complex Relationships in the Digital Age* (New York: Oxford University Press, 2019).

24 R. C. Fraley and M. E. Heffernan, "Attachment and Parental Divorce: A Test of the Diffusion and Sensitive Period Hypotheses," *Personality & Social Psychology Bulletin* 39 (2013): 1199–213.

25 M. Gindes, "The Psychological Effects of Relocation for Children of Divorce," *Journal of the American Academy of Matrimonial Lawyers* 15 (1998): 119–148.

26 J. Cheadle, P. Amato, and V. King, "Patterns of Nonresident Father Contact," *Demography* 47 (2010): 205–225.

27 V. King and J. Sobolewski, "Nonresident Fathers' Contributions to Adolescent Well-Being," *Journal of Marriage and Family* 68 (2006): 537–557.

28 A. Steinbach, "Children's and Parents' Well-Being in Joint Physical Custody: A Literature Review," *Family Process* 58 (2019): 353–369.

29 K. L. Modecki, M. J. Hagan, I. Sandler, and S. A. Wolchik, "Latent Profiles of Nonresidential Father Engagement Six Years after Divorce Predict Long-Term Offspring Outcomes," *Journal of Clinical Child and Adolescent Psychology* 44 (2015): 123–136.

30 M. Coleman, L. Ganong, L. Russell, and N. Frye-Cox, "Stepchildren's Views about Former Step-Relationships following Stepfamily Dissolution," *Journal of Marriage and Family* 77 (2015): 775–790; Lowenstein, "Attachment Theory and Parental Alienation."

31 Lowenstein, "Attachment Theory and Parental Alienation."

32 E. K. Holmes, K. C. Dunn, J. Harper, W. J. Dyer, and R. D. Day, "Mother Knows Best? Inhibitory Maternal Gatekeeping, Psychological Control, and the Mother-Adolescent Relationship," *Journal of Adolescence* 36 (2013): 91–101.

33 L. Halcomb, "Who Counts as Family? Gamete Donation and the Construction of Family Forms in Medical Markets," *Journal of Family Issues* 41 (2019); V. Jadva, L. Lamba, K. Kadam, and S. Golombok, "Indian Egg Donors' Characteristics, Motivations and Feelings towards the Recipient and Resultant Child," *Reproductive Biomedicine and Society Online* 1 (2015): 98–103.

34 E. Di Nucci, "IVF, Same-Sex Couples and the Value of Biological Ties," *Journal of Medical Ethics* 42 (2016): 784–787.

35 S. Golombok, C. Murray, V. Jadva, F. MacCallum, and E. Lycett, "Families Created through Surrogacy Arrangements: Parent-Child Relationships in the First Year of Life," *Developmental Psychology* 40 (2004): 400–411.

36 S. Golombok, E. Ilioi, L. Blake, G. Roman, and V. Jadva, "A Longitudinal Study of Families Formed through Reproductive Donation: Parent-Adolescent Relationships and Adolescent Adjustment at Age 14," *Developmental Psychology* 53 (2017): 1966–1977; S. Imrie and S. Golombok, "Long-Term Outcomes of Children Conceived through Egg Donation and Their Parents: A Review of the Literature," *Fertility and Sterility* 110 (2018): 1187–1193.

37 Golombok et al., "Longitudinal Study of Families."

38 Golombok et al., "Longitudinal Study of Families"; Imrie and Golombok, "Long-Term Outcomes."

39 S. Altenhofen, R. Clyman, C. Little, M. Baker, and Z. Biringen, "Attachment Security in Three-Year-Olds Who Entered Substitute Care in Infancy," *Infant Mental Health Journal* 34 (2013): 435–445; S. Erich, H. Kanenberg, K. Case, T. Allen, and T. Bogdanos, "An Empirical Analysis of Factors Affecting Adolescent Attachment in Adoptive Families with Homosexual and Straight Parents," *Children and Youth Services Review* 31 (2009): 398–404; A. E. Goldberg and K. R. Allen, "Same-Sex Relationship Dissolution and LGB Stepfamily Formation: Perspectives of Young Adults with LGB Parents," *Family Relations* 62 (2013): 529–544; F. Lionetti, "What Promotes Secure Attachment in Early Adoption? The Protective Roles of Infants' Temperament and Adoptive Parents' Attachment," *Attachment & Human Development* 16 (2014): 573–589.

40 Goldberg, *Open Adoption and Diverse Families.*

41 K. Raby and M. Dozier, "Attachment across the Lifespan: Insights from Adoptive Families," *Current Opinion in Psychology* 25 (2019): 81–85.

42 Raby and Dozier, "Attachment across the Lifespan"; Altenhofen et al., "Attachment Security in Three-Year-Olds."

43 Erich et al., "Empirical Analysis of Factors."

44 É. A. Feugé, L. Cossette, C. Cyr, and D. Julien, "Parental Involvement among Adoptive Gay Fathers: Associations with Resources, Time Constraints, Gender Role, and Child Adjustment," *Psychology of Sexual Orientation and Gender Diversity* 6 (2019): 1–10.

45 A. L. McConnachie, N. Ayed, S. Foley, M. E. Lamb, V. Jadva, F. Tasker, and S. Golombok, "Adoptive Gay Father Families: A Longitudinal Study of Children's Adjustment at Early Adolescence," *Child Development* 92 (2021): 425–443.

46 V. King, "The Antecedents and Consequences of Adolescents' Relationships with Stepfathers and Nonresident Fathers," *Journal of Marriage and Family* 68 (2006): 910–928.

47 M. Kalmijn, "Adult Children's Relationships with Married Parents, Divorced Parents, and Stepparents: Biology, Marriage, or Residence?," *Journal of Marriage and Family* 75 (2013): 1181–1193.

48 M. V. Antokolskaia, "Parenting in Stepparent Families: Legal Status versus de Facto Roles," *Child and Family Law Quarterly* 27 (2015): 271–284. (In 36 percent of cases they took a secondary role, in 14 percent they took on a tertiary role, after

the resident and nonresident parent, and in 30 percent of cases they were cast as simply the partner of the caretaking parent.)

49 Coleman et al., "Stepchildren's Views about Former Step-Relationships."

50 Coleman et al., "Stepchildren's Views about Former Step-Relationships"; L. Ganong, C. Sanner, and M. Coleman, "Divorce and Stepgrandparenthood," in *Grandparenting: Influences on the Dynamics of Family Relationships*, ed. B. Hayslip Jr. and C. A. Fruhauf (New York: Springer, 2019), 111–129.

51 Ganong, Sanner, and Coleman, "Divorce and Stepgrandparenthood."

52 I. Padavic and J. Butterfield, "Mothers, Fathers, and 'Mathers': Negotiating a Lesbian Co-parental Identity," *Gender & Society* 25 (2011): 176–196 (i.e., the notion that their bonds are simply not as strong).

53 A. E. Goldberg, *Lesbian and Gay Parents and Their Children: Research on the Family Life Cycle* (Washington, DC: American Psychological Association, 2010); Goldberg, *Open Adoption and Diverse Families.*

54 Goldberg, *Lesbian and Gay Parents.*

55 This is in contrast to couples who use reciprocal in vitro fertilization (IVF), allowing one partner to carry a child using the other partner's eggs.

56 Chestfeeding is the process of feeding a child milk from a person's chest, also called breastfeeding or nursing (but chestfeeding can be used by people of any gender identity).

57 J. B. Downing and A. E. Goldberg, "Lesbian Mothers' Constructions of the Division of Paid and Unpaid Labor," *Feminism & Psychology* 21 (2011): 100–120; A. E. Goldberg and M. Perry-Jenkins, "The Division of Labor and Perceptions of Parental Roles: Lesbian Couples across the Transition to Parenthood," *Journal of Social and Personal Relationships* 24 (2007): 297–318.

58 N. Gartrell, A. Banks, J. Hamilton, N. Reed, H. Bishop, and C. Rodas, "The National Lesbian Family Study: 2. Interviews with Mothers of Toddlers," *American Journal of Orthopsychiatry* 69 (1999): 362–369; A. E. Goldberg and J. Z. Smith, "Perceived Parenting Skill across the Transition to Adoptive Parenthood among Lesbian, Gay, and Heterosexual Couples," *Journal of Family Psychology* 23 (2009): 861–870; A. E. Goldberg, A. M. Moyer, and L. A. Kinkler, "Lesbian, Gay, and Heterosexual Adoptive Parents' Perceptions of Parental Bonding during Early Parenthood," *Couple and Family Psychology: Research and Practice* 2 (2013): 146–162.

59 A. E. Goldberg, J. B. Downing, and C. C. Sauck, "Perceptions of Children's Parental Preferences in Lesbian Two-Mother Households," *Journal of Marriage and Family* 70 (2008): 419–434.

60 K. R. Sweeney, A. E. Goldberg, and R. L. Garcia, "Not a 'Mom Thing': Predictors of Gatekeeping in Same-Sex and Heterosexual Parent Families," *Journal of Family Psychology* 31 (2017): 521–531.

61 R. Gaunt, "Maternal Gatekeeping: Antecedents and Consequences," *Journal of Family Issues* 29 (2008): 373–395.

62 B. Hayman and L. Wilkes, "De Novo Families: Lesbian Motherhood," *Journal of Homosexuality* 64 (2017): 577–591; N. Surtees and P. Bremner, "Gay and Lesbian

Collaborative Co-parenting in New Zealand and the United Kingdom: 'The Law Doesn't Protect the Third Parent,'" *Social & Legal Studies* 29 (2020): 507–526.

63 Gartrell et al., "National Lesbian Family Study: 2."

64 N. Gartrell, H. Bos, H. Peyser, A. Deck, and C. Rodas, "Family Characteristics, Custody Arrangements, and Adolescent Psychological Well-Being after Lesbian Mothers Break Up," *Family Relations* 60 (2011): 572–585.

65 Goldberg and Allen, "Same-Sex Relationship Dissolution."

66 M. A. Saini, L. M. Drozd, and N. W. Olesen, "Adaptive and Maladaptive Gatekeeping Behaviors and Attitudes: Implications for Child Outcomes after Separation and Divorce," *Family Court Review* 55 (2017): 260–272.

67 Goldberg and Allen, "Same-Sex Relationship Dissolution."

68 M. Siegel, C. Assenmacher, N. Meuwly, and M. Zemp, "The Legal Vulnerability Model for Same-Sex Parent Families: A Mixed Methods Systematic Review and Theoretical Integration," *Frontiers in Psychology*, March 16, 2021.

69 K. Acosta, "In the Event of Death: Lesbian Families' Plans to Preserve Stepparent–Child Relationships," *Family Relations* 66 (2017): 244–257; Siegel et al., "Legal Vulnerability Model."

70 A. Malmquist, S. Anderson, and J. Salomonsson, "Life Finds a Way: Young Adults with Lesbian Mothers Reflect on Their Childhood Prior to Legal Recognition of Same-Sex Parents in Sweden," *Frontiers in Psychology* 11 (April 15, 2020) (e.g., they became separated from their nonlegal parent when their parents divorced, inheritance became an issue if their nonlegal parent passed away).

71 Surtees and Bremner, "Gay and Lesbian Collaborative Co-parenting."

72 Surtees and Bremner, "Gay and Lesbian Collaborative Co-parenting."

73 M. Pallotta-Chiarolli, E. Sheff, and R. Mountford, "Polyamorous Parenting in Contemporary Research: Developments and Future Directions," in *LGBTQ-Parent Families*, ed. A. E. Goldberg and K. R. Allen (New York: Springer, 2020), 171–183.

74 Goldberg, *Lesbian and Gay Parents and Their Children*; R. Hertz, M. Nelson, and W. Kramer, "Sperm Donors Describe the Experience of Contact with Their Donor Conceived Offspring," *Facts, Views, and Vision: Issues in Obstetrics, Gynecology, and Reproductive Health* 7 (2015): 91–100 (indeed, a frequent concern for female couples embarking on insemination with a known donor is the potential for fuzzy boundaries and unclear roles).

75 Surtees and Bremner, "Gay and Lesbian Collaborative Co-parenting."

76 Surtees and Bremner, "Gay and Lesbian Collaborative Co-parenting."

77 Hertz, Nelson, and Kramer, "Sperm Donors Describe the Experience of Contact."

78 A. E. Goldberg and K. A. Allen, "Donor, Dad, or . . . ? Young Adults with Lesbian Parents' Experiences with Known Donors," *Family Process* 52 (2013): 338–350; F. Tasker and J. Granville, "Children's Views of Family Relationships in Lesbian-Led Families," *Journal of LGBT Family Studies* 7 (2011): 182–199.

79 N. Gartrell, A. Deck, C. Rodas, H. Peyser, and A. Banks, "The National Lesbian Family Study: 4. Interviews with the 10-Year-Old Children," *American Journal of Orthopsychiatry* 75 (2005): 518–524.

80 Gartrell et al., "National Lesbian Family Study: 4."
81 A. Koh, G. van Geusekom, N. Gartrell, and H. Bos, "Adult Offspring of Lesbian Parents: How Do They Relate to Their Sperm Donors?," *Fertility and Sterility* 114 (2020).
82 Acosta, "In the Event of Death."
83 Acosta, "In the Event of Death."
84 Siegel et al., "Legal Vulnerability Model."
85 Malmquist, Anderson, and Salomonsson, "Life Finds a Way."
86 Malmquist, Anderson, and Salomonsson, "Life Finds a Way" (e.g., ensuring legal protections in the event of death).
87 Coleman et al., "Stepchildren's Views about Former Step-Relationships"; Ganong, Sanner, and Coleman, "Divorce and Stepgrandparenthood"; Surtees and Bremner, "Gay and Lesbian Collaborative Co-parenting."
88 N. Cahn and J. Carbone, "Custody and Visitation in Families with Three (or More) Parents," *Family Court Review* 56 (2018): 399–409.
89 Chateauneuf, Turcotte, and Drapeau, "Relationship between Foster Families and Birth Families."
90 King and Sobolewski, "Nonresident Fathers' Contributions to Adolescent Well-Being."

2

Same-Sex Parents

A Case Study from Italy

CORINNA SABRINA GUERZONI

The development of assisted reproductive technologies (ARTs), combined with social and juridical changes within family structures, has reinvented family reproduction and kinship practices. Contemporary forms of procreation, family, and parenthood (including increasingly complex networks of parental figures—biological parents, adoptive parents, donors, birthmothers, surrogates, and social parents) offer new insights to the study of parental dynamics.

Today, family compositions are more complex and varied, ranging from single-parent to multiparent configurations,[1] same-sex-parent families, heterosexual-parent families, and families with stepparents. However, despite the increased variation in family forms, biogenetic connection retains a certain relevance in Western societies. This is especially true in Italy, which, consistent with Sarah Franklin's theoretical reasoning,[2] allows biological data to prevail over any other parental relationship. For most European and American kinship systems, parenthood is primarily bilateral, which means that a person's lineage is often associated or traced through a bilateral (mother-father) genealogy, generally represented by sharing biogenetic substances (blood or genes). In other words, the so-called natural model consisting of two parents differentiated by genders continues "to colonize our conceptual and emotional imagery of parenting";[3] it remains a sort of "zombie" concept.[4]

To better understand the Italian approach to social parents and the implications of this approach for the lives of family members, this chapter takes a deep dive into one family form that often includes at least one social parent: Italian families headed by same-sex couples. I focus on this form since, as we will see through the course of this chapter, parenting by lesbian, gay, bisexual, and transgender (LGBTQIA+) people in Italy is not fully recognized by law but can be achieved, in some cases, through a series of legal battles.

Italian same-sex families, and other relationships established by ARTs, show a disconnection among biogenetic kinship, legal kinship, and intentional, practical, and everyday kinship.[5] In Italy, parenting by LGBTQIA+ people,[6] better known as *omogenitorialità*, develops within two strong, dominant ideologies: the primacy of the so-called natural family—nuclear, heterosexual[7]—and the existence of a parenting model based on gender complementarity, namely the idea that a family could be composed of only a father and a mother.[8] The Italian context is particularly interesting. Italy does not have any law expressly recognizing gay parenting; at birth, only biological parents are officially identified as legal parents. For example, Italian law 40/2004 bars access to fertility treatments for same-sex people. Thus, the only possible solution for LGBTQIA+ people to have biological children is to access ARTs abroad. In addition, the Italian adoption law—184/1983—does not expressly allow adoptions for same-sex couples. As a result, generally speaking, only the biological parent is defined as the legal parent of a child born through IVF. In this context, social parents, to be legitimized as such, face long legal battles, often characterized by unpleasant and anxious situations without certainty of a positive result. This chapter explores how LGBTQIA+ social parents live in this context heavily influenced by heteronormative systems in which the nonbiological parent is not officially recognized as a parent.

Italian Same-Sex Parenting Struggling Against Heteronormativity

In 1989, Denmark became the first country to offer a legal framework for recognizing same-sex couples, which has since become more and more common in Europe. Other European countries have not reached the same level of rights regarding the introduction of marriage and the recognition of parental status for same-sex couples.[9] Northern European countries pioneered the now common trend of enacting laws allowing same-sex marriage.[10] By contrast, the timing of same-sex marriage among southern states varies. Italy represents a peculiarly hostile legal regime with regard to same-sex parents. And in addition to legal hurdles, these families also experience social stigma and prejudices. In the public sphere, Italian same-sex families are often described as "unnatural." Here, the word "natural" is used as a synonym for "legitimate" and "unnatural" for "illegitimate."

In the Italian context, political and juridical recognition of same-sex parenting is a top priority of gay activists,[11] as more and more gay people become parents through transnational reproduction. As noted above, in most cases Italy fully recognizes only the biological parent in a same-sex-parent family. In 2015, however, the European Court of Human Rights ruled that Italy violated the European Convention on Human Rights by not recognizing same-sex couples' right to family life. In 2016, following a long parliamentary dispute, same-sex relationships were officially recognized and regulated with the introduction of civil unions. The debate on the regulation of same-sex relationships has now moved to focus on gay and lesbian parenting and specifically to the question of whether a same-sex partner can become a parent through adoption (the so-called stepchild adoption for same-sex couples). Stepchild adoption—namely coadoption by the social parent—was at the core of the 2016 political debate about same-sex relationships. But in the end, the provision that would have expressly allowed same-sex partners to complete coparent adoptions was removed from the civil union law. Thus, today in Italy, the law allows for recognition of the loving bond between the adults in a same-sex relationship but does not expressly recognize the filiation link between both parents and their children.

This legislative process and the ultimate removal of the stepparent adoption provision from the civil union legislation prior to its enactment show "the homophobic regime incorporated in some social and political components."[12] As a result of this failure, current Italian legislation is poorly adapted to parenting by LGBTQIA+ couples.[13] Under the current law, generally speaking only biological parents are legally recognized, while the so-called nonbiological or social parents are not. Indeed, despite the growing number of same-sex families,[14] gay parenting remains a social category that is yet to be defined, as it is a form that exists in fact but is not yet fully recognized from either a legal or a social point of view. As Italian anthropologist Simonetta Grilli argues, gay parenting is a social category that is still being materialized since it exists on a social level but has less cultural and especially legal recognition since gay parenting is still subject to numerous social stigmas.[15]

Transparency, Traces, Visibility

Gay parenting is not a fully legitimate family composition under the existing Italian legal kinship system,[16] which does not recognize same-sex-parent families. The Italian legal system generally recognizes the rights and responsibilities only of biological parents, and legal protections for nonbiological parents are often elusive.

Living as legally invisible, social gay parents seek to protect themselves by leaving as many traces as possible of their commitment as parents, both for care and for the economic support of the child. Grilli reflected on this "institutional work" that LGBTQIA+ families must engage in;[17] they are in the process of being "described," "shown," and finally fully "recognized."[18] As one social mother explained, "We collect papers." As her comment suggests, it is important for the nonbiological parent to store any and all possible records of their existence. This documentation includes things such as payment receipts, wills, and the written testimony of friends, relatives, and neighbors. The ability to perform one's own parenting is entrusted with the possibility of passing as good parents,[19] with the implementation of a series of tactics that attempt to gain recognition and legitimacy of a family on the public level.

Some incremental legal advancements have been made. For example, courts have granted adoptions in situations not expressly recognized by law in the context of other types of relationships. The first stepchild adoptions were granted in the context of cases involving divorced or widowed parents who wanted their new partner recognized as a legal parent. In those cases, often there was an absence of a second original legal parent.

Later, some courts applied this procedure to same-sex families. In other words, stepchild adoption was not initially conceived of as a form of legal protection specifically for gay parents. It was first developed in other contexts. Only later did the Italian Supreme Court apply this process to same-sex couples. This decision was based on an extensive interpretation of the law regulating adoption, which has been part of the Italian legal system since 1983 (law 184/1983, article 44). This law allows adoption in specific cases, such as social parents within same-sex families.

This so-called jurisprudence in action has allowed for the recognition of the relationship between the social parent and the biological child of their same-sex partner. In 2014, judge and former president of the Juvenile Court of Rome Melita Cavallo was the first to apply stepchild adoption to social gay parenting, opening the way to dozens of other proceedings.[20] Since this ruling, stepchild adoption has been requested by many same-sex families. However, the outcomes of such requests depend on a series of variables that make up the elements of the stepchild adoption request. Thus, while several juvenile courts have granted stepparent adoptions to same-sex couples,[21] many similar requests have been systematically rejected. In a restrictive and heteronormative context, not only can similar cases lead to the recognition of kinship or not, but the same person may or may not be recognized as a parent depending on the place of residency and according to specific conditions (such as the genders of the parents).

In previous work on gay parenting,[22] I showed how some practices are crucial for social parents in their quest to be fully recognized as legal parents, and how same-sex families performed what I defined as the policy of being transparent.[23] By the term "transparency," I mean giving a place to biogenetic connection, while also highlighting all the actions undertaken by social parents to be recognized by the rest of their community. To use Goffmanian language, I say that the background of the intimacy of reproduction has been brought into the light to be shown to, and strategically shared with, the community.[24] In other words, in their quest for legal recognition, social parents must demonstrate that they have been present since the beginning of the reproductive journey. They do so by collecting traces, leaving documents, and showing their continuous presence. This requires them to authenticate a precise *transparency of conduct*, or a systematic organization of moments and circumstances to make all the steps clear, documented, visible, and shareable. These *transparency practices* also include all the actions taken to make their presence as visible as possible in the eyes of the community.

Transparent policy becomes particularly crucial in the cases in which same-sex parents request recognition of their social parenthood before courts. Since there are no laws that explicitly recognize both same-sex partners as parents of children born within a homosexual relationship at birth, one way to accord recognition to the other parent is asking a court to grant a stepchild adoption. This represents the expansion of the legal-political apparatus into the privacy of people's lives.[25] While on the one hand there is a political need for visibility as a route to recognition, on the other hand, by invoking these legal procedures, the families become subjects increasingly under attack as targets of political campaigns and social struggles. In this way, the demand for rights can be a double-edged sword that affects these family configurations that are legally vulnerable.

Social Lesbian Motherhood

In this section, I focus on lesbian motherhood and on cases in which lesbian mothers sought to obtain legal recognition of their social relationships with their children. These stories show how lesbian mothers seek to prove the legitimacy of their relationships. They also illustrate the vulnerable legal status of nonbiological same-sex partners and the lack of consistency in the law on the ground.

The first story is that of a lesbian couple who successfully obtained legal recognition of the so-called social mother after six years of juridical fights. Camilla (the birth mother) and Maria were together for more than six years when they decided to have a baby through IVF in Spain. Luca was born in Italy, and on his birth certificate only the biological mother Camilla is listed as his legal mother. I report below a short interview collected with Maria, the social mother: "I cannot stand [the fact] that I needed to show that I am the other mother. For us it was clear, and for Luca too. He calls me 'mom.' But for the Italian bureaucracy I was like a ghost, I didn't exist, I was nothing. It hurt me so many times when I needed to show that I was his mother even if I hadn't given birth to him. Before the recognition, I was living in fear: 'What is going to happen to Luca if Camilla dies?' I didn't have any rights." In this interview, Maria described the fear she felt when she was not fully recognized as Luca's mother. Her position as a parent was not reflected in a change to her legal identity. Indeed, Maria, like most gay social parents in Italy, needed to have written authorization from the birth mother for any formal situation, from appointments at the pediatrician to the school, in which she wished to be recognized as Luca's mother. Maria continued,

> You know, I needed her authorization for everything. For example, I couldn't go to the pediatrician alone with my son without having this document. I needed also to show that I was there since the beginning. We followed some friends' suggestions on how to collect useful information for our case. I had to collect proof that I was his mother. We took selfies right before the embryo transfer to show that I was there. During the delivery I was there as well. I collected all of Luca's drawings in which the teachers listed Camilla and me as "moms." I tried to be the "super-parent" and be present in any possible meetings at school or at his football games. It was exhausting because I needed to collect as many forms of proof as I could to show the relationship with my son. But in most cases, how could I do that? I mean, I hadn't taken any videos when I changed his diaper, or when he was sick and I was there, or when he had a fever, or all the times I rocked him to sleep!

Maria described all the efforts that she undertook to prove the relationship with her child. She emphasized how exhausting and emotionally difficult it was to have to prove something that for her was a fact of life. This excerpt from an interview describes only a few of the many documents and other forms of proof that gay social parents need to in order to be fully recognized. Maria and Camilla were one of the first same-sex couples to obtain legal recognition of both parents' relationships with their child. In addition to having to document their relationships for a judge, the family also had to be followed by a social worker and a psychologist who evaluated their environment and analyzed the relationship between Luca and Maria. Speaking of the effects of this process on their family, Camilla added,

> It has been very hard for us, especially for her [Maria]. The psychologist asked for an observation of Maria and Luca together. She wanted to see how they played together, which I understand. I understand that it can give a lot of information on how a child is feeling comfortable. But we were like on the stage. Maria was feeling nervous about it, and she was acting like a robot. Luca probably felt it, and he was crying. He cried all

> the time; he probably felt that something was weird. And we were already seeing a denial from the judge. In that specific moment I felt that we were discriminated just for our sexual orientation. I don't think that they ask the same thing for all the heterosexuals out there who used IVF to conceive. That's so stupid!

As described above, in the stepparent adoption process, social service officials must verify the existence of a relationship between the adopter and the adopted. From the data I collected, social services do not have any standard protocols for stepchild adoption within same-sex families. As a result, the recognition processes differ from one case to another. For example, in the same city, Rome, another person I interviewed, Chiara, described the varied approaches different social workers took. Chiara, one of the social parents, testified,

> For one of my friends, it was very easy. The social worker arrived in their house, took coffee with them and then he said: "Oh thank you, I am sorry to be here to do this check. I know you are as much as a parent as your partner, but I need to be here and check that." In our case it has been so hard, and we literally live in the same city. We have scheduled eight meetings, and we already had the first three meetings. My partner and I went to the social worker's office. We had two-hour sessions with a psychologist and a social worker, and I assure you that the meeting that we had was not an interview. It was more a therapy session, the most judgmental that you may have. I know the difference because I have been in therapy for seven years. We received such stupid questions, they asked a lot of questions about the relationship between me and my family, about my coming out and how my parents reacted to it. We never talked about our son. And every time that we tried to drive their attention there, on the relationship between me and my child, they were not listening and insisting on "How did your parents react to your homosexuality?" "How did they take it?" . . . I mean, all the questions were more on our relationship rather than the relationship that I have with my son.

Many of the social parents whom I interviewed explained how stressful this situation was for them, especially because they did not know what to expect from this evaluation. Sara, another social mother, also found the interviews with social workers upsetting: "It was very painful for me. While the psychologist was asking questions, I felt very stressed, because I felt judged. And the situation was also ambiguous, because my daughter is seven years old, and I was there to adopt her. You know what I mean? I was there to adopt my own daughter, the daughter that I have been raising since the first minute that I had her in my arms. We wanted her, we wanted her together. I need to go through all of that just because we are two moms." Sara's words are in line with other stories collected with social parents. Social parents stressed how the stepchild adoption process is not an appropriate process for their family structure because they are required to ask for the intervention of the Juvenile Court to recognize a parental status that, in their view, already exists. Moreover, the process evaluates their suitability as parents, when they are in fact already parents. According to the social parents whom I interviewed, their role cannot be compared with that of other adoptive parents since they always had a parental relationship with their children. Many couples (quite reasonably) hesitate to access stepchild adoption precisely because they feel judged regarding their own family intimacy. Teresa, a social parent from northern Italy, added,

> I had a discussion with a social worker before the meeting that we have scheduled with my daughter. I asked her to avoid using the word "adoption" with my nine-year-old daughter. And trust me, I had to convince her. I didn't want her to mention that, I mean, my daughter calls me mom. I thought it was brutal to say to her that I was adopting her. I am already her mom, and I didn't want to confuse my daughter. I mean, I am her mother, I am not her legal mother yet. But I am definitely not an adoptive mother.

Teresa had several different consultations with social workers, and in these consultations she argued that they were not acting properly in the terms of her family configuration. She added, "In our [same-sex] families we deal with social workers who generally deal with other situations, such as adoptions. Sometimes they have this attitude, and they are fussy about a thousand issues. But we are not like adoptive parents who welcome a new member into the family. My daughter has known me since day zero. We are families with children, we desired them, we had them, and we are already raising them. Why don't they evaluate heterosexuals who had kids through IVF?" The arbitrariness of the collection of information relating to the existence of a relationship between the social parent and the child of the homosexual couple serves as an example of the unpredictability of the process. In some cases, the requests for recognition by same-sex parents were accepted, while in other cases they were rejected.

These stories show how Italian lesbian nonbiological parents often feel that their existence is erased. They are required to produce voluminous forms of proof to document and "prove" the existence of their family. They have to open up their homes and their lives to officials to be evaluated, and ultimately they have to prove to a court that they are fit to be a parent, even though they already are. And having done all of this, their request may or may not be granted, based on no clear set of rules or criteria.

Social Gay Fatherhood

Most Italian gay fathers become parents by accessing surrogacy in the United States,[26] and especially in California, known as one of the most "surrogacy friendly states"[27] with the most favorable legislation for these kinds of cases. But while these families are able to access surrogacy in the United States, they continue to face hurdles in getting their families recognized when they return to Italy. Over the years, numerous Italian lawyers have proposed different solutions for their clients regarding the registration in Italy of the foreign birth certificate. Some attorneys have suggested listing only the genetic father on the child's original U.S. birth certificate, while others have suggested that both fathers should be listed on it. These are important decisions because in many cases U.S. birth certificates with two fathers listed on it have been described as incompatible with the Italian legal system and are therefore void. In such cases, those families were unable to register their children as Italian citizens.[28]

Starting from the Court of Trento's ruling of February 23, 2017, followed by others, an important transition in jurisprudence has taken place. In the February 2017 ruling, the Court of Trento recognized the right of a couple of gay fathers to be both listed as "fathers" in Italy, without any distinction between the biological parent and the social one, accepting *de facto* two fathers. Despite this fundamental step, other offices continued to deny recognition of birth certificates on which two fathers were listed. In addition, the transcription of the U.S. birth certificate in Italy does not imply the direct recognition of the parental role of the persons indicated on the birth certificate itself. For these reasons, many attorneys suggested an easier way: ask for a birth certificate with only one father on it, register the baby in Italy, and only after the baby is recognized as an Italian citizen, request an amendment of the birth certificate to add the second father.[29] Matteo, a gay father, described this complex process of navigation in a context full of numerous denials and continuous changes of direction:

> We asked to our U.S. lawyer to make some changes through our journey because the situation in Italy is so complex. It changes if you live in one city rather than another one, or if a new court ruling is out. At first, we asked to have both [of us] on the birth certificate. Then we heard that a judge denied the stepchild adoption to some friends, and we got scared. We asked to have the birth certificate with only the biological father on it, and only after having registered our daughter in Italy, we asked for the amendment [to the birth certificate] with both fathers on it. Without any legal and official law that truly protect our children, we are like ghosts for our state. We go through this process because we fear losing her. So, we asked to have only Saverio [the biological father] on the birth certificate. We are now thinking if we want to start the stepchild [adoption], but we don't know yet. Everyone assumes that we are rich because we had our daughter through surrogacy, but I am not sure. I am afraid that we don't have enough money to do that. We spent all our savings on this huge project.

Gay fathers face a different set of hurdles and challenges, not only the legal system that denies specific rights but also the social stigma linked to surrogacy and gay fatherhood. Roberto, another father, faced discrimination and stigmatization the day that he went to register his son at the registry office. He mentioned that he argued with an employee because she refused to transcribe the U.S. birth certificate:

> She began by asking me where his mother was. I explained that my son doesn't have any mother. So, she asked me if I was a widower. She seemed confused that I was there without a woman near me. While I was handing his U.S. passport, I told her that the woman who carried the pregnancy hadn't recognized him as her son. I specifically avoided [using the term] "surrogacy," because I know all the bad prejudices around it here in Italy. I was vague. I hoped that she was not going to ask any further questions. The employee took the passport, and while she was checking it, she commented: "Ah, okay. I see what we have here. You are one of those rich gay men who went in America to buy a baby. Aren't you ashamed of having exploited a woman? Do you know that surrogacy is illegal in Italy? Do you know that it is an abominable practice? A family is composed by a mother and a father. No, I can't. I don't feel like registering this child today." I was in front of her, and I felt like I committed a crime. She humiliated me in front of a lot of people, and she made me feel like a terrible person. I was scared to argue back, so that day I left. I didn't want to have many eyes on me, especially because we know that surrogacy is a double-edged sword for a family like mine.

This episode demonstrates how the zombie concept of natural family unfolds in employees' practices who, in the absence of any specific laws that recognize social parents within same-sex families, can arbitrarily decide if, how, and when to register a foreign birth certificate. This fact not only has consequences on the sociocultural level but also produces effects on the actual transcription of a foreign birth certificate in Italy and on the attitude of the social workers who meet these families.

The fear of making mistakes is present in any bureaucratic action, from the registration of the birth certificate to the request for the stepchild adoption. One couple I interviewed included Mirko, a social father living in southern Italy, and his husband Giovanni, who had twins through surrogacy in California. They used ova from a donor that were fertilized using semen from both men. As a result, each man was a genetic parent of one of the two resulting children. They obtained U.S. birth certificates for their children listing both men as fathers. Upon their return to Italy, they asked to both be registered as parents on the birth certificates since they knew that their mayor was open to doing so. Mirko said,

> We have been lucky, and we were positive about our situation because we heard about the first case of recognition of double fatherhood. We had our twins in California and we had a birth certificate in which we were both listed as parents. It has been very easy for us. We live in Sicily and our mayor was ok with registering our twins. As soon as we came back, we worked to obtain full recognition. We had the birth certificates, a good lawyer, our twins were registered, and we obtained the stepchild adoption when our twins were two years old. We had friends who waited until their son was six years old. Their lawyers suggested that to them because they needed to show the existence of a long-term relationship, but we knew that we had to try before any negative court ruling regarding a denial of a stepchild adoption request that could have changed the scenario, like something that the judge could use against us.

Mirko, like many interviewees, underlined how, in the absence of a national law, even a denied stepchild adoption can have negative impacts against the LGBTQIA+ community at large because other judges can rely on those denials as precedents.[30] Fortunately for Mirko, they did not experience that outcome and were able to successfully register the birth certificate. They later completed stepparent adoptions for the twins, a process that went quite smoothly.[31] During the adoption process, Mirko and Giovanni had only two meetings with the social worker. Their petition was successful, and they have both been recognized as fathers. As Mirko feared, though, after some positive cases, in 2018 a number of courts denied requests by gay male couples for stepparent adoptions.

Gay male fathers, even when recognized as legal parents by foreign jurisdictions, remain vulnerable in Italy. Some are able to have their legal relationships recognized in Italy, but even in these cases the process is expensive, families remain vulnerable in the interim, and their relationships remain invisible under the law. In some cases, families' attempts at legal protection are denied altogether, and all families face challenges arising from the social stigma attached to the practice of surrogacy.[32]

Conclusion

Today, in the absence of adoption or any other legal recognition, social parents within same-sex parenting do not have any family rights since their kinship ties remain legally unrecognized. In this context, social parents struggle daily against uncertainty, stigma, and the absence of specific protocols. From their point of view, they are the parents of their children. The lack of legal recognition does not alter how they undertake parental duties on a day-to-day basis. Parenting is not the direct and immediate consequence of the birth of children; rather, it is the outcome of the construction of a reproductive project consisting of multiple obstacles.

While Italy remains less protective for LGBTQIA+ families as compared to other countries explored in this book, as discussed throughout this chapter, we can see that there may be some room for legal action at regional and local levels to achieve recognition of kinship ties. A prominent example was the Italian Supreme Court's first authorization of coparent adoption in 2016. In order to bolster their claims for social and legal recognition, social parents used different strategies to prove their role as parents: collecting papers, being visible, and showing their commitment emerged as key symbolic resources to seek legal recognition of their status. But this process is subject to the discretion of social workers, psychologists, and judges. As a result, the process can seem arbitrary. This arbitrariness can have profound impacts on the effective recognition of social parenting and on the social parents' wider kinship network.

In addition, even where the adoption is granted, there are some important limitations to its protection. A stepchild adoption is not a full adoption; instead, it is a process applied in so-called special cases, as homosexual parents are often labeled. When granted, the adoption judgment does result in full recognition of the social parent's parental rights. However, it also has some important shortcomings, such as with regard to the effects of the adoption on the adopter's family of origin. For example, after a stepchild adoption is granted, the adopter's parents and siblings do not become legally related to the adopted child. In this way, while the process does provide some protection to some social parents (i.e., those who have the privilege of winning a lawsuit), this law does not fully protect children born and raised in same-sex families.

The analysis of the stories collected in this chapter shows the difficulties experienced by LGBTQIA+ parents who live daily within a heteronormative system that continues to refuse to enact legislation that would guarantee protections to these families.

NOTES

1 Didier Le Gall and Yamina Bettahar, *La pluriparentalité* (Paris: Presses universitaires de France, 2001); Agnes Martial, "Multi-parenthood and Contemporary Family Forms in French Studies," *Antropologia* 6, no. 2 (2019): 13–26.

2 Sarah Franklin, *Biological Relatives: IVF, Stem Cells, and the Future of Kinship* (Durham, NC: Duke University Press, 2013).

3 Rosa Parisi, "Processi di normalizzazione e regimi di verità. Raccontare la famiglia: note a margine di una ricerca sull'omoparentalità," *Voci* 9 (2014): 58–68, 61.

4 Ulrich Beck and Elisabeth Beck-Gernsheim, *Individualization* (Thousand Oaks, CA: Sage, 2002).

5 Florence Weber, *Le sang, le nom, le quotidien. Une sociologie de la parenté pratique* (Paris: Aux Lieux d'être, 2005).

6 In contemporary societies, gay parenting testifies to some trends within the most varied forms of parental relations, such as the primacy of the emotional dimension over the purely biological one, the desired and researched choices of filiation, and the clear dissociation between sexuality and reproduction.

7 Remotti Francesco, *Contro natura. Una lettera al papa* (Rome: Laterza, 2008).

8 Anne Cadoret, *Genitori come gli altri: omosessualità e genitorialità* (Milan: Feltrinelli, 2008).

9 Kees Waaldijk, John Asland, et al., "More or Less Together: Levels of Legal Consequences of Marriage, Cohabitation and Registered Partnership for Different-Sex and Same-Sex Partners. A Comparative Study of Nine European Countries," *Documents de travail* 125 (2005); Kees Waaldijk, "The Right to Relate: On the Importance of 'Orientation' in Comparative Sexual Orientation Law," *Duke Journal of Comparative & International Law* 24 (2013): 161–199.

10 Marie Digoix, "Mariage pour tous: Expériences scandinaves," *P@ges Europe*, January 28, 2013.

11 Alice Sophie Sarcinelli and Charlotte Simon, "'With Your Head Held High': Italian and Belgian Lesbian Parented Families' Claims and Strategies to Obtain Kinning Rights," *Antropologia* 6 (2019): 63–82. For example, on June 7, 2022, the Rete Lenford Network–Avvocatura per I diritti LGBTI+ (Association of Lawyers) and Famiglie Arcobaleno (Rainbow Families) associations proposed the first law written by the associations and not by Parliament. The bill aims to protect LGBTQI+ families and looks at the right to adoption and access to medically assisted procreation. There are four fundamental points of the bill: (1) egalitarian marriage; (2) recognition at birth for sons and daughters of same-sex couples; (3) access to adoptions for single people, regardless of sexual orientation and gender identity, and same-sex couples; and (4) access to medically assisted procreation paths for single women and female couples.

12 Simonetta Grilli and Rosa Parisi, "At the Edge of Reproductive Rights: Some Reflections on the Public and Institutional Debate on Same-Sex Unions and Same-Sex Parenting in Italy," in *Plural Kinship Spaces: Qualitative Approaches of*

Contemporary Intimate and Public (Re)Configurations, ed. Alice Sophie Sarcinelli, Fanny Duysens, and Élodie Razy (Louvain: L'Harmattan, 2020), 185.

13 Chiara Saraceno, *Coppie e famiglie. Non è questione di natura* (Milan: Feltrinelli, 2012); Chiara Saraceno and Manuela Naldini, *Sociologia della famiglia* (Bologna: Mulino: 2021).

14 Monica Bonaccorso, *Mamme e papà omosessuali. Primo saggio italiano sulla famiglia omosessuale* (Rome: Editori Riuniti, 1994); Margherita Bottino and Daniela Danna, *La gaia famiglia. Che cos'è l'omogenitorialità* (Trieste: Asterios, 2005); Chiara Lalli, *Buoni genitori. Storie di mamme e di papà gay* (Milan: Il Saggiatore, 2009).

15 Simonetta Grilli, *Antropologia delle famiglie contemporanee* (Rome: Carocci, 2019).

16 Janik Bastien Charlebois, "Au-delà de la phobie de l'homo: quand le concept d'homophobie porte ombrage à la lutte contre l'hétérosexisme et l'hétéronormativité," *Reflets* 17, no. 1 (2011): 112–149, 114, describes heteronormativity as "the diffusion of theories that consider heterosexuality the standard mode of sexual development and, as a consequence, see homosexuality as a deficit that requires explanation" (translation by the author).

17 Simonetta Grilli, *Antropologia delle famiglie contemporanee* (Rome: Carocci, 2019).

18 Janet Finch, "Displaying Families," *Sociology* 41 (2007): 65–81.

19 Harold Garfinkel, *Studies in Ethnomethodology* (New York: John Wiley, 1967).

20 Court of Minors of Rome, sentence no. 299 of July 10, 2014, applied stepchild adoption in the so-called particular cases (law 184/1983). The Rome Juvenile Court recognized for the first time in Italy the social parenting done by the partner of a child's biological mother, conceived abroad through IVF as part of the couple's joint procreative project.

21 Marco Farina, "Same-Sex Adoptions: The Italian Case," *Italian Law Journal* 3 (2017): 207–220.

22 Corinna S. Guerzoni, *Sistemi procreativi. Etnografia dell'omogenitorialità in Italia* (Milan: Franco Angeli, 2020).

23 In this chapter I refer to some data that I collected through two different ethnographic research projects focused on gay parenting in Italy (2012; 2014–2017). All names are pseudonyms.

24 Simonetta Grilli, "D'autres familles. L'homoparentalité en Italie," *Ethnologie française* 2 (2016): 289–298.

25 Stephen Hicks, *Lesbian, Gay and Queer Parenting: Families, Intimacies, Genealogies* (New York: Palgrave Macmillan, 2011); Ken Plummer, *Intimate Citizenship: Private Decisions and Public Dialogues* (Seattle: University of Washington Press, 2003); Marilyn Strathern, *Kinship, Law and the Unexpected: Relatives are Always a Surprise* (Cambridge: Cambridge University Press, 2005).

26 According to the literature, most Italian gay fathers went to the United States for their surrogacy journey. See, for example, Roberto Baiocco, Nicola Carone, and

Vittorio Lingiardi, "Italian Gay Fathers' Experiences of Transnational Surrogacy and Their Relationship with Surrogate Pre- and Postbirth," *Reproductive Bio-Medicine Online* 34 (2016): 181–190; Guerzoni, *Sistemi procreativi*; Zsuzsa Berend and Corinna S. Guerzoni, "Reshaping Relatedness? The Case of US Surrogacy," *Antropologia* 6 (2019): 82–100.

27 Heather Jacobson, *Labor of Love: Gestational Surrogacy and the Work of Making Babies* (New Brunswick, NJ: Rutgers University Press, 2016); Corinna S. Guerzoni, "Alla ricerca della 'fertilità.' Immaginari e percorsi riproduttivi di pazienti transfrontalieri italiani," *AM Rivista della Società italiana di antropologia medica* 43–46 (2018): 151–176.

28 This situation makes it impossible to obtain the Italian ID necessary to have access to all the benefits reserved for citizens, such as a pediatrician, etc.

29 This request requires additional documentation for the stepchild adoption.

30 In 2020 and 2021, after a flurry of administrative and judicial rulings recognizing some social parents as legal parents, there was backlash due to four negative rulings that made the legal battles in same-sex families more complicated. Specifically, the Constitutional Court (sentence no. 32/2021) rejected the recognition of a social mother while ruling on the insufficiency of stepchild adoption for the purpose of the adequate protection of the interest of the minor and consequently inviting the legislator to fill the regulatory gap. While on the one hand this decision underlines the need to enact a law to protect same-sex families, on the other hand it opens the way to a series of possible negative outcomes due to the interpretability of this verdict in which the social mother has been denied. Currently, stepchild adoption appeal, taken for granted up to that moment, is in an even more uncertain terrain.

31 Stepchild adoption recognizes only the parental relationship of social parents; in this case both social fathers were registered as the legal parents of their non-biological children. However, according to the law under analysis, the children, despite having the same biogenetic connection (the same ova donor), having been born from the same woman (the gestational surrogate), and having been adopted by each social father, are not legally recognized as brothers to each other by the Italian state.

32 In Italy surrogacy is prohibited and is often described as an immoral practice. I analyzed Italian narratives on surrogacy in Corinna S. Guerzoni and Tatiana Motterle, "Sul corpo delle surrogate. Analisi del discorso pubblico italiano sulla gestazione per altri," *Gender/Sexuality/Italy* 5 (2018): 1–22.

3

Stepparents

A Social Science Perspective

MARIE-CHRISTINE SAINT-JACQUES AND MARION ADAMISTE

Two significant shifts in the history of families led to the emergence of stepfamilies: widowhood and, far more common nowadays, parental separation or divorce. The considerably shorter life expectancy in previous centuries left many children without a father or mother.[1] The stepfamily of yore referred to the concept of remarriage, a widespread practice from the sixteenth century to the nineteenth. In recent decades, the formation of stepfamilies in Western societies has flowed from the decreased influence of the Church on individual behavior, the rise in feminism, and more liberal morals influencing expectations in couple relationships.[2] If the relationship is not fulfilling and satisfying, many parents will decide to separate. However, a separation does not mean the end of a parent's love life. In fact, separated parents very often repartner.[3] All of these parents bring a new adult into their child's life and, as will be seen in this chapter, that person may take on varying degrees of parental responsibilities. Because the new adult is not biologically related to and generally has not adopted their partner's child, they are referred to as a social parent. Stepparents are among the most common social parents in the family setting of today's children, and yet they receive little social or legal recognition. However, the tide may be turning.

The goal of this chapter is to better understand this situation by examining the social and cultural context underpinning stepfamilies, the development of roles and relationships in stepfamilies, and some of the consequences of the lack of legal status for stepparents for children's well-being.[4] To properly contextualize the issue, the concept of stepfamilies will be defined and a few demographic indicators provided.

Although the insights from the chapter apply more broadly, it examines Canada as an example of stepparenthood.

What Is a Stepfamily?

A stepfamily is defined as a couple with at least one child born or adopted in a former union.[5] At least one member of the couple is neither the biological nor adoptive parent of one of the children. Stepfamilies in turn may be classified as simple or complex. A simple stepfamily is "a stepfamily in which all children are the biological or adopted children of one, and only one, married spouse or common-law partner, and whose birth or adoption preceded the current relationship."[6]

Blended stepfamilies (also called complex stepfamilies) fall into three categories: (1) a couple with a child/children of one member of the couple only and a child/children born or adopted in the current union; (2) a couple in which each partner has at least one child from a previous union and one child together; and (3) a couple in which both partners have a child/children from a previous union.

The notion of stepfamily has evolved over time to reflect the greater diversity in contemporary stepfamilies as well as the desire for an inclusive definition.[7] An inclusive definition means that "stepfamily" includes couples who either are legally married or cohabit, without distinction about gender. The proportion of couples who cohabit either permanently or before getting married has grown steadily since the 1980s,[8] and it appears to be higher in second unions.[9] Last, children born of previous unions may live with their parent and stepparent either full-time or part-time, which means that many children move between their biological parents' homes.[10]

Extent of the Phenomenon

It is not easy to quantify or compare the extent of the stepfamily phenomenon given the different definitions used, the units of analysis considered (family, couples, or children), and other variables such as the age of children or sibling type involved. Even though some children live with both of their biological parents, they are classified as living in a stepfamily because they have half siblings or stepsiblings, that is, children from their parents' previous unions.[11] That being said, according to the last two population censuses of Canada, roughly 10 percent of children aged birth to fourteen were living in a stepfamily.[12] France reports similar trends,[13] whereas in the United States the proportion of children living in a stepfamily is slightly lower.[14] Stepfamilies account for 5 percent of all families in England and Wales, and three in four stepfamilies include dependent children.[15] The number of stepfamilies is growing in the thirty-seven member countries of the Organisation for Economic Co-operation and Development.[16] These statistics are recognized as underestimating the real proportion of children living in stepfamilies, as censuses often define family on the basis of residence.[17] Children may actually divide their time between the homes of both of their parents.

The issue is also worth examining from a longitudinal perspective. For example, 30 percent of children in Québec have lived with a stepparent by age seventeen.[18] The children transitioned to a stepfamily at the average age of 6.5. Considering only children born outside a union, the average age at the time of transition was 3.8.[19] The young age of children when they enter a stepfamily matters, as it will likely affect their relationship with the stepparent. Children with separated parents have a high probability of becoming part of a stepfamily. In Québec, 47 percent of mothers and 49 percent of fathers of children aged thirteen and under formed stepfamilies with a new partner within five years following separation; after ten years, the share rose to 87 percent.[20] In a survey of recently separated parents conducted in 2018 and 2019, 43 percent of the parents had repartnered two years following separation. Of those parents, 41 percent were living with their new partner all of the time and 41 percent some of the time, each partner having their own home.[21]

Logically, the proliferation of stepfamilies in the past few decades, the fact that a significant proportion of children experience stepfamily life, and the fact that many stepparents carry out parental responsibilities every day should bring stepparents out of the shadows. However, the reality is that stepparents receive little social or legal recognition.[22] There are several contributing factors at play. In keeping with the goal of this chapter, we examine the social and cultural context of stepparenting and the myriad ways in which the status of stepparent is evolving, stepparents play their roles, and relationships develop in stepfamily households.

Barriers to Stepparent Recognition

Social and Cultural Context

The difficulty recognizing the importance of the bonds between stepparents and stepchildren lies in the broader issue of filiation. The very existence of stepfamilies, adoption, and same-sex parents demonstrates that being a parent is about more than biology[23] and that the social and legal dimensions are crucial.[24] However, in Western societies the concept of family is firmly rooted in a culture that values intact two-parent families, and families that do not meet that norm are viewed through a deficit perspective. Such a perspective carries cultural beliefs held by people ranging from families to psychosocial practitioners, judges, mediators, lawmakers, and politicians. Those beliefs influence how families see themselves. For example, laws and public policies help define and shape the concepts of normal and deviant.[25] Giving greater legitimacy to the status of stepparents could help reduce loyalty conflicts, normalize the stepfamily experience, and recognize the specific contribution of stepparents. However, as highlighted by Maclean, Drake, and McKillop, current social policies send conflicting messages to stepfamilies.[26] For example, several countries include the stepparent's income in family income but do not recognize rights or responsibilities for stepparents.

Some public opinion polls demonstrate an openness to giving greater recognition to the stepfamily experience.[27] In a survey of twelve hundred Quebecers, stepfamilies were generally not considered to have less value than intact two-parent families, but they were certainly described in more negative terms.[28] On the basis of various indicators, people recognized and agreed that stepparents assume certain parenting roles. For example, a majority of Quebecers believed that a stepparent who takes care of their partner's child should be able to consult a doctor for a minor health problem. Two-thirds of the respondents said that, in the event of a separation, a stepparent who has lived a significant amount of time with their stepchild should have visitation rights. Although there was less consensus, half of the respondents believed that a stepparent should be able to adopt their stepchild or should provide for the stepchild's financial needs.[29] Half of the respondents felt that a stepparent should not be able to authorize major surgery for the stepchild. People are therefore open to expanding stepparents' rights but not to giving them all of the rights of parents. There is no monolithic opinion. Holtzman also reported a diverse portrait of what constitutes a family in the eyes of university students. Her research revealed changing conceptions of the family and that young adults utilize both traditional and socially expansive definitions.[30]

Mason et al. interviewed stepcouples in the United States to get their opinions on how legislation could give them better support. Once again, the results painted a diverse portrait. Whereas a large group wanted greater authority for the stepparent, a second group wanted more public recognition, more support, and more public awareness and education about stepfamilies. A third group believed that their problems were their own and that the law could do nothing to help. In addition, there was an almost unanimous wish for continued contact with stepchildren in the event of divorce or their partner's death. Several stepparents had even considered seeking primary custody or adopting the child in the event of the death of one of the child's parents but decided not to pursue that option because of the existence of the nonresident biological parent.[31]

The norm of a two-parent family is also deeply ingrained in family law, which is at odds with the logic of a world in which a growing number of children are being raised by multiple parental figures. The majority of children in stepfamilies have another parent, in addition to the stepparent's partner. Consequently, except in very specific circumstances, because the child has another parent who wants to continue serving as a parent, a stepparent cannot adopt and thereby have a legal bond with a stepchild, at least not under Québec's current adoption system. And because they cannot adopt the child, they cannot share parental authority because only parents can exercise such authority. In Québec, as in many other parts of the world, the law does not allow parental responsibilities to be shared among more than two parents.[32] According to both Goubau and Chabot and Willems and Sosson, the law is highly resistant to the concept of multiparenthood, as the current legal system tends to follow the traditional two-parent model.[33] Moreover, recognition of the stepparent status is generally not grounded in an openness to multiparenthood, but rather in recognition of the substitute parent role played by some stepparents. In contrast to Québec, Ontario (whose family law regime is based on common law) is more inclined to recognize and protect multiparent families.[34] Therefore, one of the barriers to recognizing the rights of stepparents is the "two-parent family" legal standard, which does not match the reality of many families.

The Heterogeneous Reality of Stepfamily Roles and Relationships

Another barrier to recognition of the stepparent-stepchild relationship lies in the fact that stepfamilies are not homogeneous. In fact, the multiple realities of stepfamily life intersect on various levels, from the trajectories of stepfamily formation to the status and roles of stepparents within the family.

Diverse Family Trajectories

The diversity in family trajectories is manifested primarily in the conjugal and parental trajectories to stepfamily formation, with the nature, sequence of constituent events, and stability of stepfamily unions varying widely.[35] Some parents repartner with another parent, giving them dual status of parent and stepparent within the stepfamily. In other cases, a separated parent forms a stepfamily with a partner who does not have children. The partner may or may not go on to become a parent in the new union. In addition, some stepfamilies are relatively stable, while others constitute just one of many episodes in the conjugal and parental trajectory. At the time of stepfamily formation, some adults may already have experience in married life, parenting or even stepparenting, while others have just stopped living with their parents. The pathways to stepfamily formation are therefore fairly diverse, which can influence the role stepparents play in their stepchildren's lives.

Diversity in Stepparent Status and Roles

Unlike other social parents (who may or may not have a legal bond with the child), such as adoptive parents, parents of children conceived by gamete donation, adults who have children as part of a parental project involving more than two parents, and coparents who are not lovers, stepparents have a relationship with their partner's children first and foremost because they want to be in a couple with their partner. Indeed, a person generally becomes a stepparent as part of a conjugal project, not necessarily a parental project. Furthermore, part of the reason for the diversity is that the stepparent role is not quite socially defined yet.[36] This diversity can be more deeply understood by examining the status conferred on stepparents within the stepfamily from the perspective of those involved: young and adult stepchildren, the parents, the stepparents, and the nonresident parent.[37] Several such studies highlight the heterogeneity of the stepparent status based on stepparenting practices or how they are represented, which can be considered on a continuum.

At one end of the continuum lie situations where the stepparent plays no parental role whatsoever. There is no meaningful bond between the stepchildren and stepparent. The latter is perceived as someone who is part of the child's environment but is not considered to be a family member or parent. The stepparent may be thought of as the parent's spouse only, but the relationship may also be marked by rejection or indifference. At the other end of the continuum lie situations where the stepparent is treated on the same footing as a parent and clearly plays a role in the family life. For example, some stepfathers are seen as having an obligation to assume paternal responsibilities.[38] As well, two-thirds of children who reported having close relationships with their stepfathers considered their stepfathers as parents.[39] Somewhat fewer stepdaughters felt the same way about their stepmothers, although some saw their stepmother as a member of the family and even a second mother.[40] Data collected from a cohort study of Québec children followed from birth revealed that one in one hundred children aged nineteen identified their stepmother as their primary mother figure, and nearly three in one hundred identified their stepfather as their primary father figure.[41] Last, a number of studies report on a middle ground, where the stepparent's role is that of a friend, mentor, family member, or caring adult, while making a clear distinction between the stepparent's role and that of the parent, even establishing a parental hierarchy. For example, children felt close to their stepparent but did not see them as a parent.[42]

The diversity in stepparent roles is common across cultures, including the United States, New Zealand, Japan,[43] Québec,[44] France,[45] and Finland.[46] Numerous studies demonstrate the heterogeneous nature of stepparent status and roles negotiated between the parties involved. An analysis of those studies leads to four observations. First, the arrival of a stepparent disrupts the coparenting relationship established between the child's parents following separation.[47] Moreover, some former spouses might fear that they are being replaced as a parent and try to limit the stepparent's involvement.[48] Second, depending on the stepfamily, stepparents may or may not be involved in the coparenting system. Some parents (be it the one in a stepcouple or the other parent) tend to make the stepparent an active participant in the coparenting team, whereas others limit the team to the parents only.[49] Other stepparents view themselves as a mentor or friend to their stepchildren, rather than as a parental figure.[50] This diversity in status and roles is seen among both stepfathers and stepmothers. For example, studies of stepfathers revealed that some carry out the functions of a father or similar to those of a father,[51] whereas others view themselves as an additional parent; that is, they provide support to the existing "parenting team." Crohn's work shows that stepmother-stepdaughter relationships vary just as widely as stepfather-stepchild relationships, with stepmothers' roles described as anything from "another mom" to "a friend."[52]

Third, the role played by stepparents included in the coparenting system is in line with multiparenthood or substitute parenthood. In both cases, the stepparent is a parental figure, but in the former the stepparent works side by side with the parents: together, they form a parenting threesome or even foursome,[53] and the stepparent is part of a team that considers children to benefit from having more than two parental figures. In the logic of substitute parenthood, the stepparent is an important parental figure who makes up for the fact that the child's other parent is virtually absent or disengaged or, in the parent's view, has trouble effectively playing their parental role.[54] In some cases, the stepparent is the only coparent supporting the parent.[55] In addition, the stepparent may be not only a substitute for the nonresident parent but also a substitute for the stepparent's own partner. Such is the case, for example, where a stepmother allies with a mother who thinks the child's father is not really involved in the parenting process.[56] Fourth, regardless of the extent of stepparent involvement, the child's parent often remains the ultimate decision maker,[57] setting the boundaries of the stepfather's involvement.[58] For example, in shared-custody families, mothers view themselves as having primary responsibility for their children.[59]

The contribution of stepparents to everyday child-rearing takes different forms and, once again, varies considerably among stepparents and among stepfathers and stepmothers.[60] Stepparents are commonly primary caregivers to their stepchildren,[61] contributing to everyday parenting tasks such as helping with homework, transporting children, and making meals, in the same way as biological parents. They may also be active participants in the stepchildren's upbringing without necessarily taking the lead, by giving advice, sharing decision making, or supporting the parent in administering discipline. Studies show that the roles played by stepparents can also depend on stepparents' personality and strengths as well as those of their partner.[62] Stepparents who act as substitute parents have a greater tendency to step into roles traditionally occupied by parents, such as parent-teacher meetings, child discipline, and general participation in all aspects of child-rearing. However, many stepparents who are a parental figure to their stepchildren are careful not to take the parent's place.[63]

Contributing Factors to the Observed Diversity

Multiple factors influence the status and roles of stepparents as well as the quality of the stepparent-stepchild relationship. Some are temporal, such as how long the stepfamily has existed, the stepchildren's age when they transitioned to a stepfamily,[64] and their stage of development. Nor is the stepparent's role static; rather it changes over time as the stepparent develops ties with the child and as the cohabiting parent's and other parent's views of the stepparent's involvement change. For example, some mothers might initially want to exclude the stepmother but come around over time. The relationship between stepchildren and their stepparent is influenced by the effort each one makes to build a relationship. Stepparents do not let rejection deter them.[65] Stepchildren are key actors in the development of bonds and not merely reactive to stepparents' behaviors.[66] Children who initially had a difficult relationship with their stepparent but eventually decided to get closer to them had a stepparent who was determined to build a positive relationship despite the child's rejection.[67] Shared parenting time and the amount of time spent with the stepparent are also factors shaping the stepparent's role.[68] For example, a stepparent may be more involved if children are in shared custody, and a nonresident stepmother will be less likely to play a mothering role.[69] In addition to temporal factors, events may occur in the family life course that force the stepparent to assume parental roles, such as exercising authority.[70] Other factors include gender, affinities, the relationship with each of the biological parents, the resources allocated to the child, and the fact of supporting children from a previous union. In addition, stepparents (there is more literature on stepfather families in this regard) have a greater tendency to take on a substitute parent role where the other biological parent is not very involved or is even absent.[71]

A Few Consequences of the Lack of Social and Legal Recognition of the Stepparent Status

The substantiated diversity in stepparent status and roles calls for qualifying the consequences of the little social and legal recognition given to stepparents. The overall finding, however, is that there is a paradox between the experience of a substantial number of stepfamilies and the current family law system. In fact, several studies demonstrate that many stepparents, parents, children, and sometimes the nonresident parent see the stepparent as a parental figure.[72] But while stepparents may play a significant role in stepfamily life, they have no legal rights or legitimate authority with regard to schooling, health care, social services, recreational opportunities, and other institutions that deal with families,[73] because in Canada and Québec family laws fall short of fully recognizing multiparenthood.[74] At the international level, recognition and protection of the stepparent-stepchild relationship vary widely across jurisdictions. The observed differences relate to the existence of a specific legal status, rights, and obligations.[75] There is a gap between some of the functions some stepparents fulfill and the lack of parental authority granted to them. As highlighted by various researchers, the diversity in family arrangements has challenged family law since the late twentieth century.[76] Family law lags behind social change.[77]

Another paradox lies in the little importance given to stepparents' and stepchildren's investment in their relationship during their life together. This investment is sometimes related to family and societal expectations of the stepparent and stepchild (establishing a respectful, harmonious and meaningful relationship), with the result that some children form a close bond with their stepparent, who has become a very significant person in their life over time. Malia points out that child development research, especially relating to children going through family transitions brought about by parental separation, clearly supports the contention that, in contrast to traditional legal options, stepfamily members generally will benefit from law reforms that facilitate multiple and secure parental relationships.[78] Such reforms foster the psychological, emotional, and economic well-being of children and reduce reliance on state welfare. Stepparents can make a difference in the economic well-being of their stepchildren.[79] Although expectations about stepparents' financial obligations toward their stepchildren vary,[80] the financial resources provided by a stepparent can help prevent children's economic vulnerability, not only during the stepcouple union but also after it ends. For that to happen, laws and policies must be grounded in a definition of family that is inclusive[81] and does not allow for differential treatment of children from the same sibling group based on the fact that some have legal ties to the parental figures and others have social ties.

Furthermore, in the event of the end of the stepcouple union, the stepparent-stepchild relationship might not be protected. It will be argued that the relationship should not continue because there is no bond of filiation between the stepparent and stepchild and that the children's everyday lives are complicated enough just trying to maintain contact with their parents. However, the complexities of the stepparent-stepchild relationship do not begin with the end of the couple union: they existed from the start. The goal of giving greater recognition to the stepparent-stepchild relationship is to fulfil children's needs for stability and maintenance of bonds of attachment. This is especially important given that stepcouples tend to break up at a higher rate than couples in their first unions.[82] It is also important to note that according to several legal experts, contact is the right of the child, not of the stepparent.[83] In addition, the right to maintain contact is not tantamount to custodial or access rights, including visitation and sleepovers. Contact may be in the form of phone calls or video chats.

Placing greater importance on the stepparent-stepchild relationship in family law comes with challenges,[84] one of which concerns our ability to properly differentiate between situations so as to account for the diverse ties between a stepparent and stepchild. In particular, it is important to distinguish between (1) a stepparent who plays a supporting role when the stepfamily is formed and whose relationship with the child is essentially defined through the relationship with the child's parent; (2) a stepparent who actually performs parental functions, is viewed by the child as a parental figure in addition to the biological parents, to whom the child has become close, and with whom a total severing of ties would be detrimental to the child; and (3) a stepparent who serves as a substitute or replacement parent (following the other parent's death or disengagement) by exercising parental responsibilities (relational and economic) in a continuous and permanent manner and who claims the child as their own. This stepparent stands *in loco parentis* to the child.

It is seemingly not easy to distinguish a highly involved, generous stepparent from a stepparent who claims the stepchild as their own. However, the distinction is important because the rights and obligations of stepparents and stepchildren are quite different. Moreover, Malia foresees considerable social resistance to recognition of stepparents' social responsibility.[85]

Furthermore, it is important to stress the fact that some research, findings, and practitioner input on parental separation and intimate partner violence highlight the need to be vigilant of situations where children might be instrumentalized in a stepcouple breakup.[86] This dynamic sometimes occurs following parental separation, but children can also be instrumentalized when a stepcouple separates.

Conclusion

The emotional and social ties between a stepchild and stepparent can vary considerably across stepfamilies. Furthermore, many stepparents carry out some, but not necessarily all, parental functions. The question is whether this makes them any less of a parental figure, especially in the stepchild's eyes. The lack of social and legal recognition of stepparents testifies to our difficulty imagining that children could have more than two parental figures. This way of thinking makes children vulnerable by potentially depriving them of resources that contribute to their well-being. It also does an injustice to social parents fully invested in their partner's children. The increase in stepfamilies should be an incentive to look for ways to ensure greater continuity, coherence, and respect with the best interests of the child in mind.

NOTES

1 André Burguière, Christiane Klapish-Zuber, Martine Segalen, and Françoise Zonabend, *Histoire de la famille*, vol. 2 (Paris: Armand. Colin, 1986); Martine Segalen, *Sociologie de la famille*, 2nd ed. (Paris: Armand Colin, 1988).

2 Renée B. Dandurand, *Le mariage en question: essai sociohistorique* (Québec: Institut québécois de recherche sur la culture, 1988).

3 Marie-Christine Saint-Jacques, Arnaud Régnier-Loilier, and Philippe Pacaut, "Diversité conjugale et familiale chez les parents québécois récemment séparés: aller au-delà du prisme de la cohabitation," in *La séparation parentale et la recomposition familiale dans la société québécoise: les premiers moments*, ed. Marie-Christine Saint-Jacques, Caroline Robitaille, Amandine Baude, Élisabeth Godbout, and Sylvie Lévesque (Québec: Presses de l'Université Laval, 2022).

4 Some parts of this chapter are a synthesis of a text previously published in French. See M.-C. Saint-Jacques, "Reconnaître socialement et juridiquement le statut de beau-parent pour protéger les droits des enfants," in *La jeunesse au carrefour de la famille, de la communauté, du droit et de la société Youth at the Crossroads of Family, Community, Law and Society*, ed. P. Noreau, D. Goubau, M.-C. Saint-Jacques, and S. Van Praagh (Québec: Éditions Thémis, 2021).

5 Such families are most commonly called stepfamilies or, to a lesser extent, blended families. Although these are two distinct concepts, they are sometimes used synonymously, which creates confusion in the literature. Heather Juby, Nicole Marcil-Gratton, and Céline Le Bourdais, with the collaboration of Paul-Marie Huot, "A Step Further in Family Life: The Emergence of the Blended Family," in *Report on the Demographic Situation in Canada*, catalogue no. 91-209-XIE, ed. Alain Bélanger, Yves Carrière, and Stéphane Gilbert (Ottawa: Statistics Canada, 2006).

6 Statistics Canada, *Portrait of Children's Family Life in Canada in 2016*, catalogue no. 98-200-X2016006 (Ottawa: Minister of Industry, 2017), 8.

7 Margaret Howden, "Stepfamilies: Understanding and Responding Effectively," AFRC Briefing (Australian Family Relationships Clearinghouse, 2007), 6.

8 Larry Bumpass and Hsien-Hen Lu, "Trends in Cohabitation and Implications for Children's Family Contexts in the United States," *Population Studies* 54 (2000): 27.

9 Suzan D. Stewart, *Brave New Stepfamilies: Diverse Paths toward Stepfamily Living* (Thousand Oaks, CA: Sage, 2007); Jay Teachman, "Complex Life Course Patterns and the Risk of Divorce in Second Marriages," *Journal of Marriage and Family* 70 (2008): 294.

10 Saint-Jacques, Régnier-Loilier, and Pacaut, "Diversité conjugale."

11 Aude Lapinte, "Un enfant sur dix vit dans une famille recomposée," INSEE première, no. 1470 (Ottawa: Statistics Canada, 2013).

12 Statistics Canada, *Portrait of Families and Living Arrangements in Canada 2011,: Families, Households and Marital Status*, catalogue no. 98-312-X2011001 (Ottawa: Census of Population, Minister of Industry, 2012); Statistics Canada, *Portrait of Children's Family Life.*

13 Lapinte, "Un enfant sur dix."

14 Rose M. Kreider and Renée Ellis, "Living Arrangements of Children: 2009. Current Population Reports" (Washington, DC: U.S. Census Bureau, 2011), 70–126; Kelly R. Raley and Megan M. Sweeney, "Divorce, Repartnering, and Stepfamilies: A Decade in Review," *Journal of Marriage and Family* 82 (2020): 81.

15 Chris W. Smith, "Census Analysis: How Do Living Arrangements, Family Type and Family Size Vary in England and Wales?" (London: Office for National Statistics, 2014).

16 OECD, "Treating All Children as Equal: Why Policies Should Adapt to the Diversification of Family Living Arrangements," Policy Brief on Child Well-Being, vol. 240 (Paris: OECD, 2019).

17 Catherine Castagner Giroux, Céline Le Bourdais, and Philippe Pacaut, "Séparation parentale et recomposition familiale: Esquisse des tendances démographiques au Québec," in *Séparation parentale, recomposition familiale: Enjeux contemporains*, ed. Marie-Christine Saint-Jacques, Caroline Robitaille, Annick Stamand, and Sylvie Lévesque (Québec: PUQ, 2016), 11–34.

18 Québec is the largest province in Canada in terms of area and, after Ontario, the second most populated (8,604,495 inhabitants). Statistics Canada, "Annual Demographic Estimates: Canada, Pronvinces and Territories" (Ministry of Industry, 2021), catalogue no. 91-215-X, ISSN 1911-2408.

19 Hélène Desrosiers and Karine Tétreault, *Les trajectoires familiales diversifiées des jeunes nés au Québec à la fin des années 1990*, Collection Portraits et Trajectoires, no. 23 (Québec: ISQ, 2018).

20 Heather Juby, Céline Le Bourdais, and Nicole Marcil-Gratton, *Linking Family Change, Parents' Employment and Income and Children's Economic Well-Being: A Longitudinal Perspective* (Ottawa: Department of Justice Canada, 2003).

21 Saint-Jacques, Régnier-Loilier, and Pacaut, "Diversité conjugale."

22 Gwendoline Motte, "Multiplication of Potential Social and Emotional Ties," in *Adults and Children in Postmodern Societies: A Comparative Law and Multidisciplinary Handbook*, ed. Jehanne Sosson, Geoffrey Willems, and Gwendoline Motte (Cambridge: Intersentia, 2019); Saint-Jacques, "Reconnaître socialement et juridiquement."

23 Marie-France Bureau, *Le droit de la filiation entre ciel et terre: Étude du discours juridique québécois* (Cowansville: Éditions Yvon Blais, 2009).

24 Hélène Belleau, "Être parent aujourd'hui: la construction du lien de filiation dans l'univers symbolique de la parenté," *Enfances, Familles, Générations* 1 (2004).

25 Sarah E. C. Malia, "Balancing Family Members' Interests Regarding Stepparent Rights and Obligations: A Social Policy Challenge," *Family Relations* 54 (2005): 298; Mellisa Holtzman, "Defining Family: Young Adults' Perceptions of the Parent-Child Bond," *Journal of Family Communication* 8 (2008): 167; Erica De'Ath, "Stepfamily Policy from the Perspective of a Stepfamily Organisation," *Marriage and Family Review* 26 (1997), in Malia, "Balancing Family Members' Interests."

26 Miriam J. Maclean, Deirdre Drake, and Diane McKillop, "Perceptions of Stepfathers' Obligations to Financially Support Stepchildren," *Journal of Family and Economic Issues* 37 (2016): 285.

27 Marie-Christine Saint-Jacques, Élisabeth Godbout, and Hans Ivers, "People's Opinions and Stereotypes about Stepfamilies," *Journal of Family Issues* 41 (2020): 2136.

28 Saint-Jacques, Godbout, and Ivers, "People's Opinions and Stereotypes about Stepfamilies."

29 Maclean, Drake, and McKillop, "Perceptions of Stepfathers' Obligations."

30 Holtzman, "Defining Family."

31 Mary A. Mason, Sydney Harrison-Jay, Gloria M. Svare, and Nicholas H. Wolfinger, "Stepparents: De Facto Parents or Legal Strangers?," *Journal of Family Issues* 23 (2002) 507.

32 Geoffrey Willems and Jehanne Sosson, "The Future of Legal Relationships between Adults and Children," in Sosson, Willems, and Motte, *Adults and Children in Postmodern Societies*, 825–856.

33 Dominique Goubau and Martin Chabot, "Recomposition familiale et multiparentalité: Un exemple du difficile arrimage du droit à la famille contemporaine," *Cahiers de droit* 59 (2018): 889; Willems and Sosson, "Future of Legal Relationships."

34 Willems and Sosson, "Future of Legal Relationships."

35 Juby, Le Bourdais, and Marcil-Gratton, *Linking Family Change*; Marie-Christine Saint-Jacques, Ana Gherghel, Sylvie Drapeau, Marie-Hélène Gagné, Claudine Parent, Caroline Robitaille, and Élisabeth Godbout, "La diversité des trajectoires de recomposition familiale," *Politiques sociales et familiales* 27 (2009): 96.

36 Marie-Christine Saint-Jacques and Sylvie Drapeau, "Dans quel type de familles grandiront les enfants québécois en 2020? Un examen de la diversité familiale et des défis qui y sont associés," in *La famille à l'horizon 2020*, ed. Gilles Pronovost, Chantal Dumont, and Isabelle Bitaudeau (Québec: Presses de l'Université du Québec, 2008), 101–143; Irène Théry, "Le temps des recompositions," in *Familles: permanence et métamorphoses*, ed. J.-F. Dortier (Auxerre Cedex: Sciences Humaines Éditions, 2002), 59.

37 Constance R. Ahrons, "Family Ties after Divorce: Long-Term Implications for Children," *Family Process* 46 (2016): 53; Lies Blyaert, Hanna Van Parys, Jan De Mol, and Ann Buysse, "Like a Parent and a Friend, but Not the Father: A Qualitative Study of Stepfathers' Experiences in the Stepfamily," *Australian and New Zealand Journal of Family Therapy* 37 (2016): 119; Helen M. Crohn, "Five Styles of Positive Stepmothering from the Perspective of Young Adult Stepdaughters," *Journal of Divorce & Remarriage* 46 (2006): 119; Didier Le Gall and Claude Martin, "Transitions familiales, logiques de recomposition et modes de régulation conjugale," in *Les recompositions familiales aujourd'hui*, ed. Marie-Thérèse Meulders-Klein and Irène Théry (Paris: Nathan, 1993), 137; Claudine Parent, Madeleine Beaudry, Marie-Christine Saint-Jacques, Daniel Turcotte, Caroline

Robitaille, Marie Boutin, and Catherine Turbide, "Les représentations sociales de l'engagement parental du beau-père en famille recomposée," *Enfances, familles, générations* 8 (2008): 154; Lawrence H. Ganong, Marilyn Coleman, and Tyler Jamison, "Patterns of Stepchild–Stepparent Relationship Development," *Journal of Marriage and Family* 73 (2011): 396; Marie-Christine Saint-Jacques, "L'ajustement des adolescents et des adolescentes dans les familles recomposées: étude des processus familiaux et des représentations des jeunes" (doctoral thesis, Université de Montréal, 1998); Maria Schmeeckle, Roseann Giarrusso, Du Feng, and Vern L. Bengtson, "What Makes Someone Family? Adult Children's Perceptions of Current and Former Stepparents," *Journal of Marriage and Family* 68 (2006): 595.

38 Parent et al., "Les représentations sociales."

39 Ahrons, "Family Ties after Divorce."

40 Crohn, "Five Styles of Positive Stepmothering."

41 Data compiled from final master file E20 of the ÉLDEQ (2017), Gouvernement du Québec, Institut de la statistique du Québec, calculations by Marie-Christine Saint-Jacques and Hans Ivers (2019).

42 Blyaert et al., "Like a Parent and a Friend"; Shannon E. Weaver and Marilyn Coleman, "A Mothering but Not a Mother Role: A Grounded Theory Study of the Nonresidential Stepmother Role," *Journal of Social and Personal Relationship* 22 (2005): 477.

43 Based on the analysis by Lawrence H. Ganong and Marilyn Coleman, *Stepfamily Relationships: Development, Dynamics and Interventions*, 2nd ed. (New York: Springer, 2017).

44 Saint-Jacques, "L'ajustement des adolescents"; Parent et al., "Les représentations sociales."

45 Sylvie Cadolle, "Les belles-mères, entre idéal de coparentalité et asymétrie homme/femme," *Dialogue* 3 (2013): 35; Le Gall and Martin, "Transitions familiales"; Claude Martin, "Transitions familiales—Évolution du réseau social et familial après la désunion et modes de régulation sociale" (doctoral thesis, Université de Paris VIII Vincennes à Saint-Denis, 1992).

46 Minna Murtorinne-Lahtinen and Kimmo Jokinen, "Stepmothers in Narratives: Negotiations on Relatedness," *Families, Relationships and Societies* 7 (2018): 285.

47 Karl Adamsons and Kay Pasley, "Coparenting Following Divorce and Relationship Dissolution," in *Handbook of Divorce and Relationship Dissolution*, ed. M. A. Fine and J. H. Harvey (Mahwah, NJ: Erlbaum, 2006), 241; Donna Hendrickson Christensen and Kathryn D. Rettig, "The Relationship of Remarriage to Post-divorce Co-parenting," *Journal of Divorce & Remarriage* 24 (1996): 73; Julie Tremblay, Sylvie Drapeau, Caroline Robitaille, Émile Piché, Marie-Hélène Gagné, and Marie-Christine Saint-Jacques, "Trajectoires de coparentalité post-rupture conjugale. Une étude exploratoire qualitative," *La revue internationale de l'éducation familiale* 33 (2013): 37.

48 Claire Cartwright and Kerry Gibson, "The Effects of Co-parenting Relationships with Ex-spouses on Couples in Step-Families," *Family Matters* 92 (2013): 18; Mari-

lyn Coleman, Mark A. Fine, Lawrence H. Ganong, Kimberly J. M. Downs, and Nicole Paul, "When You're Not the Brady Bunch: Identifying Perceived Conflicts and Resolution Strategies in Stepfamilies," *Personal Relationships* 8 (2001): 55; L. J Doodson, "Understanding the Factors Related to Stepmother Anxiety: A Qualitative Approach," *Journal of Divorce & Remarriage* 55 (2014): 645.

49 Marion Adamiste, "Couple recomposé et parents séparés: comprendre l'exercice de la coparentalité au sein des familles recomposées" (doctoral thesis, École de psychologie, Université Laval, 2022); Lawrence Ganong, Marilyn Coleman, Tyler Jamison, and Richard Feistman, "Divorced Mothers' Coparental Boundary Maintenance after Parents Repartner," *Journal of Family Psychology* 299 (2015): 93; Dawn O. Braithwaite, M. Chad McBride, and Paul Schrodt, "'Parent Teams' and the Everyday Interactions of Co-parenting in Stepfamilies," *Communication Reports* 16 (2003): 93; Paul Schrodt, "Coparental Communication with Nonresidential Parents as a Predictor of Couples' Relational Satisfaction and Mental Health in Stepfamilies," *Western Journal of Communication* 74 (2010): 484.

50 Blyaert et al., "Like a Parent and a Friend"; Rex Forehand, Justin Parent, Andrew Golub, and Megan Reid, "Male Cohabiting Partners as Primary Coparents in Low-Income Black Stepfamilies," *Journal of Child and Family Studies* 24 (2015): 2874; Ganong et al., "Divorced Mothers' Coparental Boundary Maintenance."

51 Kari Lee Adamsons, Kay Pasley, and Marion O'Brien, "An Ecological Approach to Father Involvement in Biological and Stepfather Families," *Fathering* 5 (2007): 129; Sylvie Cadolle, "Séparation des parents et passage à l'âge adulte fragilisé," in *Précarités et éducation familiales*, ed. Chantal Zaouche-Gaudron, Claire Safont-Mottay, Olivia Troupel-Cremel, Véronique Rouyer, and Myriam De Léonardis (Toulouse: Érès, 2009), 39; William Marsiglio, "When Stepfathers Claim Stepchildren: A Conceptual Analysis," *Journal of Marriage and Family* 66 (2004): 22; Parent et al., "Les représentations sociales"; Gloria M. Svare, Sydney Jay, and Mary Ann Mason, "Stepparents on Stepparenting: An Exploratory Study of Stepparenting Approaches," *Journal of Divorce & Remarriage* 41 (2004): 81.

52 Helen Crohn, "Young Women Recall Their Positive Relationships with Their Mothers and Stepmothers," *Dissertation Abstracts International Section A: Humanities and Social Sciences* 66 (2005): 1957; Crohn, "Five Styles of Positive Stepmothering."

53 Adamiste, "Couple recomposé et parents séparés"; Braithwaite, McBride, and Schrodt, "'Parent Teams.'"

54 Adamiste, "Couple recomposé et parents séparés"; Linda M. Burton and Cecily R. Hardaway, "Low-Income Mothers as 'Other Mothers' to Their Romantic Partners' Children: Women's Coparenting in Multiple Partner Fertility Relationships," *Family Process* 51 (2012): 343; Forehand et al., "Male Cohabiting Partners"; Ganong et al., "Divorced Mothers' Coparental Boundary Maintenance"; Martin, "Transitions familiales"; Claudine Parent and Caroline Robitaille, "Portrait de familles recomposées: analyse du discours de conjoints et de conjointes vivant en famille recomposée," *Intervention* 122 (2005): 102; Saint-Jacques, "L'ajustement des

adolescents"; Michelle Sweet, "Formation and Features of a Stepparent Identity" (PhD diss., Institute for Clinical Social Work, 2002).

55 Adamiste, "Couple recomposé et parents séparés"; Forehand et al., "Male Cohabiting Partners."

56 Ganong et al., "Divorced Mothers' Coparental Boundary Maintenance."

57 Parent et al., "Les représentations sociales."

58 William Marsiglio and Ramon Hinojosa, "Managing the Multifather Family: Stepfathers as Father Allies," *Journal of Marriage and Family* 69 (2007): 845; Parent et al., "Les représentations sociales"; Adamiste, "Couple recomposé et parents séparés"; Karen Ripoll-Núñez, Karen Martinez Arrieta, and Angela Maria Giraldo Gallo, "Decisiones sobre crianza de los hijos en familias reconstituidas," *Revista Colombiana de Psicología* 22 (2013): 163.

59 Nicolas Favez, Eric D. Widmer, Minh-Thuy Doan, and Hervé Tissot, "Coparenting in Stepfamilies: Maternal Promotion of Family Cohesiveness with Partner and with Father," *Journal of Child and Family Studies* 24 (2015): 3268; Ganong et al., "Divorced Mothers' Coparental Boundary Maintenance."

60 Ripoll-Núñez, Arrieta, and Gallo, "Decisiones sobre crianza"; Kristin Hadfield and Elizabeth Nixon, "Comparison of Relationship Dynamics within Stepmother and Stepfather Families in Ireland," *Irish Journal of Psychology* 33 (2012): 100.

61 Mason et al., "Stepparents"; Hadfield and Nixon, "Comparison of Relationship Dynamics"; Murtorinne-Lahtinen and Jokinen, "Stepmothers in Narratives."

62 Adamiste, "Couple recomposé et parents séparés."

63 Blyaert et al., "Like a Parent and a Friend"; Hadfield and Nixon, "Comparison of Relationship Dynamics."

64 Ganong, Coleman, and Jamison, "Patterns of Stepchild–Stepparent Relationship Development"; Annkatrine Liegmann Gates, "Stepmothers' Coparenting Experience with the Mother in Joint Custody Stepfamilies," *Journal of Divorce & Remarriage* 60 (2019): 253.

65 Ganong, Coleman, and Jamison, "Patterns of Stepchild–Stepparent Relationship Development"; Gates, "Stepmothers' Coparenting Experience."

66 Ganong and Coleman, *Stepfamily Relationships*.

67 Ganong, Coleman, and Jamison, "Patterns of Stepchild–Stepparent Relationship Development."

68 Ahrons, "Family Ties after Divorce."

69 Weaver and Coleman, "Mothering but Not a Mother Role," 477.

70 Gates, "Stepmothers' Coparenting Experience."

71 Parent et al., "Les représentations sociales"; Gloria M. Svare, Sydney Jay, and Mary Ann Mason, "Stepparents on Stepparenting: An Exploratory Study of Stepparenting Approaches," *Journal of Divorce & Remarriage* 41 (2004): 81; Ganong et al., "Divorced Mothers' Coparental Boundary Maintenance"; Crohn, "Five Styles of Positive Stepmothering."

72 Mason et al., "Stepparents"; Adamiste, "Couple recomposé et parents séparés"; Forehand et al., "Male Cohabiting Partners"; Ahrons, "Family Ties after Divorce";

Saint-Jacques, "L'ajustement des adolescents"; Adamiste, "Couple recomposé et parents séparés"; Braithwaite, McBride, and Schrodt, "'Parent Teams'"; Ganong et al., "Divorced Mothers' Coparental Boundary Maintenance"; Marsiglio and Hinojosa, "Managing the Multifather Family."

73 Pamela J. Henry and James McCue, "The Experience of Nonresidential Stepmothers," *Journal of Divorce & Remarriage* 50 (2009): 185; Claudine Parent and Madeleine Beaudry, "Le développement de l'insatisfaction conjugale dans un contexte de recomposition familiale," *Revue canadienne de santé mentale communautaire* 21 (2002): 153; Claudine Parent and Caroline Robitaille, "Statut et rôle parental des beaux-pères dans les familles recomposées; Intervention sociale en protection de la jeunesse," in *Éthique et Famille*, vol. 1, ed. Edwidge Rude-Antoine and Marc Piévic (Paris: L'Harmattan, 2011), 101; Claudine Parent, Marie-Christine Saint-Jacques, Madeleine Beaudry, and Caroline Robitaille, "Stepfather Involvement in Social Interventions Made by Youth Protection Services in Stepfamilies," *Child and Family Social Work* 12 (2007): 229.

74 Dominique Goubau, "Le statut du tiers 'significatif' in les familles recomposées," *Développements récents en droit familial* 340 (2011), www.caij.qc.ca.

75 Motte, "Multiplication of Potential Social and Emotional Ties."

76 Jason D. Hans, "Stepparenting after Divorce: Stepparents' Legal Position regarding Custody, Access, and Support," *Family Relations* 51 (2002): 301; Claudine Parent, Amélie Poulin, and Caroline Robitaille, "Regard critique sur un rôle inventé: le rôle beau-parental," in *Séparation, monoparentalité et recomposition familiale*, ed. Marie-Christine Saint-Jacques, Daniel Turcotte, Sylvie Drapeau, and Richard Cloutier (Québec: Les Presses de l'Université Laval, 2004), 127; Comité Consultatif Sur Le Droit De La Famille, Alain Roy (prés.), *Pour un droit de la famille adapté aux nouvelles réalités conjugales et familiales* (Québec: Ministère de la Justice du Québec, 2015), www.justice.gouv.qc.ca.

77 Goubau and Chabot, "Recomposition familiale et multiparentalité."

78 Malia, "Balancing Family Members' Interests."

79 Mason et al., "Stepparents"; Forehand et al., "Male Cohabiting Partners"; Ganong and Coleman, *Stepfamily Relationships*.

80 Maclean, Drake, and McKillop, "Perceptions of Stepfathers' Obligations."

81 OECD, "Treating All Children as Equal."

82 Marie-Christine Saint-Jacques, Caroline Robitalle, Élisabeth Godbout, Claudine Parent, Sylvie Drapeau, and Marie-Hélène Gagné, "The Process Distinguishing Stable from Unstable Stepfamily Couples: A Qualitative Analysis," *Family Relations* 60 (2011): 545.

83 Comité Consultatif Sur Le Droit De La Famille, *Pour un droit de la famille*.

84 Saint-Jacques, "Reconnaître socialement et juridiquement."

85 Malia, "Balancing Family Members' Interests."

86 Claudette Guilmaine, *Vivre une garde partagée : une histoire d'engagement parental* (Montréal: Éditions du Chu Sainte-Justine, 2009); Janet Johnston, Vivienne Roseby, and Kathryn Kuehnle, *In the Name of the Child: A Developmental Ap-*

proach to Understanding and Helping Children of Conflicted and Violent Divorce (New York: Springer, 2009); Regroupement des maisons pour femmes victimes de violence conjugale, "Droit de la famille: viser la protection des femmes et des enfants" (brief, Commission citoyenne sur le droit de la famille, June 14, 2018), 22–23; Maryse Rinfret-Raynor, Myriam Dubé, Christine Drouin, Nicole Maillé, and Elizabeth Harper, "Violence conjugale post-séparation en contexte d'exercice des droits d'accès post-séparation," in *Violences faites aux femmes*, ed. Suzanne Arcand, Dominique Damant, Sylvie Gravel, and Elizabeth Harper (Québec: Presses de l'Université du Québec, 2008), 185.

4

Nonparental Primary Caregivers

A Case Study from the United States

KRISTINA BRANT

Extended family members and close friends who are like family (i.e., *fictive kin*) have long assumed important child-rearing responsibilities in the United States, particularly among families from ethnic minority and/or economically disadvantaged backgrounds.[1] In recent years, however, there has been an increase in the number of relatives and fictive kin who act in *primary* caregiving roles without a biological parent present.[2] In large part this increase has stemmed from the U.S. opioid crisis, which has increased rates of substance use disorder and drug overdose deaths among parents.[3] In such situations, nonparental primary caregivers may gain some rights and responsibilities regarding the child if they are granted guardianship or legal custody, and they may become a legal parent if they adopt the child. However, many of these caregivers never have their roles formalized in any way by the state; these nonparental primary caregivers serve as social parents but lack recognition as legal parents.

This chapter begins with a review of the prevalence and importance of relative and fictive kin caregivers in the United States. I then turn to a case study to highlight some of the challenges faced by these nonparental primary caregivers who serve only as social parents, lacking legal rights and recognition. Drawing on primary data with relatives and fictive kin who step in to raise children amid parental substance use disorder, I highlight *why* relative and fictive kin caregivers often take on caregiving roles without legal recognition and *how* that lack of legal recognition can harm family well-being. I also consider how biological parents in these situations can become social parents themselves when their rights are terminated but they remain a presence in the caregiver's and child's lives.

Ultimately, this work sheds light on the hardships that result when social and legal institutions do not recognize the labor shouldered by social parents and the importance of these parent-child bonds.

The Caregiving Roles of Relatives and Fictive Kin

Traditionally, social science and legal scholarship on "the family" has privileged one normative family type—the "Standard North American Family," or SNAF, which consists of a husband and wife in their twenties to forties who live with their biological children in a nuclear household. Nevertheless, relatives and fictive kin have long played an important role in family life and child-rearing, forming multigenerational (i.e., grandparents living with parents and children), skipped generation (i.e., grandparents living with children without parents), and extended family households (i.e., other family members living with children with or without parents).

Historically, the prevalence of these household types has been higher among families of color and low-income families.[4] This pattern has both historical and cultural roots: studies ranging from the mid-twentieth century to the present day have documented the significant parenting involvement of grandmothers in Black communities, of extended family members and fictive kin, particularly women, in Indigenous families, and of extended family members in diverse populations of immigrants, such as Chinese and Latino families, who often bring to the United States cultural norms of multigenerational living.[5] The initiation of multigenerational, skipped generation, and extended family living arrangements can also be motivated by economic need. Studies have shown, for example, that depressed economic conditions and housing crises lead families to "double up" to save on housing and child care costs.[6]

In recent years, however, the prevalence of multigenerational, skipped generation, and extended family households has increased across all racial and class groups; today, roughly 35 percent of U.S. youth will live in one of these household types at some point before age eighteen.[7] Demographic shifts, like an increased share of immigrant children, policy shifts like reduced welfare support and increased parental incarceration, and structural shifts like declining economic opportunities have each contributed to a rise in these living arrangements among marginalized groups.[8] But we have also seen rises among more economically advantaged groups, for example due to cultural shifts like declines in marriage rates and increases in single parenthood.[9]

In the above scenarios, forming one of these household types serves as a "family adaptive strategy," whereby a family shifts child-rearing responsibilities to adapt to a challenge like financial vulnerability or divorce.[10] However, these living arrangements may also be imposed onto families by the state. If the state deems a parent unfit to raise their child, perhaps due to extreme poverty or substance use, they may initiate a child-protection case and place the child with relatives or a close family friend.[11] Depending on the rules imposed on the family by the court, the parent may be allowed to live with the caregiver and child—creating a multigenerational or extended family household—or they may be denied that privilege—creating a skipped generation household. Considering that Black, Indigenous, and low-income parents are disproportionately surveilled by the child welfare system, its influence has also likely contributed to the high prevalence of these household types among these groups.[12]

When a child's biological parents are present, as in a multigenerational household, coresiding relatives typically play an important supplemental or partial caregiving role.[13] However, when parents are not present, as in a skipped generation household, relatives become the child's primary caregiver.[14] Research on families with such "nontraditional" household structures typically considers these two groups separately and comparatively. One study focusing on grandparent health, for example, found that grandparents who are primary caregivers (in skipped generation households) have worse self-reported health than supplemental or partial caregivers (in multigenerational households).[15] A recent literature review on child health demonstrated that children in skipped generation households are generally found to have worse physical and socioemotional health outcomes than children in multigenerational households.[16]

By comparing families with coresiding relative caregivers and families with primary relative caregivers, this line of work tends to present the latter—relative-headed households—as a homogenous group. Yet despite looking the same descriptively, families in relative-headed households can occupy diverse legal arrangements, as relatives who serve as primary caregivers are not seen and recognized equally by the state.

Some primary caregivers may hold limited legal rights and responsibilities through an appointment of guardianship or an award of custody, and some may become a legal parent through adoption and thus hold full legal rights over the child. However, absent such a proceeding, other primary caregivers may hold no legal ground at all. This latter group may conduct all the physical and emotional labor of a parent, but they are not recognized as such on paper.

In my fieldwork, service providers have suggested that the proportion of nonparental primary caregivers in this latter group may be increasing. Yet research considering the reasons why nonparental primary caregivers end up as social, but not legal, parents and the implications of this social parenthood status remains limited.[17] In the section that follows, I build out our understanding of nonparental primary caregivers as social parents using a case study of kin and fictive kin serving as caregivers amid the U.S. opioid crisis. While caregivers with guardianship or legal custody are also social (as opposed to legal) parents, I focus specifically on those primary caregivers who are in the most legally vulnerable position—lacking any kind of legal recognition in their caregiving roles.

Social Parents in the U.S. Opioid Crisis

Over the past two decades, the United States has experienced a widespread and increasingly deadly opioid crisis. The crisis can be traced to the early 2000s, when overprescribing norms led to an influx of legal yet very addictive prescription opioids into U.S. communities.[18] After realizing the addictive nature of these substances, health care providers attempted to rein in prescription numbers.[19] However, opioid use disorder was already widespread, and people were compelled to turn to more accessible and potent alternatives: first heroin, then illicitly manufactured fentanyl, and most recently amphetamines laced with fentanyl.[20]

While rates of opioid use disorder and opioid-related overdose have increased across age groups, they are highest for individuals at peak childbearing and parenting age.[21] Consequently, growing evidence suggests that the opioid crisis has fundamentally shifted the structure of families: specifically, ever greater numbers of kin and fictive kin have taken on primary caregiving roles for children whose parents use opioids.[22] Two recent studies, for example, show how localities with higher opioid overdose death rates and higher opioid prescription rates possess higher rates of children living with adults other than their parents.[23] In one county in Appalachian Kentucky—the proclaimed "epicenter" of the opioid crisis—a 2020 elementary school survey showed that 34.8 percent of students were being raised by a nonparental primary caregiver, without a biological parent present.

In the event of a parent's overdose death, a relative or close family friend would typically assume permanent care of the child, if the other parent is either not living or not available. Yet opioid use disorder is far more common than overdose fatalities, and thus it is more likely that a parent is—temporarily or over a longer period of time—unable to care for the child. In 2019, opioid-related overdose deaths peaked at 50,000; yet that same year an estimated 9.7 million people misused prescription opioids (including fentanyl) and 745,000 used heroin.[24] In families where parents are currently experiencing opioid use disorder or are in recovery, relatives and family friends often serve as social parents. Many of these nonparental primary caregivers have taken on their child-rearing responsibilities informally, and even if they care for the child for years, they may never pursue guardianship, legal custody, or adoption in the court.

Through four years of ethnographic fieldwork in rural Appalachian Kentucky, including 164 in-depth interviews with nonparental primary caregivers, biological parents who use(d) opioids, and representatives of the criminal justice, child welfare, and social support systems in which these families are embedded, I sought to understand how families navigate parental opioid use disorder and related shifts in child caregiving responsibilities. In many of these families, opioid use had created social parents—be that a relative or fictive kin caregiver who had informally assumed primary caregiving responsibilities but lacked legal rights, or a biological parent who had lost legal rights to their child but maintained a social bond with them. I first focus on the experiences of the former group—nonparental primary caregivers who lack legal recognition. Drawing on the stories of six relative and fictive kin caregivers in my sample, I outline why caregivers take on social parent roles and how these nonlegal arrangements can impact both caregivers and children.

Reasons for Relatives' and Fictive Family Members' Social Parenting

I identified three reasons why relatives and fictive kin not only take on, but also stay in, nonlegal roles, despite assuming the majority of caregiving responsibilities. First, nonparental caregivers may fear seeking legal recognition (i.e., filing for custody), instead choosing to avoid the legal system at all costs. Grandparents, for example, may fear that a judge could deem them unfit to care for their grandchild, perhaps because they "failed" in raising their own child (the biological parent). Other relatives and fictive kin may fear that the court could prioritize family reunification in a way that privileges a biological parent but denies the importance of their own parenting roles. Multiple school staff explained that they had seen more caregivers avoiding the legal system, typically because a friend, family member, or neighbor of the caregiver had been denied in their attempts to formalize their own caregiving roles in the past.

Doris, for example, has cared for her eleven-year-old grandniece, Becca, for Becca's entire childhood. Becca's mom, McKayla, had left Becca with Doris as an infant, fleeing the county due to multiple warrants for possession and trafficking. Doris and her mother (Becca's great-grandmother) had also raised McKayla due to Doris's sister's own issues with substance use. On the one hand, Doris worried that this intergenerational pattern could hurt her image in the eyes of the court. She told me, "They [social workers] make you look like a bad parent, don't you think?" However, on the other hand, Doris also worried that opening a case could lead Becca's dad to come back into the picture and demand rights himself. Because of her suspicions of his abusive nature, Doris wanted to avoid that possibility at all costs. Consequently, Doris felt stuck in her nonlegal parenting role; while she had been the one constant caregiver in Becca's life, she felt that the only way to ensure her future with Becca was to avoid the legal system.

Second, nonparental caregivers may face fear of retribution from the biological parent, should they push for legal recognition themselves. Under our current legal system, a caregiver seeking legal recognition can place the biological parent's parental status at risk—a result that the biological parent often does *not* want, otherwise they would have transferred legal custody in the first place. If caregivers' desires are to ensure, first and foremost, that the child is safe, rocking the boat by seeking legal rights could cause them to lose the ability to care for that child (or other children) at all. For this reason, they may feel compelled to silently continue in social parenting roles without seeking legal recognition.

When I met Stephanie, she had been the primary caregiver for her teenage niece, Amber, for nearly three years. Stephanie's own upbringing had been rife with domestic violence and trauma, and these experiences pushed her brother—Amber's father—to develop an opioid use disorder. Stephanie's parents had been granted legal custody of Amber and her brother—their grandchildren—but Stephanie knew that their household was unsafe. Eventually, Stephanie convinced her parents to allow Amber to come live with her, and they signed a sheet of notebook paper to give Stephanie educational and medical rights. Stephanie wanted legal recognition of her parenting role, and she was certain that a judge would rule in her favor if it came down to a fight. However, Stephanie realized that in doing so, not only would her parents cut her off from Amber's brother, whom they were still caring for, but her siblings would also cut her off from their children—Amber's cousins. Stephanie explained, "I know that I'd win, but at what cost? I would lose all connection with my remaining niece and nephews, all connection. And they need me too." Remaining in her social parenting role but without seeking legal protection for that status ensured she would not be cut off from the rest of her family.

Finally, nonparental caregivers may face obligations to both the child they are caring for and the child's biological parent that make them reluctant to seek legal recognition. For example, a caregiver might fear that the parent losing custody could cause emotional harm to the biological parent or create lasting damage to either the caregiver's relationship with the biological parent or the relationship between the parent and child. While gaining legal recognition could benefit the caregiver and the child, the caregiver may choose to avoid doing so, fearing that repercussions for the biological parent may be too great.

This was the case for Peggy, whom I met shortly after she had served as an informal relative caregiver for her grandson. Years earlier, Peggy had suffered from an opioid use disorder herself when she was a single mother. During this time, Peggy's own parents had assumed legal custody of her children. Once in recovery, Peggy endured a lengthy, frustrating, and demoralizing legal battle before finally getting her children back in her care. Years later, Peggy's daughter, Emily, had become a single mother and developed an opioid use disorder herself. Having experienced the emotional process of losing and regaining legal custody herself, Peggy did not want to impose that trauma on Emily. Peggy wanted to ensure that Emily's son—her grandson—was safe, but she did not want to seek legal recognition if that meant removing recognition from Emily. She told me, "I wanted to make sure that relationship stayed intact . . . I endured enough trauma and hate throughout my life to where I don't ever want to see anybody treated like that." Peggy convinced Emily to go to treatment, and when she felt that Emily was able to care for her grandson again, Peggy helped transition primary caregiving responsibilities back to Emily. Peggy prioritized Emily retaining legal rights as a parent, even when she was struggling; she did not want Emily to feel that her identity as a parent was being taken from her. In doing so, however, she needed to serve as an informal caregiver herself.

Implications of Relatives' and Fictive Family Members' Social Parenting

Doris, Stephanie, and Peggy each would have liked legal recognition of their parenting role, but they were held back by fear and constraints imposed by the current system that establishes legal recognition. Yet this exclusion from legal recognition carries serious implications for caregivers' and children's well-being. I found that nonparental primary caregivers in social parenting roles faced three common challenges. First, these caregivers (and their children) can suffer emotionally without the promise that their parenting role will persist. Several informal caregivers were concerned that the biological parents might attempt to take the children from their care and end their relationship with the children. Such concerns could engender considerable stress, not simply because caregivers and children had formed attachments but because some caregivers worried that the biological parents could not yet parent on their own.

Angela, for example, had acted as the primary caregiver for her boyfriend's niece, Janie, for nearly eight years. While Janie's parents had both dealt with substance use issues in the past, Angela believed that they were both in recovery, and she would take Janie to see both parents on weekends. Recently, however, Janie's mom had been telling Janie that she planned to take her back. Angela told me, "She'd be like Janie when are you coming home? This is your home. Angela's not your family. And trying to manipulate her to the point that Janie has developed anxiety over the whole thing. . . . She's been back in therapy since the winter because of this pressure her mom is putting on her to come live with her." While Janie had been with Angela for most of her life and desired to stay there, the lack of stability and permanence weighed on both Janie and Angela. Since Janie's mom was still recognized as the legal parent, while Angela lacked legal recognition, Angela worried that Janie's mom had the legal right to assume care of Janie again.

Second, these informal caregivers may feel that the biological parent holds all the power in their relationship, lacking the ability to advocate for oneself and lacking recourse to protect oneself. If the biological parent has the ultimate say as to what will happen with the child, an informal caregiver has little power to make demands or requests of the parent. Asking for financial assistance, for example, could simply result in a threat by the parent to take the child back. If the nonparental caregiver's main desire is to ensure the child is safe in their care, they may find themselves in a vulnerable position, forced to be conciliatory and avoid conflict with the parent.

Nona and Sheryl, two sisters, had served as primary caregivers for Dylan, Nona's great-grandson, since he was three. While Derick, Dylan's father, was mostly out of the picture, he wanted to retain his status as a legal parent; Sheryl believed this was because of finances—Derick, for example, would file Dylan as a dependent on his taxes. Derick was inconsistent in visits and offered meager financial support for raising Dylan. Yet Nona and Sheryl resisted asking for help, as they were afraid it could anger him. Nona said, "He doesn't do nothing. He has [helped] occasionally, but not like he should. We can't tell him anything. . . . He's very stern about telling him anything." Nona and Sheryl felt that Derick abused their kindness—he set the rules of their family arrangement. But Nona and Sheryl felt compelled to allow this to happen; it was a concession for being able to keep Dylan safe.

Finally, informal primary caregivers lack access to many financial support programs, despite possessing the income levels or conditions that would otherwise qualify them. For example, relative and fictive kin caregivers receiving Social Security retirement or disability benefits can draw additional benefits on a child in their care only if they have adopted them. Other support programs, such as the Kentucky Family Caregiver Program, will provide financial support only to grandparents or great-grandparents who hold legal custody. Food assistance through the Supplemental Nutrition Assistance Program (SNAP) and Women, Infants, and Children (WIC) do not require a person to have legal custody; typically, simply stating that you are the primary caregiver is sufficient. However, this does not allay the fear that informal caregivers may have in approaching government services and "outing" themselves as primary caregivers.

When I met Elaine, she had recently stepped in as the primary caregiver for her two grandchildren after her daughter, who had been in recovery, relapsed. Her daughter was receiving SNAP for the children, but Elaine could not convince her daughter to pass the support to her. When I asked Elaine if she might go to the "Food Stamp office" to explain her situation and ask for assistance, Elaine told me she would not take that chance; she worried that telling the office she was caring for her grandchildren could lead to an open Child Protective Services case on her daughter. Due to her very low income, Elaine also worried that the court could place her grandchildren with another caregiver over her. While Elaine desperately needed help, she was afraid to approach governmental support services for fear of losing the children. For now, she was relying on organizational support, but in a largely poor and rural county, the available resources only barely met her needs.

Biological Parents as Social Parents

While I have thus far focused on nonparental primary caregivers who act as social parents, these are not the only caregivers who may lack legal recognition in kinship families. Biological parents who use(d) opioids may become social parents if the court rescinds their rights to care for their children. Sometimes this is through a formal termination of their parental rights. Even if official termination of parental rights has not occurred, a transfer of permanent legal custody to a relative or family friend can effectively remove a biological parent's legal authority over the child, unless they should take the case to court to regain those rights.

Yet, in either scenario, these parents may remain important caregiving figures in their children's lives, especially if they enter recovery.

At the time of her interview, Kelly, for example, was navigating her role and identity as a mother to her son without legal recognition. Not fully understanding the implications of her actions, she had voluntarily terminated her parental rights while in jail. Kelly recalled, "I thought signing my rights over would be helpful. I signed them over while I was in jail, pathetically asked at the time, 'Can this be reversed?' and was just pushed to sign the paper." Kelly had since successfully attended a long-term residential treatment program, and when I talked to her, she had been in recovery from her opioid use disorder for six years. She had reestablished a relationship with her son, but ultimately the extent of that relationship was constrained by her lack of legal recognition. Since her own parents were now the legal parents, they could choose to keep her son primarily with them. While they allowed Kelly to see her son, she grappled with the feeling that she had no claim to playing an even greater role in his life.

Conclusion

As a researcher seeking to uphold and advocate for the needs of my respondents, working with both biological parents and nonparental caregivers can seem contradictory. Even in the eyes of my respondents, the rights and recognition of these two groups seem at odds with one another. Yet this conflict arises precisely *because* of the rigid and traditional family norms we enforce in social and legal systems.

During my research, I met a single grandmother, Vivian, who had initially obtained legal custody of her grandchild amid her son and his partner's struggles with opioids. Yet once he entered recovery, the two chose to pursue joint custody. Since Vivian was unmarried, and since her son's ex-girlfriend was estranged, the two entered an agreement privileging and recognizing both grandmother and father as important parental figures in the child's life. Vivian's story pushes us to think outside of the current social and legal norms. Can social and legal systems be designed to reflect and support natural family practices, rather than enforcing "traditional" standards onto "nontraditional" arrangements? The concept of social parenthood could, for example, allow nonparental primary caregivers to *also* be recognized as parents when needing to step in amid a biological parent's challenges. For biological parents who reassume a caregiving role after entering recovery, this concept could also diminish the need for a statute that allows for restoration after the termination of parental rights.

The role of kin and fictive kin in child-rearing is not new; in fact, the increasing prevalence of nonparental primary caregivers amid today's opioid crisis mirrors a similar change that took place during the crack epidemic of the 1980s and 1990s.[25] Yet U.S. social and legal systems have still not adapted to support families facing challenges like substance use disorder.[26] The welfare state, social support systems, and legal definitions of parentage continue to privilege the SNAF form, and therefore caregivers in these alternative family forms may be excluded from legal, social, and economic support. As the number of nonparental primary caregivers continues to rise, we can support kinship families by creating more flexible social and legal systems that recognize these caregivers in addition to—rather than instead of—biological parents.

NOTES

1 Naomi Gerstel, "Rethinking Families and Community: The Color, Class, and Centrality of Extended Kin Ties," *Sociological Forum* 26 (2011): 1–20.

2 Annie E. Casey Foundation, "Stepping Up for Kids: What Government and Communities Should Do to Support Kinship Families" (2012), www.aecf.org.

3 Generations United, "Raising the Children of the Opioid Epidemic: Solutions and Support for Grandfamilies" (2018), www.gu.org; Lydia Anderson, "Opioid Prescribing Rate and Grandparents Raising Grandchildren: State and County Level Analysis" (paper, Population Association of America, Austin, TX, April 10–13, 2019); Monica Lisette Caudillo et al., "The Opioid Epidemic and Children's Living Arrangements in the United States, 2000–2018" (paper, American Sociological Association, August 7–10, 2021).

4 Esme Fuller-Thomson et al., "A Profile of Grandparents Raising Grandchildren in the United States," *Gerontologist* 37 (1997): 406–411; Philip N. Cohen and Lynne M. Casper, "In Whose Home? Multigenerational Families in the United States, 1998–2000," *Sociological Perspectives* 45 (2002): 1–20; Christina J. Cross, "Extended Family Households among Children in the United States: Differences by Race/Ethnicity and Socio-Economic Status," *Population Studies* 72 (2018): 235–251.

5 Carol Stack, *All Our Kin: Strategies for Survival in a Black Community* (New York: Basic Books, 1974); Dianna J. Shomaker, "Transfer of Children and the Importance of Grandmothers among Navajo Indians," *Journal of Cross-Cultural Gerontology* 4 (1989): 1–18; Jane L. Pearson et al., "Black Grandmothers in Multigenera-

tional Households: Diversity in Family Structure and Parenting Involvement in the Woodlawn Community," *Child Development* 61 (1990): 434–442; Kathleen S. Bahr, "The Strengths of Apache Grandmothers: Observations on Commitment, Culture, and Caretaking," *Journal of Comparative Family Studies* 25 (1994): 233–248; Andrea G. Hunter, "Counting on Grandmothers: Black Mothers' and Fathers' Reliance on Grandmothers for Parenting Support," *Journal of Family Issues* 18 (1997): 251–269; Carole B. Cox et al., "Culture and Caregiving: A Study of Latino Grandparents," in *To Grandmother's House We Go and Stay: Perspectives on Custodial Grandparents*, ed. Carole B. Cox (New York: Springer, 2000), 218–232; Laura D. Pittman, "Grandmothers' Involvement among Young Adolescents Growing Up in Poverty," *Journal of Research on Adolescence* 17 (2007): 89–116; Bridgid Mariko Conn, "A Three-Generation Study of Chinese Immigrant Extended Family Child Caregiving Experiences in the Preschool Years," *Research in Human Development* 10 (2013): 308–331.

6 Anne R. Pebley and Laura L. Rudkin, "Grandparents Caring for Grandchildren: What Do We Know?," *Journal of Family Issues* 20 (1999): 218–242; Jennifer Reid Keene and Christie D. Batson, "Under One Roof: A Review of Research on Intergenerational Coresidence and Multigenerational Households in the United States," *Sociology Compass* 4 (2010): 642–657; Natasha V. Pilkauskas et al., "The Prevalence and Economic Value of Doubling Up," *Demography* 51 (2014): 1667–1676.

7 Natasha V. Pilkauskas and Christina J. Cross, "Beyond the Nuclear Family: Trends in Children Living in Shared Households," *Demography* 55 (2018): 2283–2297; Cross, "Extended Family Households"; Pilkauskas et al., "Historical Trends in Children Living in Multigenerational Households in the United States: 1870–2018," *Demography* 57 (2020): 2269–2296.

8 Pebley and Rudkin, "Grandparents Caring for Grandchildren"; Keene and Batson, "Under One Roof"; Pilkauskas et al., "Historical Trends."

9 Pilkauskas and Cross, "Beyond the Nuclear Family."

10 Phyllis Moen and Elaine Wethington, "The Concept of Family Adaptive Strategies," *Annual Review of Sociology* 18 (1992): 233–251.

11 Kelley Fong, "Child Welfare Involvement and Contexts of Poverty: The Role of Parental Adversities, Social Networks, and Social Services," *Child and Youth Services Review* 72 (2017): 5–13; Robin Ghertner et al., "The Role of Substance Use in Child Welfare Caseloads," *Child and Youth Services Review* 90 (2018): 83–93; Laura Radel et al., "Substance Use, the Opioid Epidemic, and the Child Welfare System: Key Findings from a Mixed Methods Study" (Office of the Assistant Secretary for Planning and Evaluation, March 6, 2018), https://aspe.hhs.gov.

12 Dorothy Roberts, *Shattered Bonds: The Color of Child Welfare* (New York: Basic Books, 2002); Kelley Fong, "Neighborhood Inequality in the Prevalence of Reported and Substantiated Child Maltreatment," *Child Abuse and Neglect* 90 (2019): 13–21.

13 Pearson et al., "Black Grandmothers in Multigenerational Households."

14 Rachel E. Dunifon, *You've Always Been There for Me: Understanding the Lives of Grandchildren Raised by Grandparents* (New Brunswick, NJ: Rutgers University Press, 2018).

15 Carol M. Musil and Muayyad Ahmad, "The Health of Grandmothers: A Comparison by Caregiver Status," *Journal of Aging and Health* 14 (2002): 96–121.

16 Aalyia F. A. Sadruddin et al., "How Do Grandparents Influence Child Health and Development? A Systematic Review," *Social Science and Medicine* 239 (2019): 112476.

17 James P. Gleeson et al., "Becoming Involved in Raising a Relative's Child: Reasons, Caregiver Motivations and Pathways to Informal Kinship Care," *Child & Family Social Work* 14 (2009): 300–310; LaShawnDa Pittman, "Doing What's Right for the Baby: Parental Responses and Custodial Grandmothers' Institutional Decision Making," *Women, Gender, and Families of Color* 2 (2014): 32–56.

18 Leonard J. Paulozzi et al., "Vital Signs: Overdoses of Prescription Opioid Pain Relievers—United States, 1999–2008," *MMWR* 60 (2011): 1487–1492; Sam Quinones, *Dreamland: The True Tale of America's Opiate Epidemic* (New York: Bloomsbury, 2015); Beth Macy, *Dopesick: Dealers, Doctors, and the Drug Company that Addicted America* (Boston: Little, Brown, 2018).

19 Gery P. Guy, "Vital Signs: Changes in Opioid Prescribing in the United States, 2006–2015," *MMWR* 66 (2017): 697–704; William N. Evans et al., "How the Reformulation of OxyContin Ignited the Heroin Epidemic," *Review of Economics and Statistics* 101 (2019): 1–15.

20 Christopher Ciccarone, "Fentanyl in the U.S. Heroin Supply: A Rapidly Changing Risk Environment," *International Journal of Drug Policy* 46 (2017): 107–111; Silvia S. Martins et al., "Change in US Lifetime Heroin Use and Heroin Use Disorder: Prevalence from the 2001–2002 to 2012–2013 National Epidemiologic Survey on Alcohol and Related Conditions," *JAMA Psychiatry* 74 (2017): 445–455; Matthew S. Ellis et al., "Twin Epidemics: The Surging Rise of Methamphetamine Use in Chronic Opioid Users," *Drug and Alcohol Dependence* 193 (2018): 14–20.

21 Lawrence Scholl et al., "Drug and Opioid-Involved Overdose Deaths—United States, 2013–2017," *MMWR* 67 (2019): 1419.

22 Margot Trotter Davis et al., "Parenting a 6-Year-Old Is Not What I Planned in Retirement: Trauma and Stress among Grandparents Due to the Opioid Crisis," *Journal of Gerontological Social Work* 63 (2020): 295–315; Megan L. Dolbin-MacNab and Lyn M. O'Connell, "Grandfamilies and the Opioid Epidemic: A Systemic Perspective and Future Priorities," *Clinical Child and Family Psychology Review* 24 (2021): 207–223; Anna C. Hansen et al., "Sources of Stress and Strength: Contextualizing the Experience of Grandparents Rearing Grandchildren in Appalachia," *Journal of Intergenerational Relationships* 20 (2022): 39–59.

23 Anderson, "Opioid Prescribing Rate"; Caudillo et al., "Opioid Epidemic."

24 National Institute on Drug Abuse, "Overdose Death Rates" (2021), www.drugabuse.gov; Substance Abuse and Mental Health Services Administration, "Key Substance Use and Mental Health Indicators in the United States: Results from the 2019 National Survey on Drug Use and Health" (2020), www.samhsa.gov.

25 Linda M. Burton, "Black Grandparents Rearing Children of Drug-Addicted Parents," *Gerontologist* 32 (1992): 744–751; Meredith Minkler and Kathleen M. Roe, *Grandmothers as Caregivers: Raising Children of the Crack Cocaine Epidemic* (Thousand Oaks, CA: Sage, 1993).

26 LaShawnDa Pittman, "How Well Does the 'Safety Net' Work for Family Safety Nets? Economic Survival Strategies among Grandmother Caregivers in Severe Deprivation," *Russell Sage Foundation Journal of the Social Sciences* 1 (2015): 78–97; Brian Powell et al., "Implications of Changing Family Forms for Children," *Annual Review of Sociology* 42 (2016): 301–322; Josh Gupta-Kagan, "America's Hidden Foster Care System," Stanford Law Review 72 (2020): 841–913; Joanne L. Parise, "'Grandfamilies' amid the Opioid Crisis: An Increasing Reason to Update Pennsylvania's Outdated Intestacy Laws," *Duquesne Law Review* 58 (2020): 202–228.

II

Legal Systems in North America

5

Social Parenthood in Canada

CLAIRE HOUSTON

Canadian law is progressive in recognizing different kinds of parents. Legal parents, who enjoy all the rights and responsibilities of parenthood, may be different-sex or same-sex individuals, and children can have more than two legal parents. There is also a category of what we might call "legally recognized social parents": individuals who are not legal parents but have been awarded rights to a child—decision-making responsibility (formerly "custody") or parenting time (formerly "access")[1]—or have been ordered to pay child support. These legally recognized social parents may have rights and responsibilities in addition to the child's legal parents. Legal recognition of social parenthood acknowledges that the function of parenting is as important as genetic ties and that children's welfare is more important than parental rights. However, Canada's law of social parenthood also carries the potential for regressive effects. Because legal recognition of social parenthood often turns on judicial assessments of a child's "best interests," racial, gender, and heteronormative biases can inform the analysis. In the child support context, legal recognition of social parenthood can promote private—rather than public/state—support of children and perpetuate gender stereotypes. This chapter describes Canadian law's progressive approach to social parenthood and also explains how it may operate in a more regressive manner.

Demographic Data

Canadian families take many forms. The most recent census data, from 2016, show that while most children live with both of their legal parents (69.7 percent of children aged birth to fourteen), many children live with one parent (19.2 percent) or in a stepfamily (9.8 percent) and a small number live in foster care or group homes (1.4 percent).[2]

Same-sex parenting is becoming more common. In 2016, approximately 12 percent of same-sex couples had children living with them, an increase of roughly 3 percent since 2011.[3] More children live with female same-sex couples than with male same-sex couples.[4]

The number of multigenerational households is also growing. Multigenerational households now represent 2.9 percent of households.[5] The proportion of multigenerational households is higher in urban centers, where there is a greater concentration of newcomers to Canada and in areas with larger Indigenous populations. For example, in Nunavut, where 86 percent of residents identify as Aboriginal,[6] one in eight households was multigenerational in 2016.[7]

There are more single mothers than single fathers, although the gap is narrowing. In 2016, 81.3 percent of children in lone-parent families were living with their mother.[8] However, between 2001 and 2016, the number of male lone-parent families grew faster than the number of female lone-parent families (34.5 percent compared to 4.8 percent).[9] Male lone-parent families report, on average, higher incomes than female lone-parent families.[10]

A small but significant percentage of children live with a grandparent (0.6 percent), with another relative (0.4 percent), or in a foster home (0.5 percent).[11] It is more common for children to live in one of these family situations in the territories, Manitoba, and Saskatchewan than in the rest of Canada. These jurisdictions have the highest proportions of Indigenous children.[12] They also have a significant share of Indigenous children living without their parents.[13]

There are limited data on families created through assisted reproduction (AR), although use of AR is increasing. In 2005, there were 11,414 treatment cycles at thirty-six clinics across Canada.[14] By 2020, this number had nearly tripled to 30,764.[15]

Data on children living in polyamorous families—a small but likely growing family form—are also lacking. A 2016 survey of individuals in polyamorous relationships found that 23.2 percent of respondents reported at least one child under the age of nineteen living full-time in their household. A further 8.7 percent of respondents said that at least one child under nineteen lived in their household part-time.[16]

Legal Recognition of Parents

Legal parentage in Canada is governed by provincial and territorial statutes, while parenting rights and responsibilities—including decision-making responsibility, parenting time, and support obligations—are set out in provincial and territorial statutes and the federal Divorce Act. Legal parentage is a status that confers rights on parents and children, including with respect to inheritance, health care, and citizenship.[17] Parenting rights and responsibilities typically flow from legal parentage but may also attach to social parents.

Depending on the province or territory, legal parentage may be established at conception or birth through a genetic tie, marriage, or a marriage-like relationship (usually determined by cohabitation for a specific length of time) or a parentage agreement. Postbirth, legal parentage may be established through adoption or court declaration. Depending on the circumstances, certain bases of parentage may trump others. Most provinces and territories start by defining a child's legal parents as the birth mother[18] and the genetic father. Most provinces and territories also presume that a birth mother's male spouse or spouse-like partner is a legal parent, regardless of biology. In several provinces, these presumptions extend to same-sex spouses or partners of birth mothers.[19] All provinces and territories recognize parentage through adoption, including adoption by stepparents.

Parentage may also be established by court declaration. In most provinces and territories, a court may declare an individual to be a child's legal parent from birth, so long as the order is in the child's "best interests." In Ontario and British Columbia, declarations of parentage have been used to recognize a third legal parent. For example, in *AA v. BB*,[20] the Ontario Court of Appeal held that it was in the best interests of the child to declare the same-sex partner of the child's biological mother a third legal parent where the partner intended to parent the child along with the child's mother and biological father (a male friend of the couple who had donated the sperm). Similarly, in a recent British Columbia case, the court found that it was in the best interests of the child to declare the parents' polyamorous partner to be the child's third legal parent.[21]

Parentage by agreement is relatively new and has been introduced in only a handful of provinces.[22] There are two types of agreements: surrogacy agreements (where the birth mother is *not* an intended parent) and parentage agreements (where the birth mother is an intended parent). These agreements cover situations involving conception by AR or sexual intercourse. They must be in writing,[23] and entered into prior to the child's conception. Ontario and Saskatchewan limit the number of legal parents by agreement to four.[24]

Parenting rights and responsibilities typically flow from legal parentage. However, legal parentage does not guarantee parenting rights or responsibilities, although it generally imposes financial support obligations.[25]

Social parents may also have parenting rights and responsibilities, either in addition to or instead of legal parents. The federal Divorce Act and provincial and territorial statutes define parenting rights and responsibilities in terms of time spent with a child (i.e., parenting time), authority to make decisions respecting the child's upbringing (i.e., decision-making responsibility), and financial support obligations. Legal parents share parenting rights and responsibilities. However, under the Divorce Act and provincial and territorial statutes, a court will award parenting time and decision-making responsibility based on a "best interests" assessment to only one individual or equally or unequally to multiple individuals. While courts may award or withhold parenting time and decision-making responsibility to a parent, legal parents and some social parents usually cannot avoid support obligations. Thus, individuals may have support obligations without any corresponding parenting rights.

Legal Recognition of Social Parents: Three Common Contexts

Same-Sex Couples

Individuals in same-sex relationships may be legal parents or legally recognized social parents. The legal status of same-sex parents depends on when the child was conceived or born[26] and how the child was conceived. Same-sex couples may rely on parentage presumptions and parentage agreements to establish legal parentage by registration at birth without a court declaration or adoption order. Most provinces have statutory parentage presumptions that include same-sex partners.[27] These provide that the birth mother's spouse or spouse-like partner at the time of the child's conception or birth is presumed to be a legal parent. Thus, these parentage presumptions do not include gay men who use surrogates to conceive.

In a minority of provinces, gay male couples who use surrogacy may establish legal parentage by parentage or surrogacy agreement. Parentage agreements must be in writing and entered into prior to conception. However, in most provinces and territories, nongenetic "intended" parents (whether in a same-sex relationship, different-sex relationship, or single) who use surrogacy to conceive must apply to a court for a declaration of parentage or adoption order. Because parentage presumptions and parentage agreements apply only to same-sex partners who are involved in the child's conception or birth, those who form relationships with the child's legal parent after conception or birth are treated as stepparents.

Stepparents

Stepparents are commonly legally recognized social parents in Canada, though this status does not arise from mere cohabitation or marriage to a parent. Canadian law allows stepparents to be assigned child support obligations and awarded decision-making responsibility and parenting time when their relationship with the child's legal parent breaks down. Stepparents may also become legal parents through stepparent adoption.

The parenting rights and responsibilities of stepparents fall under federal, provincial, or territorial jurisdiction, depending on the relationship between the stepparent and legal parent. The federal Divorce Act sets out the parenting rights and responsibilities of stepparents who have been married to the child's legal parent and are divorcing the parent. Provincial and territorial statutes govern the rights and obligations of nonmarried stepparents as well as other social parents. While there are some differences among the various statutes, there is also considerable consistency.

Stepparent liability for child support usually depends on the relationship between the stepparent and the child. The federal Divorce Act provides that a stepparent who "stands in the place of a parent" may be ordered to pay child support.[28] In Ontario and other provinces, child support liability may attach to a stepparent who has "demonstrated a settled intention to treat a child as a child of his or her family."[29] Different courts have held that "stands in the place of a parent" has the same meaning as "demonstrates a settled intention" to treat the child as one's own.[30] British Columbia has taken a more restrictive approach, assigning liability only to stepparents who have contributed to the support of the child for at least one year, and where the proceeding for support is commenced within a year of the stepparent having paid support.[31] Finally, in Québec, only stepparents who have been married to the child's legal parent can be held responsible for child support.[32]

In *Chartier v. Chartier*,[33] the Supreme Court of Canada interpreted "stands in the place of a parent" under the Divorce Act. The stepfather in *Chartier* sought to avoid paying child support on the basis that he ended his relationship with the child after separating from the child's mother. The Court held that whether a person "stands in the place of a parent" depends on "the nature of the relationship" while the family was intact.[34] Several factors must be considered, and these must be viewed objectively. The stepparent's intention is one of these factors. Others include whether the child participates in the extended family as would a genetic child, whether the person provides financially for the child, whether the person disciplines the child, whether the person represents to the child and others that they are responsible as a parent, and the nature or existence of the child's relationship with the absent genetic parent. Lower courts have applied *Chartier* in disputes over support liability under provincial and territorial statutes.[35]

Since *Chartier*, many lower courts have adopted a "high threshold" for imposing child support obligations on stepparents, most of whom are stepfathers.[36] To balance concerns over fairness to stepparents, these courts place greater emphasis on the stepparent's intention. For example, in *Cook v. Cook*, a widely followed Nova Scotia decision, the court reasoned that child support obligations should only be imposed where a social parent has "intentionally acted or can be inferred to have acted so as to substantially replace the natural parent's role."[37] Other courts have adopted a lower threshold. In *Widdis v. Widdis*, a Saskatchewan court explicitly rejected the high threshold in *Cook*, saying that the focus should be on "the nature of the commitment made by the stepparent" and not whether the stepparent has replaced the natural parent.[38]

One controversial category of stepparent payor is the "mistaken father." Some Canadian courts have imposed child support obligations on men who have parented under the mistaken belief that they are the child's genetic father because these men have demonstrated a settled intention to treat the child as their own.[39] For example, in *Day v. Weir*, a man paid support for approximately fifteen years after being told by the genetic mother that he was the genetic father.[40] The parties never cohabitated and the man had limited or no contact with the child for years. The court acknowledged that the man and child did "not [have] a strong relationship."[41] However, the court relied on the man's continued payment of support, his (former) belief in paternity, and "sufficient contact and involvement" to find that the man had been responsible for child support.[42]

The amount of child support that a stepparent must pay depends on other support obligations to the child. Canadian law recognizes that child support obligations of social parents are secondary to those of legal parents.[43] The Child Support Guidelines generally establish the amount of child support based on a payor's income and the number of children. This is called the "table amount." Section 5 of the guidelines grants courts discretion to reduce the table amount where the payor is a person who "stands in the place of a parent."[44] However, child support obligations are joint and several.[45] Thus, a stepparent may be responsible for the full guidelines amount where no other parent is paying support or the amount is insufficient.[46]

Stepparents may also be awarded decision-making responsibility and parenting time. Some jurisdictions have threshold criteria. For example, under the federal Divorce Act, only a stepparent who "stands in the place of a parent" may apply. In Alberta, a stepparent making a claim under the provincial statute must successfully apply to be a "guardian" before being awarded decision-making responsibility or parenting time. In most cases, an individual must have had "care and control" of the child for at least six months to be appointed a guardian.[47] In Ontario, by contrast, "any person" may apply for decision-making responsibility or parenting time with a child,[48] though there must be a close social link to succeed in such a claim.

Once a stepparent has met the threshold for applying for parenting rights and responsibilities, their claim is assessed according to the "best interests" of the child. Canadian courts have held that stepparents who stand in the place of a parent have equal claims to decision-making responsibility and parenting time. In *Johnstone v. Locke*, an Ontario court held that "all decisions with respect to custody [decision-making responsibility] and access [parenting time] are to be determined on the basis of the best interests of the child having regard to the facts in each case. Neither parental status nor stepparent status confers any presumed right or entitlement to custody or access to the child."[49] Similarly, in *Khan v. Kong*, an Ontario court stated, "The right of a biological parent is . . . a secondary consideration to the best interests of the child."[50] This sentiment has enabled courts to grant custody of children to stepparents over the objections of a legal parent if this is in a child's best interests.[51]

However, genetics may play a more significant role in parenting disputes involving two legal parents and a stepparent. In *Johnstone*, the stepmother applied for joint custody of the nine-year-old girl who was already the subject of a joint custody agreement between her genetic father and mother. The stepmother and father partnered when the child was nearly two years old and separated when the child was six. During that time, the stepmother acted as the primary caretaker of the child and the child referred to her as "Momma." In rejecting the stepmother's application, the court held that conflict between the parties precluded an order for joint custody. The court was also unwilling to order the child to move between three homes: "[The child] has always lived in two homes, never three."[52]

Similarly, in *JCB v. HJC*,[53] the Alberta Court of Appeal upheld a lower court decision dismissing a custody application by a stepfather who played a significant parental role in the child's life, deferring to the wishes of the genetic parents. The genetic parents separated shortly after the child's birth, and the mother moved in with the stepfather. For six years, the stepfather "acted as a father" to the child.[54] The mother and genetic father then agreed to place the child with the genetic father and his parents. The mother moved in with the genetic father and his parents shortly after. The lower court dismissed the stepfather's application, citing his critical and unhealthy attitude toward other members of the child's family. In a short decision dismissing the stepfather's appeal, the Alberta Court of Appeal repeated the lower court's charge: "You are not the parent. We have two parents who are doing the parenting."[55]

Nonparental Primary Caregivers

Canadian law respecting the parenting rights of individuals other than stepparents is more complex. Depending on the jurisdiction, nonparental primary caregivers may apply for decision-making responsibility or parenting time, and may be ordered to pay child support, although such awards are rare. Legislation in some jurisdictions distinguishes between nonparental primary caregivers and other third parties who do not assume a parental role (i.e., grandparents).

Some jurisdictions limit third-party child support liability. In Ontario and other jurisdictions, formal foster parents are excluded from child support liability.[56] In Alberta, child support obligations flow only to an individual who "has demonstrated a settled intention to treat the child as the person's own child" *and* "is the spouse of a parent of the child or is or was in a relationship of interdependence of some permanence with a parent of the child."[57]

Nonparental primary caretakers may be awarded decision-making responsibility and parenting time where it is in the "best interests" of the child. This is provided by statute and has been affirmed by the Supreme Court of Canada. In the 1983 case of *Racine v. Woods*, the court rejected an Indigenous, genetic mother's claim for custody of a child whom she had placed for adoption with a non-Indigenous couple.[58] The court accepted that the couple had become the child's psychological parents. Before *Racine*, genetic parents benefitted from the "parental preference" principle in custody disputes with adoptive parents.[59] According to Justice Wilson, who wrote the decision, *Racine* introduced a new era in which "the law no longer treats children as the property of those who gave them birth but focuses on what is in their best interests."[60] Two years later, in *King v. Low*, the Court dismissed another genetic mother's appeal of a custody order in favor of the child's adoptive parents but left some room for parental rights in the best "interests" analysis.[61] According to Justice McIntyre, "Parental claims must not be lightly set aside, and they are entitled to serious consideration in reaching any conclusion. Where it is clear that that the welfare of the child requires it, however, they must be set aside."[62] Most recently, in *BJT v. JD*, the Court held that while a biological connection may signal a close emotional or psychological bond between a parent and a child, "a biological tie in itself should generally carry minimal weight" in assessing a child's best interests.[63] In that case, the Court affirmed a lower court's decision to place a child with his grandmother instead of his father.

Canadian courts have interpreted the "best interests" test as precluding any presumption in favor of legal parents in disputes with nonparental primary caregivers. In *Hernandez v. Nikas*, an Ontario court awarded custody of an eight-year-old child to the child's nanny. The court found that the legal mother had "sorely abdicated her responsibilities" by abandoning the child to the nanny's care for three years and that the mother's instability, propensity for conflict, drug use, and "self-indulgent lifestyle" left her incapable of parenting the child.[64] In response to the mother's claim that "she is the child's biological mother and that should take precedence over [the nanny's] non-biological connection to the child," the court held that biology was "but one factor the court should consider."[65]

However, biology may tip the balance in favor of legal parents in custody disputes with nonparental primary caretakers. In *AL v. DK*, the child's aunt and uncle appealed a custody award to the genetic father.[66] At trial, the father successfully challenged an agreement in which he and the mother transferred custody to the aunt and uncle. After three years in the care of her aunt and uncle, the six-year-old child was transferred to the custody of her father. The British Columbia Court of Appeal upheld the trial judge's order. Two of the three judges relied on *King v. Low*. According to Justice Newbury, *King* supported the principle that, "other things being equal, children belong with one or both of their parents, and unless there are grave reasons for concern about the well-being of the children with both of their parents, not even grandparents have a right to intervene."[67]

Courts may also defer to legal parents when considering nonparental caretakers' claims for parenting time. In *DLC v. GES*, the Saskatchewan Court of Appeal overturned an access order in favor of the genetic mother's close male friend.[68] The mother became pregnant with twins using in-vitro fertilization. The friend supported the mother emotionally and financially in getting pregnant and during the pregnancy, and he cared for the children after birth. In overturning the access order, the court held that "an emotional bond between an applicant and a child" was not sufficient to order access "in this kind of case."[69] In endorsing a higher standard for nonparental caretaker access, the court respected the rights of legal parents, especially vulnerable legal parents: "Single parents, in particular, often need assistance from friends and others in caring for their children. Those caregivers will frequently develop a strong attachment to children and *vice versa*. But . . . it would be a serious overstep to impose court-sanctioned visiting rights as a consequence of such relationships."[70]

Discussion

Canadian law provides that individuals who assume a parent-like relationship to a child may acquire parenting rights and responsibilities. By extending parenting rights and responsibilities to social parents, the law appropriately recognizes the importance of nongenetic, caretaking relationships to children. It also expands the traditional meaning of "parent." While progressive in principle, the law can also have regressive effects, depending on when and how it is applied.

First, legal recognition of social parents may disproportionately threaten the rights of marginalized legal parents. Following the Supreme Court of Canada's decision in *Racine* and other courts' rejection of a custody presumption in favor of legal parents, judges can downplay the rights of genetic parents when interpreting the "best interests" standard. In Canada, this has greater significance for Indigenous parents whose children are more likely to live with alternative caregivers or in a multigenerational household. It may also disproportionately impact women, who head most lone-parent families and often need to rely on alternative caregivers for assistance.

Second, the "best interests" standard for resolving disputes between genetic parents and social parents can be interpreted to perpetuate traditional assumptions about parentage. Following the Supreme Court of Canada's decision in *King*, and other courts' endorsement of genetic parents as natural guardians, judges can elevate the rights of genetic parents when interpreting "best interests." This has significance for social parents and children in "alternative" family forms. For example, *Johnstone* and *JCB*, cases involving more than two parents, can be read as supporting a two-parent ideal. The court in *JCB* reasoned that "two parents [are] doing the parenting." The judge in *Johnstone* rejected three-way custody in part because the child had always lived in two homes. (Children of two separated parents are regularly expected to transition from one home to two.) A few jurisdictions now recognize more than two legal parents, thanks in part to advocacy by parents in "nontraditional" family forms. Heteronormative assumptions about the primacy of the two-parent family may undermine these family forms.

Finally, legal recognition of social parenthood privatizes dependency and reinforces gendered assumptions about parenting. In the child support context, extending liability to social parents relieves the state of financial responsibility for children, thus reinforcing the assumption that supporting children is an individual—rather than a collective—responsibility.[71] In the case of "mistaken fathers," the need to locate a private payor may be so strong that even men who do not voluntarily "stand in the place of a parent" may be liable. This privatization of dependency has gender equality implications, since most single parents are mothers, and most child support claims against social parents are brought by legal mothers against stepfathers. By directing single mothers to seek support from stepfathers, the law endorses the traditional, heterosexual, two-parent family and female dependency. Where a stepfather/stepchild relationship grows distant or ends after family dissolution, as in *Chartier*, extending child support liability in these cases also risks perpetuating the view that fathering is primarily about financial provision.

Cataloging the limitations of Canada's law of social parenthood is not meant to negate its progressive potential. Legal recognition of social parenthood elevates the significance of caretaking and accepts that children's best interests can be served in alternative family forms. However, acknowledging the limitations of Canada's approach is important, especially as the legal category of parent continues to expand. A few Canadian jurisdictions now recognize more than two legal parents and "intentional" parents. Inevitably, the boundaries of these categories will be contested, and disputes will arise within different family forms (e.g., how should parenting responsibility be divided among three legal parents?).[72] In resolving these conflicts, traditional assumptions about the family and neoliberal commitments to individual responsibility should not be allowed to undermine the progressive goal of supporting all children, parents, and families.

NOTES

1 In 2021, Canada's Divorce Act was amended to replace the terms "custody" and "access" with "decision-making responsibility" and "parenting time."

2 Statistics Canada, "Portrait of Children's Family Life in Canada in 2016" (August 2, 2017), www.statcan.gc.ca.

3 Statistics Canada, "Same-Sex Couples in Canada in 2016" (August 2, 2017), www.statcan.gc.ca.

4 Statistics Canada, "Same-Sex Couples and Sexual Orientation . . . by the Numbers" (last modified June 25, 2015), www.statcan.gc.ca.

5 Statistics Canada, "Percentage of Multigenerational Households, Canada, Provinces and Territories, 2016" (last modified August 2, 2017), www.statcan.gc.ca.

6 Statistics Canada, "Focus on Geography Series, 2016 Census" (last modified April 10, 2019), www.statcan.gc.ca.

7 Statistics Canada, "Family Day 2019 and the Diversity of Families in Canada" (last modified February 18, 2019), www.statcan.gc.ca.

8 Statistics Canada, "Portrait of Children's Family Life."

9 Statistics Canada, "Portrait of Children's Family Life."

10 Statistics Canada, "Single-Earner and Dual-Earner Census Families by Number of Children" (last modified August 16, 2021), www.statcan.gc.ca.

11 Statistics Canada, "Portrait of Children's Family Life."

12 Statistics Canada, "Portrait of Children's Family Life."

13 Annie Turner, "Living Arrangements of Aboriginal Children Aged 14 and Under" (Statistics Canada, last modified August 11, 2016), www.statcan.gc.ca.

14 Mary Jane Mossman et al., *Families and the Law: Cases and Commentary*, 3rd ed. (Concord, ON: Captus Press, 2019), 17.

15 Canadian Assisted Reproductive Technologies Registry (CARTR) Plus, "Final Treatment Cycle and Pregnancy Outcome Data for 2020" (Ottawa: Better Outcomes Registry & Network Ontario, 2020). These data likely provide an underestimate of the number of ART treatment cycles in Canada as there are now more than thirty-six fertility clinics across Canada.

16 John-Paul Boyd, *Polyamory in Canada: Research on an Emerging Family Structure* (Calgary: Canadian Research Institute for Law and the Family, 2017), 5. Statistics Canada does not track polyamorous relationships.

17 *AA v. BB*, 2007 ONCA 2 at para. 14.

18 Ontario uses the term "birth parent" to account for the different gender identities of individuals who give birth. See Children's Law Reform Act, RSO 1990, chap. C-12, sec. 1(1) (hereafter cited as CLRA).

19 See, e.g., Family Law Act, SBC 2011, chap. 25, sec. 27(3).

20 *AA v. BB*, 2007 ONCA 2.

21 British Columbia Birth Registration No. 2018-XX-XX5815, 2021 BCSC 767.

22 Ontario, British Columbia, and Saskatchewan allow parentage agreements: CLRA, chap. C-12; and Family Law Act; Children's Law Act, 2020, SO 2020, chap. 2.

23 But see *MRR v. JM*, 2017 ONSC 2655, where an Ontario court granted a declaration of nonparentage in a case where the parties failed to put their parentage agreement in writing.
24 Saskatchewan Children's Law Act, 2020, SO 2020, chap. 2, sec. 61(2).
25 See British Columbia's Family Law Act, which presumes that only legal parents who have lived with a child may exercise parenting responsibilities and parenting time, while all legal parents are responsible for child support: Family Law Act, secs. 39, 40 and 147. The requirement that a parent live with a child in order to exercise parenting responsibilities and parenting time disproportionately impacts fathers: see *Phillips v. BC Ministry of the Attorney General*, 2019 BCHRT 76.
26 Parentage presumptions deem individuals in a relationship with the birth mother at the time of the child's birth legal parents. See, e.g., CLRA, sec. 7(2).
27 A judge recently declared parts of Manitoba's Family Maintenance Act unconstitutional on the basis that the legal definition of parentage excluded same-sex parents and therefore violated the equality provision of Canada's Charter of Rights and Freedoms. See Katie May, "Manitoba to Update 'Parent' Law," *Winnipeg Free Press*, November 12, 2020, www.winnipegfreepress.com.
28 Divorce Act, secs. 15.1(1) and 2(1).
29 Family Law Act, sec. 1(1).
30 See, e.g., *Kincaid v. Arsenault*, 2002 CarswellOnt 1346.
31 Family Law Act, sec. 147(4).
32 Québec law does not extend child support liability to common law stepparents. However, married stepparents are liable under the Divorce Act.
33 *Chartier v. Chartier*, 1999 SCR 242.
34 *Chartier v. Chartier*, para. 39.
35 See, e.g., *Forsyth v. Santinhos*, 2019 ONCJ 847.
36 Nicholas Bala, "Who Is a 'Parent'? 'Standing in the Place of a Parent' & Canada's Child Support Guidelines S. 5" (July 12, 2007), Queen's University Legal Studies Research Paper No. 07-11, https://papers.ssrn.com.
37 *Cook v. Cook*, 2000 CarswellNS 20 at para. 33.
38 *Widdis v. Widdis*, 2000 SKQB 441 at para. 12.
39 Other courts have refused to impose child support obligations on "mistaken fathers." See, e.g., *TW v. SL*, 2017 SKQB 45, where the "mistaken father" was not ordered to pay child support because he had never intended to act as a father toward a child that was not his own.
40 *Day v. Weir*, 2014 ONSC 5975, contra *TW v. SL*, 2017 SKQB 45 at para. 74.
41 *Day v. Weir*, 70.
42 *Day v. Weir*, 70.
43 See British Columbia's Family Law Act, sec. 147(5)(a): "If a stepparent has a duty to provide support for a child under subsection (4), the stepparent's duty . . . is secondary to that of the child's parents and guardians."
44 SOR/1997–175, sec. 5.
45 *Chartier* at para. 42.

46 See, e.g., *Duffy v. Boisvert*, 2017 BCSC 500.
47 Family Law Act, SA 2003, chap. F-45, sec. 23.
48 CLRA, sec. 21(2).
49 *Johnstone v. Locke*, 2012 ONSC 719 at para. 96.
50 *Khan v. Kong*, 2007 CarswellOnt 8983 at para. 232, aff'd 2009 ONCA 21.
51 See *JL v. RL*, 2017 NBBR 151, where a court awarded custody of two children to the genetic mother's same-sex partner.
52 *Johnstone* at 114.
53 *JCB v. HJC*, 2015 ABCA 90.
54 *JCB v. HJC*, para. 1.
55 *JCB v. HJC*, para. 7.
56 Family Law Act, 2, sec. 1(1).
57 Family Law Act, sec. 48(1)(a) and (b).
58 *Racine v. Woods*, 2 SCR 173 (1983).
59 See, e.g., *Martin v. Duffell*, SCR 737 (1950); *Hepton v. Maat*, SCR 606 (1957); and *McNeilly v. Agar*, SCR 53 (1958).
60 *Racine* at 174.
61 *King v. Low*, 1 SCR 87 (1985).
62 *King v. Low*, para. 27.
63 *BJT v. JD*, 24 SCC (2022), para. 101.
64 *Hernandez v. Nikas*, 2017 ONSC 162 at paras. 93 and 94.
65 *Hernandez v. Nikas*, paras. 75 and 76.
66 *AL v. DK*, 2000 BCCA 455.
67 *AL v. DK*, para. 25, citing *Seymour v. Seymour*, BCJ No 1970 (1994). See also *KEL v. SAL*, 2018 ONSC 1309, in which the biological father was awarded custody over the maternal grandparents.
68 *GES v. DLC*, 2006 SKCA 79.
69 *GES v. DLC*, para. 65.
70 *GES v. DLC*, para. 65.
71 Carol Rogerson made this point with respect to stepparent child support obligations: "The Child Support Obligations of Step-Parents," *Canadian Journal of Family Law* 18 (2001): 9.
72 Fiona Kelly argues that resolving multiparent parenting disputes may not be more complicated or complex than resolving parenting disputes between two parents: "Multiple-Parent Families under British Columbia's New Family Law Act: A Challenge to the Supremacy of the Nuclear Family or a Method by Which to Preserve Biological Ties and Opposite-Sex Parenting?," *UBC Law Review* 47 (2014): 565, 574–575.

6

Social Parenthood in Mexico

SOFÍA TREVIÑO FERNÁNDEZ

In Mexico, as well as in other jurisdictions in Latin America, the narrow legal categories that recognize legal parenthood and parental rights have never been able to capture family diversity or how children receive care and affection in a plurality of ways. Traditional civil law frameworks of parentage/filiation do not cover the role of extended family, stepparents, and people who effectively assume parental responsibilities. However, recent legal and social transformations surrounding family life, which include the increased use of assisted reproduction and constitutional protections for LGBTQ family formation, have put pressure on the civil codes that currently govern parent-child relationships. While codes and statutory law have mostly stagnated in regard to social parenthood, case law at the Supreme Court level has increasingly recognized the lived realities of families in Mexico.

Demographic Data

Almost without exception, studies of Latin America include general observations on the importance of family in the region.[1] While family remains central to economic and social life, family patterns have changed. In the past twenty years, marriage rates in Mexico have almost halved,[2] while cohabitation has steadily risen.[3] Simultaneously, divorce has increased steeply,[4] particularly after the introduction and expansion of no-fault divorce beginning in 2008.[5] There has also been an increase in both homes with single parents and children living with unmarried cohabitating partners.[6] Around 3.7 percent of the total child population does not reside with either of their biological parents.[7]

These family changes have not been distributed equally among socioeconomic groups. Around one in five children experiences a father's migration by age fifteen, a phenomenon that disproportionally impacts rural communities and children born to less-educated mothers.[8] Even if cohabitation has increased in all sectors of society, it is still more prevalent in low-income families.[9] While higher-income women have delayed marriage, are having children later, and face lower probabilities of divorce,[10] the same is not true for lower-income women.[11]

Family diversity has also become more visible. According to the 2020 census, more than 300,000 self-identified same-sex couples live together, an increase of around 38 percent from 2010. Almost half of these same-sex couples are raising children, 58 percent within marriage. Although there is no official information on whether their children are biological, formally adopted, or born through assisted reproduction (AR), we now know that more than 62,000 unmarried, same-sex couples also raise children in Mexico.

The social normalization of AR has benefited not just same-sex couples; single people and different-sex couples have also accessed these technologies. While we do not know how many children in Mexico are conceived using AR, the increased demand has led to a swift rise in providers. By 2018, around one hundred authorized clinics across twenty-one states and most public health care systems offered some sort of AR services.[12]

Finally, information about children without legal parental care in Mexico is unreliable. However, while caregiving by extended family remains a very common practice,[13] government data also point toward an inefficient adoption system and prevailing institutionalization for children without family care. Official information acknowledges that between 2014 and 2020 only seventy-three national and international adoptions were granted in Mexico City;[14] in contrast, more than thirty thousand children were officially registered in institutions or social assistance centers in Mexico, most of which are private.[15]

Legal Recognition of Parents

Mexico is a federal country with thirty-two subnational units, including Mexico City. While there is some relevant federal legislation on the protection of children's rights, family law is mostly understood to be under each state's purview. Therefore, there are thirty-two different codes or family law statutes across the country that regulate the most important aspects of parent-child relationships. State courts have jurisdiction over family law cases, however through a constitutional remedy called *amparo*, federal courts—including the Supreme Court—can review state courts' decisions. Under certain circumstances,[16] Supreme Court amparo precedents can become binding to all judges, and via mechanisms of constitutional abstract review, the court can strike down state law in decisions that bind all state authorities.

Though regulation on parentage does vary across states, some general principles can be delineated. The recognition of parental rights and responsibilities—custody, visitation, child support, immigration status, access to social security benefits, medical decision making, etc.—always depends on the recognition of legal parental status through filiation or the establishment of legal guardianship (*tutela*). Formal guardianship is established only in the absence of both parents and (in their absence) grandparents, either by death or by the judicial termination of their rights. Even if distinctions between marital and nonmarital children are textually forbidden, most codes and statutes still rely on marital presumptions to establish legal parenthood, and some codes have introduced strong language and protections for biological bonds.

Generally, filiation is established by marital presumption, recognition, investigation, or adoption. The first three mechanisms have come to presuppose a biological relationship with the child.[17] This is evidenced by the unfettered authorization of judicial investigation of paternity and maternity by any evidentiary means, including DNA testing.[18] Most codes extend the marital presumption to children born within nonmarital cohabitation (*concubinato*) and regulate adoption separately. There is debate among Mexican civil law treatise authors[19] on whether adoption can be considered filiation precisely because it lacks the biological/genetic link. Though some codes still limit filiation inquiries to children born to unmarried women, these restrictions can no longer be enforced based on case law regarding the doctrine of "biological truth."[20] This strong biological understanding is also present in civil law treatises that stipulate that filiation "could only originate naturally from the biological fact of birth," shaping professional narratives around family bonds in Mexican law.[21]

However, all states have maintained a rarely used provision from the original nineteenth-century code that allows for some recognition of the act of parenting—or de facto parenthood. Used for suing to have paternity recognized mostly concerning inheritance disputes, the provision on "possession of son or daughter status" (*posesión del estado de hijo*) served as a basis to prove filiation in the absence of birth certificates. Therefore, it was not, per se, a "source" of filiation but rather evidence of the underlying bond. Doctrinal work describes it as "not based on a normative regime, . . . [it has] its origin in factual situations; traditionally, [it derives from] the treatment, name, and fame, . . . not from official records, but from the facts of daily reality."[22] For treatise writers, the possession of a "constant state" proved the filiation of children born in marriage. Evidence would be required of the husband's family and society consistently recognizing them as a child of the marriage and, in addition, of their use of his surname, with his consent, or of the potential father providing them with "subsistence, education, and establishment."

"Fame" was crucial to the provision: the social recognition of what was then understood to be the parent-child relationship.[23] After eliminating considerations for illegitimacy in the early twentieth century, the provision would also apply to children born out of wedlock. With time, the civil registry's expansion, and the appearance and increased use of DNA testing, this provision became somewhat dead law—that is, until the Supreme Court recently revived it (see below).

Overall, with very limited exceptions, codes provide no protections, rights, or responsibilities for people who effectively act as parents but lack biological or genetic ties. Additionally, codes change slowly. Few codes or family law statutes provide for AR,[24] and when the phrase "assisted reproductive technologies" does appear, it is usually mentioned only as a source of filiation and is explicitly or implicitly limited to heterosexual couples. Only two states, Sinaloa and Tabasco, regulate surrogacy, and do so in very restrictive ways; limited to heterosexual couples that can provide medical certification of infertility. As the Supreme Court explained in a recent case,[25] the lack of regulation in parentage law does not mean that AR is not used by either single people or different-sex or same-sex couples; it means only that all involved (parents, donors, surrogates, children) are unprotected in cases of conflict.

Legal Recognition of Social Parents: Three Common Contexts

Same-Sex Couples

Same-sex couples and their children face many obstacles to establish legal parenthood, particularly for the person who lacks a biological relation with the child. Only twenty-one of the thirty-two states in Mexico recognize same-sex marriage in the codes and filiation rules remain gendered. However, traditional mechanisms to establish filiation have been used by same-sex couples, including adoption.[26]

In a few cases in which the civil registry rejected applications for birth certificates, the Supreme Court ruled that denying the recognition of filiation to LGBTQ individuals due to a lack of biological connection to the child was both detrimental to the child's best interest and a violation of the constitutional principle of equality and nondiscrimination. To guarantee same-sex couples' rights to procreation and family life, the court considered that it was possible to establish filiation using AR through either recognition or marital presumption (that usually applies to cohabitating partners as well).[27]

In a case involving a female same-sex couple that wasn't allowed to register a child as their own, the court went further: the state code was unconstitutional because it reinforced heteronormative conceptions of parenthood that were incompatible with the constitutional and conventional rights to equality and family protection.[28] The court balanced the child's right to identity and the potential biological parent's rights with the interest of recognizing family diversity. First, it reiterated that, independent of the determination on legal filiation, the child maintained the right to investigate her "biological origin" and to claim—if she so wishes—the recognition of paternity from her biological father, but, meanwhile, "the full exercise of filial rights shall be safeguarded with respect to the individuals [now] at the head of her family environment."[29] Second, it was established that the biological parent (it is not known if the couple used AR)[30] may have an interest in claiming paternity and establishing filiation with the child; however, since that was only a possibility, the child's interests would be better protected by recognizing filiation with the people who effectively assumed the parental function.[31]

These court decisions are not binding to nonjudicial authorities beyond the specific case, including civil registries. While some jurisdictions will register children born through AR, the most likely scenario is that same-sex couples and their children will have to go to court or through regular adoption proceedings to establish a legal relationship with the parent or parents that lack a biological connection to the child.

Stepparents

Mexican codes provide no protections for stepparents during or after partnership with the legal parent. Adoption is available only when there is just one legal parent or when one of the legal parents loses or relinquishes their parental rights. Argentina recently became the only country in Latin America that recognizes some legal protections for stepparents while the relationship with the legal parents subsists.[32]

Nonparental Primary Caregivers

Despite the prevalent practice of extended family raising children, informal guardianship usually grants no legal rights. Accordingly, the prevailing system generally leaves many children and their primary caregivers without any defined legal status or protections. In most codes, the family law rules rooted in nineteenth-century paradigms have not been thoroughly reviewed; Mexico City's code has changed the most.

In the 2000s the city relaxed divorce rules, and in 2010 it became the first jurisdiction in Latin America to recognize same-sex marriage. Concerning social parenthood, two provisions stand out. In 2012, the original 1920s text of article 378 was amended, establishing that the person—not the woman—who cares for a child during early infancy ("who cares for the breastfeeding") and *holds the child as their own* can contradict someone else's claim to recognize the child and cannot—without a court ruling—be separated from the child.[33] Particularly phrased with gender neutral terms, the provision grants some legal protection to relationships between parents and children on the basis of parental conduct.

Additionally, in 2011, the city introduced a provision that cannot be found in other states. Under article 400, "The family, with or without kinship (*parentesco*), that has assumed the permanent care of a child" has the right to be heard in adoption proceedings and oppose them. If one of the family members chooses to adopt the child, they would be preferred vis-à-vis third parties. Interestingly, this provision refers to "the family," not the individuals who care for a child, and acknowledges not only the practice of extended family members caring for children but also people without biological or preexisting legal relationships.

Outside of Mexico City, in 2007 the state of Sonora published a new family code, which introduced a third category to the traditional bases of kinship regulation (those being consanguinity and marriage): "voluntary kinship" (*parentesco voluntario*). This new category provides for adoption and AR along with "the filiation or fostering of orphaned or abandoned minors or those who have been legally surrendered by their parents, provided that the relationship lasts for over one year with all the characteristics and purposes of the parental-filial relationship."[34]

Finally, although most children without formal or informal family care still end up in institutions, in 2014 Congress approved a federal statute on the rights of children (LGDNNA) that included alternative care provisions. In response, Mexico City passed a local statute and amended the civil code to accommodate foster families. For the first time, the practice of extended family caring for children in the absence of legal parents received some legal recognition, and the statute regulated the possibility of foster families without biological or genetic ties. By 2018 the city's system of family protection services instituted a pilot program (with somewhat disappointing results),[35] and in 2020 the federal government drafted guidelines for a national alternative care program that includes a foster family system.

Developed on the principle that alternative care systems must pursue reunification with "the family of origin," the federal program's guidelines expressly establish that filiation will not be derived from foster care arrangements. Mexico City's statute also provides that, in the case of conflict, a family judge will decide on issues regarding parental authority, custody, and visitation, but there is no clear guidance on how to apply the rules.[36] While at first glance it remains unclear whether the legal relationship between foster parents and children may extend outside the arrangement (at least in Mexico City) under article 400, foster families may be granted a preferred right to adopt children under their care.

Discussion

In contrast with codified law, in the past fifteen years the Supreme Court has revised increasingly more cases using human rights language—particularly from the Convention on the Rights of the Child (CRC)—to modify previous understandings of parent-child relationships. There are three different themes in the court's jurisprudence that reflect this evolution.

The Right to Identity and "Biological Truth"[37]

A child's right to identity—under article 4 of the Mexican Constitution and CRC articles 7 and 8—was the basis to open paternity and maternity suits. First, it became possible to attribute filiation to married men.[38] Later, paternity contestation proceedings involving children with two recognized legal parents were allowed.[39] An important body of cases established DNA testing as the prevalent means to establish filiation, even overruling legal parenthood through marital presumptions.[40] Early cases ruled that establishing a filial bond with the biological father did not violate the best interest standard even if, by default, that would take away the legal (and social) father's parental rights.[41] The court granted injunctions (amparos) for DNA testing, arguing that—in some cases—they should occur even against the child's wishes since knowing their "biological origin" was crucial to establish identity.[42]

This markedly strong biological focus on filiation soon became more nuanced. While most early cases did provide a vague reference to considering the child's best interest in determinations regarding DNA testing, it was not until 2014 that the court clarified that test results need not alter preexisting filial bonds.[43] But in the same ruling the court expressly reinforced the two-parent paradigm under the "incompatibility of opposed filiation principle": a child may have only two legal parents (with adjacent parental rights and responsibilities).[44] As a result, if a child already has two legal parents, recognition of the biological parent as a legal parent would displace the person who had been the other legal parent up until that point. The court ruled that while "biological truth" should be provided for, other considerations must be weighed to determine whether "legal filiation" must be changed.

The Doctrine on "Consolidated Social Reality"

The first case to recognize the relationship between effective caregivers and children involved a complicated adoption process in which the biological mother regretted giving up the child. The court terminated the biological mother's rights and confirmed the irregular adoption under a best interest of the child argument.[45] In cases that followed, the court provided more guidance; for example, it allowed two people to change their names to coincide with the person who raised them but with whom they did not share a biological/genetic bond. The court developed the right to identity and held that "in law there does not necessarily have to be correspondence between the biological reality and the legal fact, since a multiplicity of circumstances outside of genetics, those of a psychosocial nature, must be considered,"[46] ruling that "from a legal point of view, the father and mother are those persons who assume and comply with the set of duties and benefit from the correlative rights that arise from this relationship."[47]

The court tried to settle the doctrine on "social reality" in a case involving a woman who left an infant in the care of a couple who unlawfully registered the child as their own and assumed full parental responsibility.[48] When the biological mother returned two and a half years later and sued for the recognition of maternity, the trial court ordered DNA testing, ruled that the birth certificate be changed, and granted her custody of the child. The Supreme Court overturned that decision, holding that while there is a "presumption in favor of the principle of keeping the child in their biological family" under a questionable interpretation of CRC article 9, that presumption is subordinated to the best interest of the child.[49] To determine what is best for the child, the court concluded that the family judge must consider (1) the circumstances under which the child was separated from their biological parents and (2) whether there has been a "consolidation of a family reality different from the biological reality."[50]

To establish if a "social reality" had consolidated, the court relied on attachment theory to argue, by analyzing the best interest of the child, that considering with whom the child has established a lasting emotional bond through interactions and care—independent from any biological or genetic link—is relevant, since breaking that connection has been proven to harm the child.[51] To ground the "social reality" doctrine in statutory law, the court relied on the codified *possession of son or daughter status* and claimed that while in its origins the provision was only used to prove an underlying filial bond, it was evident that the act of treating a child as one's own had received some legal recognition.[52]

The court also established a harm standard: to overrule the interest in preserving the (biological) family relationship in order to terminate parental rights or deny recognition of filiation, "it is not enough to show that the definitive separation from the [biological] parents 'will be more beneficial to the child'; it must be shown that, otherwise, the child will be placed in a detrimental situation."[53] This high standard proved to be problematic—especially when AR is involved—because it furthers the tendency of trying to match legal filiation to biological filiation by making the biological family *the* family by default.[54]

Finally, the court corrected course and added that the right to identity not only is satisfied by the recognition of biological origins but also can be guaranteed by the reaffirmation of the child's "social reality," "because it is the context in which the child grows up that determines who they are and how they are perceived by others."[55] While the ruling on "social reality" was a plurality opinion,[56] the general criteria were confirmed in subsequent cases and served as a basis for recognizing the legal status of LGBTQ parents who lacked a biological connection to their children.[57]

Intended Parenthood (voluntad procreacional)

The most recent case law involves the recognition of *voluntad procreacional* as a basis of legal parental status. When a woman sued her former husband to strip him of legal status as a parent of a child born using sperm donation, the court determined that, under a best interest principle, a child's right to their identity is protected by conserving the filial bond with the person who consented to using AR.[58] The court—trying to fill the codes' voids—developed the doctrine on intended parenthood and later applied it to cases involving same-sex couples as described above.

After a complicated evolution of the case law in the Supreme Court, there is a tendency to recognize family stability protections for people who take on parental duties and responsibilities independent of biological considerations. This approach has been developed both on the realization that it is better for children when the relationship with their caregivers is protected and on the recognition that family diversity is not safeguarded under traditional civil-law categories. Nevertheless, the law of parenthood continues to be problematic.

Social Parenthood: Looking Ahead

It is evident that the existing codes and statutes on parenthood have been pushed to a tipping point. A system that ties all parental rights to the recognition of legal parental status in filiation and simultaneously remains anchored to the two-parent paradigm will continue to leave children and diverse families unprotected, particularly in the face of changing family patterns. Without a more fluid and flexible legal understanding of parenthood, strong tension will persist between biological and nonbiological family ties, which the Supreme Court's doctrines on confrontation between "biological truth" and "social reality" already reflects. As it has before, this could lead to the termination or nonrecognition of rights and protections for people with legitimate interests—whether biological or based on parental conduct—to the detriment of children and family life.

As it stands, the statutes leave trial courts with little authority to protect the best interests of children in cases where social and biological parentage do not align. Judges must either follow the statutory directive and sever existing parental relationships or ignore the clear directives in the statutes and protect existing nonbiological parent child relationships consistent with constitutional and international human rights directives. This could, in turn, result in the recognition of multiparent families (or triple filiation), as some courts have done in Brazil and Argentina,[59] or in judges separating parental rights from parental legal status on a case-by-case basis (with all the problems this level of judicial discretion might entail). Therefore, while unlikely, there is a need for a complete overhaul of the codes' filiation system with an approach that either breaks the two-parent paradigm[60] or provides specific rules to authorize rights and protections for parent-child relationships outside of the legal parental status (or both). This change would recognize the importance of parental care, give certainty to parents and children, and rein in judicial discretion and bias in favor of all families.

NOTES

I would like to thank Karla Ripoll for her assistance with research for this chapter.

1 Manuel L. Carlos and Lois Sellers, "Family, Kinship Structure, and Modernization in Latin America," *Latin American Research Review* 7, no. 2 (1972): 95–124.

2 National Institute of Statistics and Geography (INEGI), *Estadísticas de Nupcialidad* (Marriage Statistics), www.inegi.org.mx. In 1999, the marriage rate for every thousand people was 7.6; in 2009, the rate was 4.0.

3 Julieta Pérez Amador, "Continuity and Change of Cohabitation in Mexico: Same as Before or Different Anew," *Demographic Research* 35 (October 2016): 1245.

4 INEGI, *Estadísticas de Nupcialidad.* The divorce rate for every hundred marriages doubled from 2009 to 2019.

5 See Edith Aguirre, "Do Changes in Divorce Legislation Have an Impact on Divorce Rates? The Case of Unilateral Divorce in Mexico," *Latin American Economic Review* 28, no. 1 (October 2019): 1–24.

6 Based on the 2010 and 2020 INEGI population and housing census, it increased from 1.8 to 2.3 million homes (6.5 percent of all households), 87.5 percent with single mothers and 12.5 percent with single fathers. Furthermore, based on the 2010 and 2020 INEGI population and housing census, it increased from 2.9 to 4.7 million homes (13.3 percent of all households); 1.3 percent are homes constituted by unmarried same-sex couples with children.

7 UNICEF, *Los derechos de la infancia y la adolescencia en México* (Mexico: UNICEF, 2018), 18.

8 Jenna Nobles, "Migration and Father Absence: Shifting Family Structure in Mexico," *Demography* 50, no. 4 (August 2013): 1303–1314.

9 Pérez Amador, "Continuity and Change," 1247.

10 Edith Aguirre, "The (Non)Impact of Education on Marital Dissolution" (Discussion Papers 19/15, Department of Economics, University of York, 2019).

11 Elsa Ortíz-Ávila, "Estrato sociodemográfico y patrones relacionados con la primera unión o la primera maternidad en México, 2018," *Población y Salud en Mesoamérica* 18, no. 1 (December 2020).

12 S. P. González-Santos, "A National Portrait," in *A Portrait of Assisted Reproduction in Mexico* (Cham: Palgrave Macmillan, 2020), 252 and 234.

13 Carlos and Sellers, "Family, Kinship Structure, and Modernization." "The importance of an extended family is not its composition, but rather the relationships and reciprocal obligations that it entails. . . . An extended family can also consist of *compadres*, single or married cousins, and other members of the same generation related through marriage or descent." In the INEGI 2020 census, around 2.3 million homes were formed by extended families with children.

14 This number reflects only adoptions under the National System of Family Development (DIF). SNDIF, "Estadística de Adopción" (2017), https://datos.gob.mx/busca/dataset/estadistica-de-adopcion. There is no accessible information for the state offices of family development services.

15 UNICEF, *Los derechos*, 118.
16 There are voting requirements, and mostly before 2021, a precedent needed to be confirmed multiple times to become binding.
17 See Jorge Alfredo Domínguez Martínez, *Derecho Civil: Familia* (Mexico: Porrúa, 2014).
18 See, e.g., Article 385 of Mexico City's Civil Code (Código Civil para el Distrito Federal).
19 See, e.g., Dominguez Martínez, *Derecho Civil*, 472.
20 See Supreme Court of Justice of the Nation (SCJN), First Chamber (FCH), Thesis Contradiction (CT) 430/2013, judgment rendered May 28, 2014.
21 Fausto Rico et al., *Derecho de familia* (Mexico: Porrúa, 2011), 79.
22 Dominguez Martínez, *Derecho Civil*, 546–547.
23 Dominguez Martínez, *Derecho Civil*, 547–548.
24 Only Tabasco, Sinaloa, Coahuila, Colima, Mexico City, State of Mexico, Jalisco, Michoacán, Puebla, San Luis Potosí, Querétaro, and Zacatecas mention AR in their family law codes or statutes.
25 SCJN, Plenary, Acción de inconstitucionalidad 16/2016, judgment rendered June 7, 2021.
26 See Estefanía Vela Barba, "Nuevas tecnologías reproductivas," in *Conceptos clave en los estudios de género*, vol. 2, ed. Hortensia Moreno and Eva Alcántara (CIEG-UNAM, 2018), 203–205.
27 SCJN, FCH, Amparo en revision (AR) 553/2018, judgment rendered November 21, 2018, para. 125n and ss. Here the court relied on an Inter-American Human Rights Court ruling. I/A Court H.R., *Artavia Murillo y otros (Fecundación In Vitro) v. Costa Rica*, November 28, 2012, *Fondo, Reparaciones y Costas*, paras. 142, 143, and 145.
28 Under article 1.1 of the American Convention of Human Rights. See SCJN, FCH, AR 852/2017, judgment rendered May 8, 2019.
29 SCJN, FCH, AR 852/2017, 74.
30 SCJN, FCH, AR 852/2017, 20.
31 SCJN, FCH, AR 852/2017, 73.
32 Article 604 of the 2015 Argentinian Civil Code (Código Civil y Comercial de la Nación).
33 The text in Spanish reads, "Artículo 378.—La persona que cuida o ha cuidado de la lactancia de un niño, a quien le ha dado su nombre o permitido que lo lleve, que públicamente lo ha presentado como hijo suyo y ha proveído a su educación y subsistencia podrá, contradecir el reconocimiento que alguien haya hecho o pretenda hacer de ese niño. En este caso, no se le podrá separar de su lado a menos que consienta en entregarlo o que fuere obligada a hacer la entrega por sentencia ejecutoriada."
34 Article 206 of the Sonora Family Code (Código de Familia para el Estado de Sonora).
35 Oscar Germes Castro and Alexa Cuello Miedzybrodzki, "Sistematización y evaluación de la cooperación de RELAF y UNICEF México para el desarrollo de seis programas piloto de acogimiento familiar, como parte de un proceso gradual

hacia la desinstitucionaliazción de niñas, niños y adolescentes en el país" (RELAF, 2018), www.relaf.org.

36 See Articles 492A and 494E of Mexico City's statute Ley de Cuidados Alternativos para Niñas, Niños y Adolescentes en el Distrito Federal.

37 CT 430/2013, para. 75. See also SCJN, FCH, Amparo directo en revision (ADR) 908/2006, judgment rendered April 18, 2007.

38 SCJN, FCH, CT 50/2011, judgment rendered June 1, 2011; and SCJN, FCH, ADR 2750/2010, judgment rendered October 26, 2011.

39 SCJN, FCH, CT 152/2011, judgment rendered November 23, 2011.

40 See, among others, SCJN, FCH, ADR 1601/2011, judgment rendered October 19, 2011; ADR 1321/2013, September 4, 2013; ADR 3246/2013, January 21, 2015.

41 SCJN, ADR 1603/2012, judgment rendered November 28, 2012.

42 SCJN, ADR *3759/2012*, judgment rendered February 27, 2013, para. 80.

43 CT 430/2013, paras. 77–81, 87.

44 CT 430/2013, paras. 82–85.

45 SCJN, FCH, ADR 348/2011, judgment rendered December 5, 2012.

46 SCJN, FCH, ADR 259/2013, judgment rendered October 30, 2013, 54.

47 ADR 259/2013, 53.

48 SCJN, FCH, ADR 6179/2015, judgment rendered November 26, 2016, 12. See ADR 6179/2015.

49 SCJN, FCH, ADR 6179/2015, 12.

50 SCJN, FCH, ADR 6179/2015, 16.

51 SCJN, FCH, ADR 6179/2015, 23. Among others, the court cites the work of John Bowlby, *A Secure Base: Parent-Child Attachment and Healthy Human Development* (London: Routledge, 1988).

52 SCJN, FCH, ADR 6179/2015, 37.

53 SCJN, FCH, ADR 6179/2015, 15 and 29.

54 CT 430/2011.

55 ADR 6179/2015, 27.

56 The case was decided by a four-to-one majority vote with three separate concurring opinions.

57 SCJN, FCH, ADR 4686/2016, judgment rendered May 3, 2017; ADR 2069/2016, November 29, 2017, and Amparo directo (AD) 34/2016, May 16, 2018.

58 SCJN, FCH, ADR 2766/2015, judgment rendered July 12, 2017, para. 143 and ss.

59 For Brazil, see S. T. F., Tribunal Pleno, RE 898.060, Relator: Min. Luiz Fux, September 21, 2016; for Argentina, see Juzgado Civil en Familia y Sucesiones Tucumán, July 2, 2020, "L.F.F. c/ S.C.O. s/ FILIACION. EXPTE No 659/17."

60 See Jens M. Scherpe, "Breaking the Existing Paradigms of Parent-Child Relationships," in *International and National Perspectives on Child and Family Law*, ed. Gillian Douglas, Mervyn Murch, and Victoria Stephens (Cambridge: Cambridge University Press, 2018), 343–359.

7

Social Parenthood in the United States

COURTNEY G. JOSLIN AND DOUGLAS NEJAIME

Many individuals in the United States are raising children to whom they are not biologically or genetically related. This chapter provides an overview of the legal parental status of these nonbiological social parents in the United States. Because parentage in the United States is largely regulated by state law, there is some state-to-state variation with regard to the legal recognition of social parenthood. Nonetheless, the trend across the United States is in favor of according at least some degree of recognition to people who are functioning as parents to children but who are not those children's biological or adoptive parents or are not married to the birth parent. Today, over half the states extend at least some parental rights to such persons.

As this chapter shows, U.S. jurisdictions increasingly authorize courts to treat these social parents as legal parents, entitled to parental rights and tasked with parental responsibilities. Such legal recognition has emerged through a range of judicial and legislative interventions—including equitable and common-law doctrines of functional parentage, rules allowing the person to be recognized as a legal parent based on publicly "holding out" the child as one's child, and statutory standards for establishing parentage that look to a range of parental conduct. We identify this shift toward legal recognition of social parents as a key part of U.S. family law's functional turn, which we endorse. The legal recognition of functional parents protects children, vindicates significant equality interests, accommodates a broad range of families, and recognizes the importance of parental care.

Demographic Data

The American family has undergone dramatic changes in the past several decades. Marriage rates are at historic lows,[1] and divorce remains common.[2] Family patterns diverge along lines of race and class.

African Americans are less likely to marry than whites,[3] and roughly 70 percent of Black children are born to an unmarried mother.[4] Higher-income, highly educated Americans adhere most closely to the conventional script of marrying and having children within marriage.[5] Low-income Americans are both less likely to marry and more likely to divorce when they do.[6] As a result, their children are less likely to live with both of their legal parents. The frequency of divorce and remarriage has produced more "blended" families—that is, households with a stepparent, stepsibling, or half sibling. Approximately one in six children in the United States lives in a blended family.[7] Hispanic, African American, and white children are equally likely to live in blended families, while a far smaller share of Asian American children live in blended families.[8]

Children are more likely than ever to have parents who are not married. Roughly 40 percent of children are born to an unmarried mother.[9] Many—but not all—of these children are born to parents who are cohabiting; for women who have never been married, approximately 62 percent of births occur within a cohabiting relationship, and for women who have been married before, 38 percent of nonmarital births occur within a cohabiting relationship.[10] In 2011, "7.7 million children were living in the same household as at least one of their grandparents."[11] In most such cases, the grandparents are acting as grandparents and the children are being parented by their parent or parents. But in some cases the parents are largely absent from the children's lives and the grandparents are acting as the children's parents.[12]

Assisted reproduction also has transformed family formation. According to the Centers for Disease Control and Prevention, more than eighty thousand children were born through assisted reproduction in 2018.[13] Notably, this figure includes only children conceived through in vitro fertilization; it does not include those conceived through a common form of assisted reproduction—insemination with donor sperm. Therefore, this number significantly undercounts the total number of children conceived through assisted reproduction. Some families using assisted reproduction are using only genetic material from the intended parents. Many families, however, are not.

Assisted reproduction has opened options not only for different-sex couples and single individuals but also for same-sex couples. As of 2016, approximately 16 percent of same-sex couples are raising children.[14] Around a quarter (22 percent) of married same-sex couples have children under age eighteen, compared to 12 percent of unmarried same-sex couples.[15] Around three-quarters of same-sex couples raising children under age eighteen are female (75 percent).[16] The majority (68 percent) of same-sex couples with children are raising a child biologically related to one of the partners.[17]

Some social parent relationships are created by virtue of government intervention. As part of the child welfare system, state actors are authorized to remove children from their parents and place them in other arrangements, including placements with foster care families. In the United States, more than 437,000 children were in foster care in 2018.[18] Of these, 32 percent were placed with relatives and 46 percent were placed with nonrelative foster parents.[19] (Ten percent were placed in congregate care.[20]) Black and Native American children are much more likely than white children to be removed from their parents and to be placed in foster care.[21]

These are just some of the varied ways in which children may end up being parented by a person who is not their biological or genetical parent.

Legal Recognition of Parents

In the United States, parentage arises primarily as a question of state, rather than federal, law. Accordingly, the recognition of social parents varies by state.

There is a relatively rigid line between people who are parents and people who are third parties. This is true in part because the federal Constitution protects the right of parents to control the upbringing of their children.[22] As a result, the Constitution has been interpreted to place some limits on when a third party can be awarded contact with a child over the objection of the child's parent or parents. That said, there are a range of circumstances under which a person who is not a parent may be extended some rights and responsibilities ordinarily accorded only to parents. For example, all fifty states permit grandparents to seek an award of contact with their grandchildren, in at least some circumstances.[23]

In the past, parental rights could be separated from parental responsibilities.[24] But today, states have generally abandoned this distinction.[25] Thus, unless their parental rights have been terminated by a court, a person who is a parent typically has all of the rights and responsibilities accorded to parents. This includes the rights to seek physical custody of or visitation with children under a best interests of the child standard and to make important decisions for a child (legal custody); and all parents have an obligation to financially support their children.

Initially, marriage was the exclusive means by which parentage was established. "A married woman who gave birth to a child was treated as a legal mother, and her husband—pursuant to the marital presumption or presumption of legitimacy—was treated as a legal father."[26] Historically, an unmarried father lacked a legal relationship with his biological child in the absence of subsequent marriage to the child's mother. In the 1960s and 1970s, the U.S. Supreme Court held that this legal regime unconstitutionally discriminated against nonmarital children and their parents.[27] These Supreme Court decisions accelerated state-level reforms as state lawmakers expanded the means through which an unmarried man could establish his parentage, including through proof of his genetic parentage.

While marriage and proof of biological parenthood remain important means by which to establish one's parental status, today most jurisdictions accord at least some degree of recognition to people who are functioning as parents to children but who are not those children's biological or adoptive parents or are not married to the birth parent.

Legal Recognition of Social Parents: Three Common Scenarios

In many U.S. states, legal doctrines are available to extend rights and impose obligations on social parents.

In some states, this recognition is accorded under equitable or common-law principles. Different states use different terms—though the most common is "de facto parentage." While the doctrines vary to some degree, they generally require both proof of the existence of an actual, bonded parent-child relationship and proof that the parental relationship was formed with the support of a legal parent. For example, a common test requires the person to show

> (1) that the biological or adoptive parent consented to, and fostered, the petitioner's formation and establishment of a parent-like relationship with the child; (2) that the petitioner and the child lived together in the same household; (3) that the petitioner assumed the obligations of parenthood by taking significant responsibility for the child's care, education and development, including contributing towards the child's support, without expectation of financial compensation [a petitioner's contribution to a child's support need not be monetary]; and (4) that the petitioner has been in a parental role for a length of time sufficient to have established with the child a bonded, dependent relationship parental in nature.[28]

In many jurisdictions, a person recognized under these doctrines is treated as a legal parent—with all of the rights and obligations that status entails.[29] Nonetheless, in some states, de facto parent recognition results in more limited rights and responsibilities.[30] In these states, the individual may be entitled to seek physical custody or visitation, but, depending on the jurisdiction, may not stand on an equal footing with a legal parent, may not be eligible for full decision-making authority, and may have no child support obligations.[31] The clear trend in the United States, though, is to treat de facto parents as full legal parents.[32] Even where a child already has two legal parents, in some jurisdictions a court may find that another person qualifies as a de facto parent.[33]

At least one jurisdiction, Michigan, limits equitable parent recognition to people who are spouses.[34] Most other jurisdictions with de facto parent doctrines or their equivalent do not categorically exclude nonmarital partners from recognition. Instead, the question turns on whether the individual formed a full and permanent parental relationship—as opposed to merely a stepparent or a grandparent relationship—with the child.[35]

A few states have codified the de facto parentage doctrine. Connecticut, Delaware, Maine, Rhode Island, Vermont, and Washington have statutory provisions providing that a de facto parent can be recognized as a legal parent if they prove a set of enumerated requirements.[36] De facto parentage under these statutory provisions does not arise automatically but requires a determination by a court. The 2017 Uniform Parentage Act (UPA), promulgated by the Uniform Law Commission and already adopted in a number of states,[37] requires a person seeking to be adjudicated a de facto parent to show that they (1) "resided with the child as a regular member of the child's household for a significant period"; (2) "engaged in consistent caretaking of the child"; (3) "undertook full and permanent responsibilities of a parent of the child without expectation of financial compensation"; (4) "held out the child as the individual's child"; and (5) "established a bonded and dependent relationship with the child which is parental in nature."[38] They must also show that the child's existing parent "fostered or supported the bonded and dependent relationship."[39] In addition, the 2017 UPA, as well as a few states, require the person claiming de facto parentage to show that "continuing the relationship between the individual and the child is in the best interest of the child."[40] If the person is recognized as a parent under this statutory provision, the person stands in parity with all other legal parents.

A number of states have an alternative statutory provision under which a social but nonmarital, nonbiological, and nonadoptive parent can be recognized. This is often referred to as the *holding out presumption*.[41] The rule creates a presumption of parentage if the person has lived with the child and represented themselves to others as the child's parent.[42] The original 1973 version of the UPA included a gender-specific "holding out" presumption, which referred to men who engaged in the required conduct.[43] The 2017 UPA updated the "holding out" presumption to be expressly gender neutral.[44] Moreover, even in states with gender-specific "holding out" presumptions, numerous courts have held that the provision must be applied equally to women.[45] Courts in many states also have held that this presumption is not necessarily or automatically overcome by evidence that the person is not the child's biological parent.[46] Importantly, some jurisdictions have both de facto parentage and a holding out presumption.

In some states, the "holding out" presumption applies to conduct that occurs at any point during the child's minority.[47] In other states, the conduct that demonstrates "holding out" must occur during the first years of the child's life.[48] A person recognized as a parent under the "holding out" presumption is treated as a legal parent, with all of the rights to custody and visitation and obligations of financial support that would be assigned to any other parent.[49]

Given that parentage can be established on a variety of grounds, including through a biological connection, based on marriage to the birth parent, or on the basis of social criteria, more than two individuals may qualify as a child's parent. Although no state expressly declares in statute that a child can have only two legal parents, it is often assumed that this is the case. This assumption is increasingly being called into question as courts are presented with cases in which more than two people have been parenting a particular child. A number of states, including California, Connecticut, Delaware, Maine, Vermont, and Washington, have enacted statutes expressly allowing a child to have more than two legal parents.[50] In some states, a judge is empowered to adjudicate an additional parent if not doing so would be "detrimental" to the child; in others, a judge may do so if it is in the child's "best interests."[51]

Multiparent arrangements arise in a diverse array of families. Commentators often focus on individuals who deliberately plan a multiparent family—for example, three individuals who consent to assisted reproduction with the intent that each of them serves as a parent to the resulting child. But multiparent families often emerge not from deliberate planning but from postbirth circumstances. In our other work, we observe that many multiparent families involve extended family members serving in a parental role for an extended period of time.[52] Even if the jurisdiction does not allow a child to have more than two legal parents, a social parent may be recognized as a de facto parent under some common-law and equitable doctrines.[53]

Same-Sex Couples

A context in which people might be parenting children to whom they are genetically unrelated involves situations where people conceive children through assisted reproduction using donated gametes. Because almost all same-sex couples who use assisted reproduction to have children rely on donated gametes, questions of social parent recognition are especially important to these families. When a female same-sex couple has a child through assisted reproduction using donor sperm, the nonbiological mother may attain parentage in a variety of ways without having to adopt her own child. If she is married to the birth mother at the time of the child's birth, she should be treated as the child's legal parent by virtue of the marital presumption of parentage.[54]

In the absence of marriage to the birth mother, the nongenetic/nongestational parent may be treated as a legal parent based on her consent to assisted reproduction. For example, under Maine's parentage law, "a person who consents to assisted reproduction by a woman . . . with the intent to be the parent of a resulting child is a parent of the resulting child."[55] In the United States, rules of this kind are described as intent-based parentage principles. While some states' recognition of legal parentage in the context of assisted reproduction applies only to married couples,[56] the trend is toward an intent-based rule that is neutral with respect to gender, sexual orientation, and marital status.[57]

A less common but nonetheless increasingly used form of assisted reproduction is surrogacy. While practically all states have laws addressing the parentage of children conceived through nonsurrogacy assisted reproduction, fewer states have laws that address the parentage of children conceived pursuant to a surrogacy arrangement. Still, the number of states that permit and regulate surrogacy—especially gestational surrogacy—is growing.[58] The clear trend is to recognize the intended parents as the legal parents at the moment of the child's birth and to not require adoption by the nonbiological intended parent.[59] Moreover, jurisdictions increasingly have allowed access to surrogacy without respect to the gender, sexual orientation, or marital status of the intended parents.[60]

In the absence of marriage to the birth mother or an applicable intent-based parentage rule, the nonbiological parent of a child conceived through assisted reproduction in a same-sex or different-sex couple might have a claim to parentage under the functional parent doctrines discussed above (including de facto parentage and the holding out presumption) if they raised the child for a significant period of time.[61]

The status of the gamete donor may in some cases also turn on functional parent doctrines. First-generation statutes regulating donor insemination typically provided that a donor is not a parent only when the sperm was used by a married woman and under the supervision of a licensed physician.[62] More recently, though, state laws have made clear that third-party donors of sperm or eggs are not parents simply because they provided genetic material.[63] A third-party gamete provider who acts as a parent, however, may have a claim to parentage based on this conduct. When both intended parents of children conceived through assisted reproduction are recognized as legal parents, the legal status of the third-party gamete provider will depend in part on whether the jurisdiction permits a child to have more than two legal parents.[64] Where the state does permit a child to have more than two legal parents, the gamete provider who has been functioning as a parent may be able to establish parenthood, not on the basis of genetic connection but instead under statutory holding out or de facto parent provisions.[65] If the state limits legal parents to a total of two, and the child already has two legal parents, then the gamete provider likely will not be recognized as a legal parent. Nonetheless, even if the state limits legal parents to a total of two, if the legal parents have allowed the gamete provider to play a parenting role for the child, that person might be entitled to some parental rights or obligations under the equitable de facto parent doctrine.

Stepparents

Stepparents are not treated as legal parents simply by virtue of their marriage to the child's parent. That said, in situations where the stepparent treats the child as *their child* (rather than as their stepchild) and the child views the stepparent as a parent (rather than as a stepparent), the stepparent may be considered a legal parent under one or more of the doctrines discussed above, including the "holding out" presumption, or statutory or common law de facto parent doctrines. If the child already has two legal parents, the legal recognition of the new spouse or nonmarital partner under these doctrines will require a legal regime that permits a child to have more than two legal parents, or two legal parents and an equitable parent who is entitled to some but not all of the rights and obligations of legal parenthood.

In a minority of states, even if the stepparent is not considered a parent, the stepparent might be entitled to seek visitation with the child after divorce.[66] These stepparent visitation statutes typically do not obligate the stepparent to provide child support.[67]

Nonparental Primary Caregivers

Many children are raised by a person other than their legal parent, and this person may become the child's psychological parent.[68] The person could qualify for parental recognition if they satisfy the relevant standard in the jurisdiction—either de facto parentage or its equivalent, or the "holding out" presumption of parentage. For de facto parentage, the person would be required to show that a legal parent fostered and supported the parental relationship between the person and the child. In addition, a few states allow courts to recognize and enforce an agreement between the original legal parent and the functional parent to grant permanent parental rights and responsibilities to the functional parent.

In some cases, the functional parent raises the child alongside a legal parent. In other cases, the functional parent raises the child in the absence of any legal parent. If, in the latter situation, the child were to return to their original legal parents after an extended period of time being raised by another caregiver, that caregiver may still be able to assert legal parentage based on de facto parentage or the "holding out" presumption. Regardless of whether the question of parental recognition arises during the child's residence with the claimant or after reunification with the legal parents, the claimant's status would require multiparent recognition if the child already has two legal parents.

Foster care, in which children live in an out-of-home placement coordinated by the state, presents a more complicated and controversial scenario. A child may be placed with a relative or nonrelative caregiver in connection with an investigation by child welfare officials. In some cases, the foster parent may hope to adopt the child and may begin the adoption process while fostering the child. At the same time, the original parent may seek reunification with the child and may oppose any attempt to terminate her parental rights.

Jurisdictions that recognize de facto parents typically require that an existing legal parent fostered and supported the parental relationship between the de facto parent and the child. Further, in many states, the doctrine requires that the individual parented the child without expectation of financial compensation. Although, in some circumstances, an individual who is a foster parent may be able to meet the standard for de facto parentage,[69] these requirements more often mean that foster parent arrangements are excluded from protection under functional parent doctrines—even if states generally do not maintain an explicit categorical exclusion.[70]

Here, we are focused on social parent doctrines that recognize an individual who is functioning as a parent. We note, however, that individuals who are not legal parents but are serving as caregivers may pursue other paths to obtain legal authority to act on behalf of the child—for example, through a guardianship action. In most circumstances, a person can become a child's legal guardian with the consent of the legal parent and would then be authorized to make decisions for the child and assume residential custody of the child.[71] In contrast to the parentage doctrines that we are addressing, a guardianship is ordinarily subject to termination at will by the legal parent.[72]

Discussion

We have identified in the United States a clear trend toward parental recognition for social parents. Indeed, in recent years, not only have states with no prior law on the matter embraced this concept, but so have a number of states that originally rejected it.[73] As the New York high court explained in 2016, its prior decision that adopted a biologically based understanding of parentage "inflicted disproportionate hardship on the growing number of [same-sex parent] families across our state."[74] That decision, the court continued, had a "negative impact on children," by denying recognition and protection to the established parent-child bonds they had formed with their nonbiological parents.[75]

Doctrines that recognize social parents, however, are not without controversy. Some courts and commentators argue that recognition of social parents impermissibly interferes with the rights of the child's other parent(s).[76] Others claim that doctrines allowing for the recognition of social parents would allow too many individuals, including those who have not actually fulfilled a parental role, to seek contact with a child.[77] We have supported and advocated the trend toward social parent recognition in our scholarly work and in legislative and litigation efforts.[78] We have done so for a variety of reasons, a few of which we identify here. With regard to the concerns noted above, we believe that the existing doctrines typically include sufficient safeguards both to protect the rights of existing legal parents and to ensure that the doctrines accurately distinguish between people who are truly functioning as a parent and those who are not.[79]

Promoting Children's Interests

First, protection for social parents promotes children's interests by securing their relationships to their psychological parents or primary attachment figures. As Joseph Goldstein, Anna Freud, and Albert Solnit explained in their foundational twentieth-century work, "Whether a person becomes the psychological parent of a child is based on day-to-day interaction, companionship, and shared experiences."[80] It does not depend on a "biological or legal relationship to the child."[81] Today, decades of research on attachment demonstrate the importance of the child's relationship to her primary caregivers or attachment figures.[82] Severing these parent-child relationships can inflict significant trauma on children—the effects of which can persist well into adulthood.[83]

Courts and legislatures that have extended parental recognition to functional parents have been animated by children's interests. As the New Jersey Supreme Court explained, "At the heart of the psychological parent cases is a recognition that children have a strong interest in maintaining the ties that connect them to adults who love and provide for them."[84] While in the United States parentage does not ordinarily turn on considerations related to the child's best interests,[85] some recent de facto parentage statutes make a best interest determination an explicit part of the standard a court is to apply. For example, following the 2017 UPA, Vermont's statute requires that, after satisfying all of the requirements in the de facto parentage statute, the claimant must also show that "continuing the relationship between the individual and the child is in the best interest of the child."[86] In this setting, the parentage determination does not turn simply on the child's best interests but instead requires a showing of six other factors as well.

Once parentage is not tethered to marriage, gender, or biology and instead aims to track the existence of parent-child relationships, a child's potential number of parents may grow. In our view, given the principles animating contemporary trends in parentage law, there is no need for a two-parent limit. Instead, the law should protect children's relationships with their parents. This position is consistent with the child-centered priorities of parentage laws that vindicate social parenthood.[87]

Family Diversity

Social parenthood doctrines respect the decisions that individuals make about family life and protect parent-child bonds that arise in a wide range of families. In doing so, these doctrines promote important constitutional values.[88] Individuals have protected liberty interests regarding a range of family formation decisions, including decisions with respect both to adult intimate relationships[89] and to childbearing and child-rearing.[90]

Extending recognition and protection to social parents furthers these constitutional interests. "A [social parenthood] rule that considers and gives effect to informal family relationships that a person chose to create promotes" constitutional commitments to autonomy in family formation.[91] The legal parent who invites another adult into their family and encourages that person to form a parent-child relationship with their child is exercising their rights with regard to the care and upbringing of their child. The social parent, too, is forming a relationship of constitutional magnitude. The important work of parenting merits protection regardless of the biological connection between parent and child.[92]

Equality

Protecting all social parenthood relationships, even when those relationships diverge from conventional norms, furthers the goals of equality and inclusion. A parentage regime designed around biological connection makes outsiders of parents and children living in a range of family configurations in the United States For example, parentage rules rooted in biological criteria harm LGBTQ parents as most LGBTQ-parent families feature at least one nonbiological parent.[93]

As New York's high court explained in 2016, given legal reforms recognizing the equality and liberty interests of LGBTQ individuals, the "foundational premise of heterosexual parenting and nonrecognition of same-sex couples is unsustainable."[94] The premise of heterosexual parenting—sexual procreation and biological parenthood—excludes same-sex couples, who ordinarily include a nongenetic parent.

It is not sufficient, the New York court held, to demand that same-sex couples marry or adopt for both partners to be recognized as parents, when the paradigmatic different-sex couple need not take formal steps: "Under [a] legal framework . . . which emphasizes biology, it is impossible—without marriage or adoption—for both former partners of a same-sex couple to have standing, as only one can be biologically related to the child. By contrast, where both partners in a heterosexual couple are biologically related to the child, both former partners will have standing regardless of marriage or adoption."[95] To treat LGBTQ parents with the dignity and respect they deserve, the government is obligated to shift from a parentage framework designed around the heterosexual family and biological relations toward a framework that makes space for nonbiological, nonadoptive, nonmarital parents.[96] Providing pathways to parentage for social parents, the New York court reasoned, was essential to "ensure[] equality for same-sex parents and provide[] the opportunity for their children to have the love and support of two committed parents."[97] In this sense, the urgent equality interests at stake in social parenthood are closely connected to the important interests in children's welfare.

NOTES

1 Sally C. Curtin and Paul D. Sutton, "Marriage Rates in the United States, 1900–2018" (National Center for Health Statistics, April 2020).

2 A. W. Geiger and Gretchen Livingston, "8 Facts about Love and Marriage in America" (Pew Research Center, February 13, 2019).

3 Pew Research Center, "The Decline of Marriage & Rise of New Families" (2010), 9, 11, 111.

4 Pew Research Center, "Decline of Marriage," 9.

5 See Gretchen Livingston, "The Links between Education, Marriage and Parenting" (Pew Research Center, November 27, 2013); Elizabeth Wildsmith, Jennifer Manlove, and Elizabeth Cook, "Dramatic Increases in the Proportion of Births Outside of Marriage in the United States from 1990 to 2016," *Child Trends*, August 8, 2018.

6 See Benjamin R. Karney, "What's (Not) Wrong with Low-Income Marriages," *Journal of Marriage and Family* 74 (2012): 413, 415; R. Kelly Raley and Larry Bumpass, "The Topography of the Divorce Plateau Levels and Trends in Union Stability in the United States after 1980," *Demographic Research* 8 (2003): 245, 256.

7 See Pew Research Center, "Parenting in America: Outlook, Worries, Aspirations Are Strongly Linked to Financial Situation" (December 17, 2015).
8 Pew Research Center, "Parenting in America."
9 Joyce A. Martin et al., "Births: Final Data for 2018," *National Vital Statistics Report* 68 (2019): 1, 5.
10 See Esther Lamidi, "A Quarter Century Change in Nonmarital Births," FP-16-03 (National Center for Family and Marriage Research, 2016).
11 Gretchen Livingston, "At Grandmother's House We Stay: One-in-Ten Children Are Living with a Grandparent" (Pew Research Center, September 4, 2013), www.pewresearch.org.
12 See, e.g., Courtney G. Joslin and Douglas NeJaime, "How Parenthood Functions," *Columbia Law Review* 123 (2023).
13 Centers for Disease Control and Prevention, "ART Success Rates" (2018).
14 Shoshana K. Goldberg and Kerith J. Conron, "How Many Same-Sex Couples in the U.S. Are Raising Children?" (Williams Institute, July 2018).
15 Goldberg and Conron, "How Many Same-Sex Couples in the U.S. Are Raising Children?"
16 Goldberg and Conron, "How Many Same-Sex Couples in the U.S. Are Raising Children?"
17 Goldberg and Conron, "How Many Same-Sex Couples in the U.S. Are Raising Children?"
18 Child Welfare Information Gateway, "Foster Care Statistics 2018" (U.S. Department of Health and Human Services, Children's Bureau, 2020).
19 Child Welfare Information Gateway, "Foster Care Statistics 2018."
20 Child Welfare Information Gateway, "Foster Care Statistics 2018."
21 See National Conference of State Legislatures, "Disproportionality and Disparity in Child Welfare" (September 28, 2020); National Indian Child Welfare Association, "2019 Report on Disproportionality of Placements of Indian Children" (2019); Jessica Dixon, "The African-American Child Welfare Act: A Legal Redress for African American Disproportionality in Child Protection Cases," *Berkeley Journal of African-American Law and Policy* 10 (2008): 109, 114–117; Dorothy Roberts and Lisa Sangoi, "Black Families Matter: How the Child Welfare System Punishes Poor Families of Color," *Appeal*, May 26, 2018.
22 *Troxel v. Granville*, 530 U.S. 57, 65 (2000) ("The liberty interest at issue in this case—the interest of parents in the care, custody, and control of their children—is perhaps the oldest of the fundamental liberty interests recognized by this Court").
23 Barbara A. Atwood, "Third-Party Custody, Parental Liberty, and Children's Interests," *Family Advocate*, Spring 2021, 48, 49.
24 See Douglas NeJaime, "The Nature of Parenthood," *Yale Law Journal* 126 (2017): 2260, 2274–2275.
25 See, e.g., *Brooke S.B. v. Elizabeth A.C.C.*, 61 N.E.3d 488, 491–492 (N.Y. 2016) (repudiating *Shondel J. v. Mark D.*, 853 N.E.2d 610 (N.Y. 2006)). But see *In re A.M.K.*, 838 N.W.2d 865 (Wis. Ct. App. 2013).

26 Douglas NeJaime, "Who Is a Parent?," *Family Advocate*, Spring 2021, 6.

27 See *Levy v. Louisiana*, 391 U.S. 68 (1968); *Stanley v. Illinois*, 405 U.S. 645 (1972); *Gomez v. Perez*, 409 U.S. 535 (1973).

28 *V.C. v. M.J.B.*, 748 A.2d 539 (N.J. 2000) (quoting *Custody of H.S.H.-K.*, 533 N.W.2d 419, 421 (Wisc. 1995)); see also *Parentage of L.B.*, 122 P.3d 161, 176–177 (Wash. 2005).

29 See, e.g., *Parentage of L.B.*, 122 P.3d 161, 177 (Wash. 2005); *Smith v. Guest*, 16 A.3d 920, 931 (Del. 2010).

30 See, e.g., *Custody of H.S.H.-K.*, 533 N.W.2d 419 (Wisc. 1995); *E.N.O. v. L.M.M.*, 711 N.E.2d 886 (Mass. 1999).

31 See *Partanen v. Gallagher*, 59 N.E.3d 1133, 1143 (Mass. 2016) (distinguishing de facto parentage from "holding out" parentage based on the rights and responsibilities entailed in each).

32 See Courtney G. Joslin, "De Facto Parentage and the Modern Family," *Family Advocate* 40 (Spring 2018): 31.

33 See Courtney G. Joslin and Douglas NeJaime, "Multi-parent Families, Real and Imagined," *Fordham Law Review* 90 (2022): 2561.

34 See *Van v. Zahorik*, 597 N.W.2d 15 (Mich. 1999).

35 See, e.g., *Kpetigo v. Kpetigo*, 192 A.3d 929 (Md. 2018); *In re Parentage of M.F.*, 228 P.3d 1270 (Wash. 2010).

36 See, e.g., Conn. Gen. Stat. Ann. § 46b-490 (2022); Del. Code Ann. tit. 13, § 8–201(c) (2020); Vt. St. tit. 15C, § 501 (2020). See also Unif. Parentage Act § 609 (Unif. Law Comm'n 2017) (hereafter cited as UPA 2017).

37 See, e.g., 15 R.I. Gen. Laws Ann. § 15–8.1–101 (2020); Vt. Stat. Ann. tit. 15C, § 101 (West 2020); Wash. Rev. Code Ann. § 26.26A.005 (West 2020).

38 UPA 2017 at § 609.

39 UPA 2017 at § 609.

40 UPA 2017 at § 609.

41 See, e.g., UPA 2017 at § 204(a)(2); Cal. Fam. Code § 7611(d) (2020).

42 See, e.g., 15 R.I. Gen. Laws Ann. § 15–8.1.401 (2020); Vt. Stat. Ann. tit. 15C, § 401 (West 2020); Wash. Rev. Code Ann. § 26.26A.115 (West 2020).

43 See, e.g., Uniform Parentage Act § 4(a)(4) (Unif. Law Comm'n 1973) ("A man is presumed to be the natural father of a child if: . . . while the child is under the age of majority, he receives the child into his home and openly holds out the child as his natural child").

44 UPA 2017 at § 204(a)(2) ("An individual us presumed to be a parent of a child if: . . . the individual resided in the same household with the child for the first two years of the life of the child, including any period of temporary absence, and openly held out the child as the individual's child").

45 See *In re Guardianship of Madelyn B.*, 98 A.3d 494 (N.H. 2014); *Partanen v. Gallagher*, 59 N.E.3d 1133 (Mass. 2016); *In re Nicholas H.*, 46 P.3d 932 (Cal. 2002); *Chatterjee v. King*, 280 P.3d 283 (N.M. 2012); *Elisa B. v. Superior Court*, 117 P.3d 660 (Cal. 2003); *In re Parental Responsibilities of A.R.L.*, 318 P.3d 81 (Colo. App. 2013).

46 See *In re Guardianship of Madelyn B.*, 98 A.3d 494 (N.H. 2014); *Partanen v. Gallagher*, 59 N.E.3d 1133 (Mass. 2016); *In re Nicholas H.*, 46 P.3d 932 (Cal. 2002); *Chatterjee v. King*, 280 P.3d 283 (N.M. 2012); *Elisa B. v. Superior Court*, 117 P.3d 660 (Cal. 2003); *In re Parental Responsibilities of A.R.L.*, 318 P.3d 81 (Colo. App. 2013); N.H. Rev. Stat. Ann. 168-B:2(V)(d); 15 R.I. Gen. Laws Ann. § 15–8.1–401 (2020); Vt. Stat. Ann. tit. 15C, § 401 (West 2020); Wash. Rev. Code Ann. § 26.26A.115 (West 2020).

47 Cal. Fam. Code § 7611(d) (2019).

48 See, e.g., 15 R.I. Gen. Laws Ann. § 15–8.1.401 (2020); Vt. Stat. Ann. tit. 15C, § 401 (West 2020); Wash. Rev. Code Ann. § 26.26A.115 (West 2020). If a state has both de facto parentage and a holding out presumption, an individual may have claims on both grounds. But if the holding out presumption requires presence from the child's birth, a person who enters the child's life after birth would be able to proceed only under the de facto parent provision.

49 See, e.g., UPA 2017 at § 201(2); *Elisa B.*, 117 P.3d at 662 (imposing support obligations on "holding out" parent).

50 See Cal. Fam. Code § 7601 (West 2020); Conn. Public Act 21–15, § 23 (2022); Del. Code Ann. tit 13, § 8–201 (West 2020); Me. Rev. Stat. Ann. tit. 19-A, § 1853 (2020); Vt. Stat. Ann. tit. 15C, § 206 (West 2020); Wash. Rev. Code Ann. § 26.26A.460 (West 2020). See also UPA 2017 at § 613, Alternative B.

51 Compare Cal. Fam. Code § 7612(c) (2020), with Vt. St. tit. 15C, § 206(b) (2020).

52 See Joslin and NeJaime, "Multi-parent Families."

53 Joslin and NeJaime, "Multi-parent Families."

54 See, e.g., UPA 2017 at § 204(a)(1); *Pavan v. Smith*, 137 S. Ct. 2075 (2017); *Henderson v. Box*, 947 F.2d 482 (7th Cir. 2020).

55 Maine Stat. tit. 19-A, §1923 (2015); see also UPA 2017 at § 703.

56 See Courtney G. Joslin, "Protecting Children(?): Marriage, Gender, and Assisted Reproductive Technology," *Southern California Law Review* 78 (2010): 1177; see also NeJaime, "Nature of Parenthood," 2367–2369 (Appendix B).

57 See, e.g., UPA 2017 at § 703; 15 R.I. Gen. Laws Ann. § 15–8.1–703 (2020); Vt. Stat. Ann. tit. 15C, § 703 (West 2020); Wash. Rev. Code Ann. § 26.26A.610 (West 2020).

58 See Courtney G. Joslin, "(Not) Just Surrogacy," *California Law Review* 109 (2021): 401.

59 Joslin, "(Not) Just Surrogacy," 433–442.

60 Joslin, "(Not) Just Surrogacy," 433–438.

61 See, e.g., *V.C.*, 748 A.2d 539; *H.S.H.-K.*, 533 N.W.2d 419; *L.B.*, 122 P.3d 161. For "holding out" cases featuring same-sex couples, see *Elisa B.*, 117 P.3d 660; *Chatterjee*, 280 P.3d 283.

62 See, e.g., Ariz. Rev. Stat. Ann. § 25–501 (2020); Ga. Code Ann. § 19-7-21 (2020); see also Uniform Parentage Act § (5)(b) (1973).

63 See, e.g., Cal. Fam. Code § 7613 (West 2020); Me. Rev. Stat. Ann. tit. 19-A, §§ 1922–1923 (2020); see also UPA 2017 at § 702.

64 See, e.g., Cal. Fam. Code § 7601 (West 2020); Del. Code Ann. tit 13, § 8–201 (West 2020).

65 See, e.g., *Jason P. v. Danielle S.*, 226 Cal. App. 4th 167 (Ct. App. 2014).

66 Jeff Atkinson, "Shifts in the Law Regarding the Rights of Third Parties to Seek Visitation and Custody of Children," *Family Law Quarterly* 47 (2013): 1, 7 (stating that, as of 2013, eight states had stepparent visitation statutes).

67 See, e.g., Cal Fam. Code § 3101(a) (West 2020); Wis. Stat. Ann. § 767.245(a) (West 2020).

68 The "Nonparental Primary Caregivers" heading is standardized across chapters; we do not mean in our chapter to suggest that functional parents are nonparents.

69 See, e.g., *In re Custody of A.F.J.*, 260 P.3d 889, 891–892, 897–899 (Wash. App. Div. 2011).

70 But see 15 R.I. Gen. Laws Ann. § 15–8.1–501 (2020).

71 See, e.g., Mich. Comp. Laws § 700.5201 (2020) ("A person may become a minor's guardian by parental appointment or court appointment. The guardianship status continues until terminated, without regard to the location from time to time of the guardian or minor ward"); Nev. Rev. Stat. § 159A.062 (2020) ("A parent of a minor may by will nominate a guardian. The person nominated must file a petition and obtain an appointment from the court before exercising the powers of a guardian").

72 See, e.g., *In re Guardianship of W.L.*, 467 S.W.3d 129 (Ark. 2015) (holding that a trial court should have terminated a guardianship when the child's legal parent revoked consent); *In re Minor Child D.I.S.*, 249 P.3d 775 (Colo. 2011) ("Just as the fit parents' decision to consent to a guardianship is presumed to be in the best interests of the child, so too their decision to seek termination of the guardianship and regain care, custody, and control of the child is presumed to be in the best interests of the child").

73 See *Conover v. Conover*, 146 A.3d 433 (Md. 2016) (overturning *Janice M. v. Margaret K.*, 948 A.2d 73 (Md. 2008)); *Brooke S.B. v. Elizabeth A.C.C.*, 61 N.E.3d 488 (N.Y. 2016) (overturning *Alison D. v. Virginia M.*, 572 N.E.2d 127 (N.Y. 1991)).

74 *Brooke S.B.*, 61 N.E.3d at 499.

75 *Brooke S.B.* at 499.

76 See, e.g., *Doe v. Doe*, 395 P.3d 1287 (Idaho 2017); John Dewitt Gregory, "Family Privacy and the Custody and Visitation Rights of Adult Outsiders," *Family Law Quarterly* 36 (2002): 163, 185.

77 See, e.g., *Jones v. Barlow*, 154 P.3d 808 (Utah 2007); Gregg Strauss, "What Role Remains for De Facto Parenthood?," *Florida State University Law Review* 46 (2019): 909.

78 See, e.g., Douglas NeJaime, "The Constitution of Parenthood," *Stanford Law Review* 72 (2020): 261; Joslin, "De Facto Parentage," 31.

79 See, e.g., *Conover v. Conover*, 146 A.3d 433, 447 (Md. 2016) ("As other courts adopting this test have recognized, these factors set forth a high bar for establishing *de facto* parent status, which cannot be achieved without knowing participa-

tion by the biological parent"); *Marquez v. Caudill*, 656 S.E.2d 737, 744 (S.C. 2008) ("[T]he [*H.S.H.-K.*] test will limit the persons who may seek to be considered a psychological parent, but it will assist those who are worthy to be called such").

80 Joseph Goldstein, Anna Freud, and Albert J. Solnit, *The Best Interests of the Child* (New York: Simon & Schuster, 1996), 12.

81 Goldstein, Freud, and Solnit, *Best Interests of the Child*, 13; see also chap. 1, "A Psychological Perspective on the Significance of Legal Recognition of Diverse Social Parent Relationships for Children," by Abbie E. Goldberg.

82 See Anne Alstott, Anne Dailey, and Douglas NeJaime, "Psychological Parenthood," *Minnesota Law Review* 106 (2022): 2363, 2373–2379 (surveying the literature).

83 See Alstott, Dailey, and NeJaime, "Psychological Parenthood," 2377–2378.

84 *V.C.*, 748 A.2d at 550.

85 Parentage is a legal determination of an adult's status with respect to a child. Once the legal parents are identified, the best interests standard structures determinations of custody and visitation. Critiques of best interests inquiries in the custody context highlight the need to keep parentage from becoming solely a determination of an individual child's best interests. Among other things, the best interests standard gives judges substantial discretion and presents a significant risk that decision makers will act in ways that prejudge unconventional families and that reflect biases based on race, class, gender, sexual orientation, disability, and marital status. See Solangel Maldonado, "Bias in the Family: Race, Ethnicity, and Culture in Custody Disputes," *Family Court Review* 55 (2017): 213; Clifford J. Rosky, "Like Father, Like Son: Homosexuality, Parenthood, and the Gender of Homophobia," *Yale Journal of Law and Feminism* 20 (2009): 257.

86 See, e.g., Vt. Stat. tit. 15C, § 501 (2020); UPA 2017 at § 609.

87 Although we note that developmental research on attachment has devoted little attention to multiparent households, there is reason to believe key insights from the literature would apply in nontraditional arrangements. See National Academies of Science, *Engineering, and Medicine, Vibrant and Healthy Kids: Aligning Science, Practice, and Policy to Advance Healthy Equity* (Washington, DC: National Academies Press, 2019), 240–241; National Academies of Science, Engineering, and Medicine, *Parenting Matters: Supporting Parents of Children Ages 0–8* (Washington, DC: National Academies Press, 2016), 3, 328. See also Alstott, Dailey, and NeJaime, "Psychological Parenthood," 2375–2376.

88 See, e.g., *Lawrence v. Texas*, 539 U.S. 558, 574, 123 S. Ct. 2472, 2481, 156 L. Ed. 2d 508 (2003). Cf. *Moore v. City of E. Cleveland, Ohio*, 431 U.S. 494, 506 (1977) (plurality opinion).

89 See, e.g., *Loving v. Virginia*, 388 U.S. 1, 12 (1967); *Lawrence v. Texas*, 539 U.S. 558, 578 (2003).

90 See, e.g., *Eisenstadt v. Baird*, 405 U.S. 438, 453 (1972); *Stanley v. Illinois*, 405 U.S. 645, 658 (1972); *Troxel v. Granville*, 530 U.S. 57, 65 (2000).

91 Courtney G. Joslin, "Autonomy in the Family," *UCLA Law Review* 66 (2019): 912, 953.

92 See NeJaime, "Constitution of Parenthood," 355.

93 NeJaime, "Nature of Parenthood," 2297.

94 *Brooke S.B.*, 61 N.E.3d at 498.

95 *Brooke S.B.* at 498.

96 Douglas NeJaime, "The Story of *Brooke S.B. v. Elizabeth A.C.C.*: Parental Recognition in the Age of LGBT Equality," in *Reproductive Rights and Justice Stories*, ed. Melissa Murray, Katherine Shaw, and Reva B. Siegel (Saint Paul, MN: Foundation Press, 2019), 245, 256.

97 *Brooke S.B.*, 61 N.E.3d at 498.

III

Legal Systems in Europe

8

Social Parenthood in England and Wales

JENS M. SCHERPE

English law regarding parenthood is a curious mixture of old and modern.[1] While the law doggedly clings to the two-parent paradigm and does not recognize more than two legal parents, the jurisdiction was one of the earliest to regulate parenthood through assisted reproductive techniques. It also allowed joint and stepchild adoption for same-sex and unmarried couples in 2002 and arguably introduced one of world's most modern regulatory framework for parental responsibility in the Children Act 1989 to allow more than two persons to hold parental responsibility. Moreover, both opposite-sex and same-sex couples can formalize their relationships as a marriage or civil partnership, and there is little difference between the two, including regarding parent-child relations. By contrast, a comprehensive regulatory framework for cohabitation / de facto relationships is missing,[2] even though these couples have access to assisted reproduction and can jointly adopt children, albeit with less favorable laws than for those who have formalized their relationships.

Demographic Data

While marriage (and civil partnership) remains the dominant family form, numbers are in decline as more people choose to live together before, or without, getting married.[3] Marriage rates for opposite-sex couples were the lowest on record in 2018, with 20.1 marriages per 1,000 unmarried men and 18.6 marriages per 1,000 unmarried women.[4] In 2020 there were some 12.9 million married opposite-sex couples in the United Kingdom (so including Scotland and Northern Ireland), with 38 percent of them living with dependent children; in the same period there were some 710,000 same-sex couple married families, of which approximately one in seven lived with dependent children.[5] In the same year, there were 3,380,000 opposite-sex cohabiting families, of which 37.4 percent had dependent children; of the 120,000 same-sex cohabitating families, only some 1.7 percent lived with dependent children.[6] In addition, 64 percent of the 2,427,000 single-mother families and 48 percent of the 430,000 single-father families lived with dependent children.[7]

Assisted reproduction is accessible to couples irrespective of their legal gender and relationship status in the United Kingdom. In 2019, almost 53,000 patients had 69,000 fresh and frozen IVF cycles and 5,700 donor insemination (DI) cycles at fertility clinics licensed by the Human Fertilisation and Embryology Authority in the United Kingdom; since the Authority started recording information in 1991, there have been around 1.3 million IVF cycles and over 260,000 DI cycles, resulting in around 390,000 babies born.[8]

Out of the approximately 12 million children living in England, on March 31, 2019, 78,150 were looked-after children (children in care) in England, compared with 69,470 in 2015;[9] almost 55,000 children and young persons were placed with foster carers.[10] In 2019, 3,570 looked after children were adopted. Of these, 430 were adopted by a single adopter; 150 by a same-sex couple and 319 by an opposite-sex couple not married or in civil partnership; 100 by a same-sex couple in a civil partnership;[11] 2,340 by an opposite-sex married couple, 170 by male married couples, and 70 by married female couples.[12]

Legal Recognition of Parents

Terminology

As the terminology used to describe the various relationships between parents/adults and children varies greatly from jurisdictions to jurisdiction, it is necessary to very briefly set out the way certain terms are used in England and Wales:[13] parentage usually refers to a person genetically/biologically[14] connected to the child; parenthood is the position of being a legal parent of a child; and having parental responsibility is a formal position with regard to the child, defined in section 3 of the Children Act 1989 as "all the rights, duties, powers, responsibilities and authority which by law a parent of a child has in relation to the child and his property."[15] As this chapter shows, formal parental responsibility is the main way in which social parenthood is recognized in England and Wales.

Legal Parenthood

Parenthood establishes kinship, and many rights and duties, but not necessarily parental responsibility for all fathers or second parents (on which see below). Unlike some jurisdictions, English law does not allow for a child to have more than two legal parents at birth or later in life (see below) and thus maintains the two-parent paradigm despite societal changes and medical advances.

Legal Parenthood at Birth—Natural Conception

Maternity is proved by parturition,[16] that is, the person[17] who gives birth always is the legal mother of the child.

As regards paternity in cases of natural conception, the *pater est quem nuptiae demonstrant* (the father is whom the marriage points out) presumption applies for married/civil partnership opposite-sex couples[18] but not for same-sex marriages/civil partnerships.[19] For couples who have not formalized their relationship,[20] paternity is presumed on the basis of the man being named as the father on the child's birth registration.[21] Both presumptions can be displaced in court proceedings to determine the paternity of a child, for example by presenting genetic evidence.[22]

Unlike some jurisdictions, English law prioritizes the "truth," and thus the courts generally will order DNA tests when exercising their discretion to order the use of blood/DNA tests under section 20 of the Family Law Reform Act 1969 as this in principle is seen as being in the best interest of the child.[23] Thus, the genetic link (whether presumed or proved) is the basis for paternity.

Legal Parenthood at Birth—Assisted Reproduction

In cases of assisted reproduction, maternity also is based on giving birth,[24] meaning that the genetic contribution is irrelevant to determine who the legal mother of a child is. Thus, even if the intended second parent is the one who contributed the ovum, this has no impact on their parental status. By contrast, if the sperm of the second intended parent is being used, they will be the legal father according to common law as the Human Fertilization and Embryology Act 2008 (HFEA) does not apply in such cases.

Paternity in donor cases and the status as so-called other parent for second female parents can be established from birth under the HFEA. However, the legal rules under the HFEA vary greatly, depending on whether the couple in question is married / in a civil partnership or not. If the second parent is in such a formalized relationship with the mother, then their parenthood will be established from birth if they consented to the assisted reproduction, independent of where and how the assisted reproduction happened.[25] By contrast, if the second parent is not in such a formalized relationship with the mother, legal parenthood will be established only if they consented *and* the assisted reproduction was undertaken in a licensed clinic in the United Kingdom.[26] Thus, if an unmarried couple conceived a child through assisted reproduction using donor sperm outside the United Kingdom or outside a licensed clinic (including so-called DIY fertilization), only the person giving birth would be the legal parent (and, where identifiable, the sperm donor) but not their partner. So, curiously, while English law in principle accepts "modern family forms" and allows acquisition of parenthood from birth for second female parents, it nevertheless insists on significant distinctions regarding parenthood based on whether the couple have formalized their relationship or not.[27]

Transfer of Legal Parenthood—Adoption and Parental Orders

A transfer of parenthood is possible only through an Adoption Order[28] or, in the case of surrogacy, through a Parental Order.[29] Both are possible for individuals as well as couples (including those who have not formalized their relationship and same-sex couples).[30] Because the number of legal parents can never exceed two in English law, the acquisition of the status of legal parent of one person therefore inevitably leads to the extinction of that status of another (unless, of course, there at the time is only one legal parent, in which case stepchild adoption is possible).

Thus, even the most intense level of parenting and commitment will not open up the possibility of being recognized as an additional legal parent (although it might do so for the acquisition of parental responsibility).

Parental Responsibility

Holders of parental responsibility have "all the rights, duties, powers, responsibilities and authority which by law a parent of a child has in relation to the child and his property," which entails bringing up the child, having contact with the child, protecting and maintaining the child, determining and providing for the child's education, determining the child's religion, consenting to the child's medical treatment, naming the child, administering the child's property and so on.[31] Crucially, one of the central features of English law on parental responsibility is that persons who are *not* the legal parents can hold it (hence parent*al* and not parent responsibility), and there can be more than two holders of parental responsibility—indeed technically there is no upper limit. As such, it is the main legal construct with which social parenthood is recognized, and Black LJ even stated in *T v. T* that "someone who has been granted parental responsibility has truly been recognized as a parent of a child."[32]

Acquisition of Parental Responsibility as Legal Parent, Stepparent, Guardian, or Special Guardian

The person[33] giving birth to the child will, as the legal mother, always automatically hold parental responsibility,[34] as will a legal father or second female parent married to / in civil partnership with the mother.[35] If no such formalized relationship exists, parental responsibility needs to be acquired by the partner,[36] which is possible by (1) registration as the child's parent (which cannot happen without the birth mother's consent), (2) formal agreement with the mother without registration as the parent, or (3) court order (Parental Responsibility Order, PRO).[37]

Persons who become legal parents through an Adoption or a Parental Order (see above) also automatically acquire parental responsibility (and then that of those previously holding it is extinguished).[38] Persons who are not the legal parents can acquire parental responsibility in a number of ways. Crucially, if another person acquires parental responsibility this does not, by itself, lead to a current holder of parental responsibility ceasing to hold that responsibility.[39] Therefore, parental responsibility generally is acquired *in addition* to that of those who already hold parental responsibility.

Stepparents (i.e., persons married to or in a civil partnership with a parent who holds parental responsibility) can acquire parental responsibility either by formal agreement with all holders of parental responsibility or by PRO.[40] Notably, this is not possible for couples who have not formalized their relationships (but see Child Arrangements Order below).

A person who is appointed as a guardian or as special guardian will acquire parental responsibility,[41] as will prospective adopters with whom a child is placed for adoption.[42] A local authority can also acquire parental responsibility for a child if the child is subject of a care order or an emergency protection order,[43] but foster parents with whom the child is placed do not. However, the local authority (or other holders of parental responsibility) can delegate the authority to take certain decisions to the foster parents.

Acquisition of Parental Responsibility through a Child Arrangements Order

For present purposes, the most important way to acquire parental responsibility is through a Child Arrangements Order (CAO). These orders allow the court to make arrangements with whom (and when) a child is going to live, spend time, or otherwise have contact.[44] When deciding whether or not a CAO should be made, the child's welfare is the court's paramount consideration, as it is for all decisions under the Children Act 1989 concerning the upbringing of a child.[45]

If a legal parent who does not otherwise have parental responsibility makes a successful application for a CAO for a child to live with them, the court *must* also make a separate PRO to give them parental responsibility;[46] if the order is about contact, then the court must *consider* making a separate PRO.[47]

If a CAO is made for persons who are not legal parents, they automatically acquire parental responsibility by virtue of the CAO.[48] However, unlike for legal parents, their parental responsibility is linked to the CAO and comes to an end when that order does because the parental responsibility is not acquired by a separate PRO.

The CAO route to parental responsibility remains the main avenue to having a legal link with the child for those who are not legal parents of the child. Acquiring parental responsibility via a CAO therefore is used particularly by new partners who are not in a formalized relationship with the parents, persons who look after (or have looked after) the child as primary caregivers, and known donors who would like to be involved in the parenting.[49]

Certain groups of people are privileged and have an entitlement to apply for a CAO (rather than having to get leave of the court to do so).[50] These include the legal parents, guardians, and special guardians of the child and those already named in a CAO,[51] but also spouses or civil partners to whom the child is regarded as a "child of the family,"[52] persons with whom the child has lived for three years and persons who are not the legal parents but have acquired parental responsibility through a CAO,[53] as well as local authority foster parents or relatives if the child lives with them for at least a year immediately preceding the application.[54]

Loss of Parental Responsibility

Parental responsibility always ends when the child turns eighteen. But a rather unique feature of English law is that mothers, irrespective of their relationship status, and fathers / second parents who are in a formalized relationship with the mother and have acquired parental responsibility at birth cannot lose it prior to that time (unless, of course, the child is adopted or subject of a Parental Order in surrogacy cases). That said, a practically rather similar result can be achieved by a court order that restricts the ability to exercise parental responsibility.[55]

By contrast, parents who had to acquire parental responsibility (because they were not in a formalized relationship with the mother) and stepparents can lose their parental responsibility by court order.[56] However, such applications are very rare and normally arise only in cases of serious physical abuse against the child (or other members of the family).[57]

If a PRO was made for a legal parent in conjunction with a CAO, the PRO cannot be revoked unless the CAO also comes to an end.[58] Moreover, unless the PRO is expressly revoked, it remains in place for the legal parent even if the CAO comes to an end.

For all other holders of parental responsibility, it comes to an end when the court order establishing it ends or when an Adoption Order or Parental Order regarding the child is made.

Meaning and Function of Parental Responsibility for Social Parenthood

Parental responsibility can be—and is—used as a flexible tool to recognize social parenthood. While it falls short of recognition as a legal parent as it does not create a permanent legal bond or kinship, and thus might seem as a "consolation prize," it nevertheless fulfils a very important function and allows for a meaningful legal relationship. As set out in section 3(1) of the Children Act 1989, it allows for full involvement in the daily life of a child, including full decision-making authority.

Another important, and rather unique, feature of English parental responsibility is that it always is individual, rather than joint. Therefore, in principle, each holder of parental responsibility may act alone and without the other holders of parental responsibility in meeting that responsibility,[59] subject only to very few statutory limitations (such as changing the surname or removing the child from the jurisdiction)[60] and not acting in a way that is incompatible with any court order made with respect to the child.[61] However, the courts have held that there is a right to be consulted on schooling, serious medical problems, and other occurrences in the child's life, but also—contrary to the express wording of the statute—that there is a duty to agree in such cases.[62]

In any event, and perhaps somewhat paradoxically, the construct of parental responsibility means that on the one hand it is regarded as important because it gives significant status to the person in question and creates an important legal bond that generates rights and duties for the benefit of the child. On the other hand, it limits the practical importance of having parental responsibility as it does not entitle actual involvement in the daily life and decision making as each holder in principle can act alone.[63] For example, this means that the resident parent / holder of parental responsibility can make almost all decisions about the child (apart from the limits pointed out above) and that the nonresident parent / holder of parental responsibility cannot intervene directly.

While there is an ongoing debate about the nature and function of parental responsibility[64] and arguably the case law is not very consistent with regard to the actual legal significance of parental responsibility, at least the way parental responsibility is construed allows for a reasonably flexible recognition of social parenthood in its many forms, contingent on this being in the best interest of the child.

Child Support

Child support is not linked to parental responsibility, and only nonresidential legal parents or parents of a "child of the family" are obliged to pay it. A "child of the family" is defined as either "child of both of them" or "any other child, other than a child placed with them as foster parents by a local authority or voluntary organization, who has been treated by both of them as a child of their family" if—and only if—the persons in question are married or in a civil partnership.[65] Therefore, one cannot be a "child of the family" if the parents are not in a formalized relationship.

Claims for child support (on behalf of the child) are not limited to persons who are the parents of or have parental responsibility for a child. The person entitled is the "person with care" of the child, defined as the person "with whom the child has his home" and "who usually provides day to day care for the child" (and "who does not fall within a prescribed category of person," which excludes local authorities and local authority foster parents—but not fosterers under private arrangements).[66]

Legal Recognition of Social Parents: Three Common Contexts

As outlined above, English law does not recognize more than two legal parents but allows for more than two persons to hold parental responsibility for a child under certain circumstances. The following "common contexts" essentially have been covered already in the explanation of the law above and thus will only be summarized here.

Same-Sex Couples

Like opposite-sex couples, same-sex couples have full access to assisted reproduction (including surrogacy) and adoption, and the same differences between formalized and nonformalized relationships of the adults also apply. Thus, being a legal parent from birth, as explained above, certainly is possible. Where the second person is not a legal parent, parental responsibility in addition to any existing parental responsibility of other persons can be acquired via a PRO (if stepparent) or a CAO. Thus, where, for example, an unmarried lesbian couple uses "DIY insemination" by a private donor to conceive a child, the woman giving birth and the donor will be regarded as the legal parents of the child, and the other woman will have to (step-)adopt the child to become a legal parent (thus ending the donor's legal parenthood), or she can acquire parental responsibility as described.

Stepparents

Where the parent is married to (or in civil partnership with) a stepparent, parental responsibility can be acquired by formal agreement with all holders of parental responsibility and—in the absence of such an agreement—by PRO if this is in the best interest of the child. If there is no such formalized relationship, then parental responsibility can be acquired via a CAO. In any event, the parental responsibility of a stepparent arises in addition to any previously existing parental responsibility.

Nonparental Primary Caregivers

All nonparental caregivers can acquire parental responsibility by a CAO in addition to existing parental responsibility. Foster carers, however, do not acquire parental responsibility as such, but the local authority can authorize them to make certain decisions for the children.

Discussion

Although the English construct of parental responsibility provides a flexible tool to deal with so-called modern family constellations and thus social parenthood, it is not without difficulties. First and foremost, there inevitably is a legal hierarchy between the status as legal parent as a superior status and parental responsibility, with the latter giving the power to act as parent rather than actually being a parent.[67] This obviously has significant legal consequences, for example with regard to succession (including inheritance tax) as well as maintenance duties, but also unescapably creates a social hierarchy that can—and in practice does—create additional problems in crisis situations as not all those involved in the parenting have equal status. This is perhaps best shown in the House of Lords decision in *Re G (Children)*,[68] which concerned a dispute about where children should reside between two women who had raised the children together but only one of them was the legal mother. In this decision Baroness Hale[69] (with whom the others concurred) outlined what she thought constituted three pathways to being "natural parent": genetic, gestational, and social or psychological parenthood.[70] This, at first glance, appears to be a novel and modern approach, as it expressly acknowledges the social and psychological contributions. Indeed, Hale cites the definition by Goldstein, Freud, and Solnit of a psychological parent as "one who, on a continuous, day-to-day basis, through interaction, companionship, interplay, and mutuality, fulfils the child's psychological needs for a parent, as well as the child's physical needs. The psychological parent may be a biological, adoptive, foster or common law parent."[71] But she then immediately follows this up by acknowledging that in the great majority of cases the natural mother combines all three ways of being a parent, whereas the father can only ever achieve a maximum of two and others might only ever have one. Indeed, in the case itself she then decided in favor of residence with the "natural mother," stating that the biological link "did count for something in the case," thus attaching decisive significance to that link rather than to both women equally being the psychological and social parents.[72] Thus, it seems biology remains the trump card.

By contrast, in known donor cases the genetic contribution does not seem to override the other interests.[73] In a number of cases, known-donor legal fathers sought greater involvement in the life of their legal children, who were primarily parented by a lesbian couple.[74] The courts struggled with finding a balance between the need to protect the child's primary family and home with the women and acknowledging the role of the biological and legal father. There is little consistency in the case law, as decisions often seemed, rightly or wrongly, fact-specific and turned in the best interest of the child. That said, there seems at least to be a trend toward acknowledging the primacy of the lesbian couple's parenting and facilitating involvement of the donor father (only) where that is in the child's best interest.[75] While this may provide for adequate outcomes in the cases concerned, ultimately it does little to provide legal certainty for this area of law.

Arguably the original concept of parental responsibility, which was hoped would "reflect the everyday reality of being a parent, and emphasize the responsibilities of all those who were placed in that position,"[76] has been somewhat changed by judicial decisions. A primary example for this is *Re S (Parental Responsibility)*,[77] where it was held by Ward LJ that it is important for the child's self-esteem and positive image of the father that "the law confers upon a committed father that stamp of approval,"[78] thus detaching parental responsibility from its function and elevating it to the level of giving some kind of "status"—while at the same time downgrading it by separating it from involving an actual parenting function. While this may usefully alleviate, to some extent, the feeling that parental responsibility often is only a consolation prize for not being able to obtain legal parenthood, it unhelpfully dilutes the original demarcation between the two legal concepts.

English law also currently precludes the recognition of more than two legal parents, with all the legal rights and duties this brings with it. Several authors have argued that the two-parent paradigm needs to be broken to reflect adequately the lived realities of many children,[79] for which the modern and wide concept of parental responsibility in English law is an insufficient substitute.

NOTES

1 Here and in the following, references to "English" law and legal concepts should be understood to refer to the law of the jurisdiction of England and Wales.

2 Cf. The Law Commission, "Cohabitation: The Financial Consequences of Relationship Breakdown" (Law COM No. 307) Cm 7182, 2007, www.lawcom.gov.uk.

3 Office for National Statistics, "Families and Households in the UK" (2020), www.ons.gov.uk/peoplepopulationandcommunity/birthsdeathsandmarriages/families/bulletins/familiesandhouseholds/2020.

4 Office for National Statistics, "Marriage in England and Wales" (2018), www.ons.gov.uk/peoplepopulationandcommunity/birthsdeathsandmarriages/marriagecohabitationandcivilpartnerships/bulletins/marriagesinenglandandwalesprovisional/2018.

5 Cf. Office for National Statistics, "Families and Households in the UK," table 9, "Married Couple Families by Type and Presence of Children."

6 Office for National Statistics, "Families and Households in the UK," table 1.

7 Office for National Statistics, "Families and Households in the UK," table 1.

8 Human Fertilisation and Embryology Authority, "UK Statistics for IVF and DI Treatment, Storage, and Donation" (May 2021), www.hfea.gov.uk/about-us/publications/research-and-data/fertility-treatment-2019-trends-and-figures.

9 Race Disparity Unit, "Adopted and Looked-After Children" (December 16, 2021), www.ethnicity-facts-figures.service.gov.uk/health/social-care/adopted-and-looked-after-children/latest.

10 Ofsted, "Fostering in England 2018 to 2019: Main Findings" (updated January 26, 2021), www.gov.uk/government/statistics/fostering-in-england-1-april-2018-to-31-march-2019/fostering-in-england-2018-to-2019-main-findings.

11 Civil partnerships were available only to same-sex couples prior to 2019, so no data for opposite-sex couples were available.

12 Race Disparity Unit, "Adopted and Looked-After Children," table E3.

13 For a wider discussion these terms, see Andrew Bainham, "Parentage, Parenthood and Parental Responsibility: Subtle, Elusive yet Important Distinctions," in *What Is a Parent? A Socio-legal Analysis*, ed. A. Bainham, S. Day Sclater, and M. Richards (Oxford: Hart, 1999), 25–46, and Jens M. Scherpe, "Breaking the Existing Paradigms of Parent–Child Relationships," in *International and National Perspectives on Child and Family Law: Essays in Honour of Nigel Lowe*, ed. Gillian Douglas, Mervyn Murch, and Victoria Stephens (Cambridge: Cambridge University Press, 2018), 343–359; see also Stephen Gilmore and Lisa Glennon, *Hayes and Williams' Family Law*, 7th ed. (Oxford: Oxford University Press, 2020), 383.

14 Scherpe uses the wider concept of biological connection to include, for example, surrogates and donors of mitochondria under parentage.

15 Parental responsibility therefore is comparable to concepts employed in other jurisdictions, such as parental control or custody.

16 *Ampthill Peerage Case* [1977] AC 547. The advent of assisted reproduction of course casts some doubt on this "simple rule"; see 3.1.2.

17 As was established, controversially, in *R (on the application of McConnell) v. Registrar General* [2020] EWCA Civ 559, this applies even if the person giving birth is legally male.

18 The common law presumption (cf. *Banbury Peerage Case* [1803–13] All ER Rep 171) was extended to civil partnerships in Legitimacy Act 1976, sec. A1(s), inserted by Civil Partnership (Opposite Sex Couples) Regulations 2019, regulation 12.

19 Marriage was opened up to same-sex couples in England in 2014. Civil partnership, which previously was the functional equivalent for same-sex couples only,

was subsequently opened up to opposite-sex couples in 2019. The legal consequences of marriage and civil partnership are almost identical.

20 There is no legal regime for the recognition of cohabitants / de facto relationships in England and Wales, unlike in Scotland.

21 Joanna Miles, Rob George, and Sonia Harris-Short, *Family Law*, 4th ed. (Oxford: Oxford University Press, 2019), 621.

22 Family Law Act 1986, sec. 55A. The usual civil standard of proof applies; Family Law Reform Act 1969, sec. 26.

23 *S v. McC and M; W v. W* [1972] AC 24; *Re H (A Minor) (Blood Test: Parental Rights)* [1997] Fam 89 (CA).

24 Human Fertilisation and Embryology Act (HFEA) 2008, secs. 33, 47.

25 HFEA 2008, secs. 35, 42.

26 HFEA 2008, secs. 36–38, 43–45.

27 This is particularly problematic in cases where unmarried couples are undergoing fertility treatment overseas. The child will be registered on the birth certificate as a child of the couple, but contrary what many couples believe, legally only the mother actually is a parent according to English law, and thus the parenthood of the other parent is vulnerable to legal challenge.

28 Adoption and Children Act 2002, sec. 46.

29 HFEA 2008, secs. 54, 54A.

30 Adoption and Children Act 2002, sec. 144(4).

31 Children Act 1989, sec. 3(1). For an attempt to identify the most important rights and duties enshrined within the concept, see, e.g., Gillian Douglas and Nigel Lowe, *Bromley's Family Law*, 11th ed. (Oxford: Oxford University Press, 2015), 337–338.

32 *T v. T* [2010] EWCA Civ 1366, [23].

33 See *R (on the application of McConnell) v. Registrar General* [2020] EWCA Civ 559.

34 Children Act 1989, secs. 2(1), 2(2)(a).

35 Children Act 1989, secs. 2(1), (1A).

36 Children Act 1989, secs. 2(2)(b), (2A)(b).

37 Children Act 1989, secs. 4, 4ZA.

38 Adoption and Children Act 2002, secs. 46, 67.

39 Children Act 1989, sec. 2(6).

40 Children Act 1989, sec. 4A.

41 Children Act 1989, secs. 5(6) and 14C(1).

42 Adoption and Children Act 2002, sec. 25. A placement can be with consent of the parents or by court order. Adoption and Children Act 2002, secs. 18ff.

43 Children Act 1989, secs. 33(3), 44(4)(c).

44 Children Act 1989, sec. 8. Before the 2014 reforms these orders were called "residence order" and "contact order," respectively. In the absence of a CAO the holders of parental responsibility can decide where the child is going to live and with whom the child is to have contact.

45 Children Act 1989, sec. 1.

46 Children Act 1989, sec. 12(1).
47 Children Act 1989, sec. 12(1A).
48 Children Act 1989, secs. 12(2), (2A).
49 On disputes arising on this, see below as well as Leanne Smith, "Tangling the Web of Legal Parenthood: Legal Responses to the Use of Known Donors in Lesbian Parenting Arrangements," (2013) 33(3) *Legal Studies* 355–381, and Alison Diduck, "If Only We Can Find the Appropriate Terms to Use the Issue Will Be Solved: Law, Identity and Parenthood," (2007) 19 *Child and Family Law Quarterly* 458–480.
50 The criteria to "have particular regard to" (in addition to the best interest of the child) for granting leave are listed in sec. 10(9).
51 Children Act 1989, sec. 10(4).
52 Defined in Children Act 1989, sec. 105. On this see also the section on child support.
53 Children Act 1989, sec. 10(5).
54 Children Act 1989, secs. 10(5A), (5B).
55 See, e.g., *Re B and C (Change of Names: Parental Responsibility: Evidence)* [2014] EWHC 3250 (Fam).
56 Children Act 1989, secs. 4(2A), 4ZA(5), 4A(3).
57 See the overview in Gilmore and Glennon, *Hayes and Williams' Family Law*, 459–461. For a recent case, see *C v. D and Another* [2018] EWHC 3312 (Fam).
58 Children Act 1989, sec. 12(4).
59 Children Act 1989, sec. 2(7).
60 Children Act 1989, sec. 13 and Child Abduction Act 1984, sec. 1.
61 Children Act 1989, sec. 2(8). An example of this would be a court order that prohibits certain medical procedures or decisions about religious upbringing without the consent of other holders of parental responsibility.
62 Space precludes a discussion of this issue, but see John Eekelaar, "Do Parents Have a Duty to Consult?," (1998) 114 *Law Quarterly Review* 337–341, and Jens M. Scherpe, "Parental Responsibility: To Consult or Consent, Is That the Question?," in *Family Matters—Essays in Honour of John Eekelaar*, ed. Jens Scherpe and Stephen Gilmore (Cambridge: Intersentia, 2022), pp. 637–653. For an overview with further references, see Miles, George, and Harris-Short, *Family Law*, 715–722.
63 For a discussion and further references, see Miles, George, and Harris-Short, *Family Law*, 691–697.
64 See the contributions in Rebecca Probert, Stephen Gilmore, and Jonathan Herring, *Responsible Parents and Parental Responsibility* (New York: Bloomsbury, 2009).
65 Children Act 1989, sec. 105.
66 Child Support Act 1991, sec. 3(3).
67 Chris Barton and Gillian Douglas, *Law and Parenthood* (London: Butterworths, 1995), 49.
68 *Re G (Children)* [2006] UKHL 43.

69 It is worth noting that Baroness Hale was the law commissioner responsible for the drafting of the Children Act 1989.

70 *Re G (Children)* [2006] UKHL 43, at [33–35].

71 *Re G (Children)*, [2006] UKHL 43, at [35]; Joseph Goldstein, Anna Freud, and Albert J. Solnit, *Beyond the Best Interests of the Child* (New York: Free Press, 1973), 98.

72 *Re G (Children)* [2006] UKHL 43, at [38].

73 Nor, as pointed out above, does the genetic contribution of the female intended parent have any legal relevance for the destination of legal parenthood at birth in surrogacy cases.

74 In all cases the children were born before the legal reforms of the HFEA that enable second legal parenthood. For a fuller exploration of known donor cases, see Smith, "Tangling the Web of Legal Parenthood" as well as Leanne Smith, "Is Three a Crowd? Lesbian Mothers' Perspectives on Parental Status in Law," (2006) 18 *Child and Family Law Quarterly* 231.

75 Cf. Smith, "Tangling the Web of Legal Parenthood," 378; see also Philipp Bremner, "Collaborative Parenting, Co-parenting and Heteronormativity: Recognising the Interests of Gay Fathers," (2017) 29 *Child and Family Law Quarterly* 293.

76 Law Commission, "Guardianship and Custody," Law Com no. 172 (London: HMSO, 1988), 2.4.

77 [1995] 3 FCR 225.

78 [1995] 3 FCR 225, 235.

79 Emily Jackson, "What Is a Parent?," in *Feminist Perspectives on Family Law*, ed. Alison Diduck and Katherine O'Donovan (New York: Routledge, 2006), 60; Thérèse Callus, "A New Parenthood Paradigm for Twenty-First Century Family Law in England and Wales?," (2021) 32(3) *Legal Studies* 347; Scherpe, "Breaking the Existing Paradigms of Parent–Child Relationships," 343–359.

9

Social Parenthood in Germany

CHRISTIANE VON BARY

While most children today live with two parents who are their genetic, legal, and social parents,[1] family forms are becoming increasingly varied in Germany. Although it has historically always been the case that adults cared for children other than those who they are genetically related to, the acceptance of unmarried and same-sex partnerships, advances in assisted reproductive technology, and a more vigilant state intervening in cases where the welfare of a child is at risk have made social parenthood both a more prevalent and a more diverse phenomenon. After addressing some demographic data, this chapter shows that the legal framework in Germany has adapted to these developments only to a limited degree and illustrates which changes are currently being discussed and continue to be necessary.

Demographic Data

The data available on social parents in Germany are limited, but a general trend is visible: a still small but growing share of the population is involved in the life of children outside the paradigm of the marital, heterosexual family on which many of the legal rules are traditionally based. The number of nonmarital families has more than doubled from 1996[2] until 2019 and now amounts to 11.5 percent of all families.[3] The percentage is significantly higher in the former East Germany,[4] but lower in families with an immigration background.[5] Same-sex-couple-headed families are on the rise, from around 3,000 in 1996[6] to 10,000 in 2018.[7] In 2018, around 15,000 children lived in families where the parents were in a same-sex marriage or registered partnership,[8] the vast majority in female same-sex-couple families.[9] Of children living in a same-sex couple family, 45 percent were born into this family, 44 percent are from previous heterosexual relationships, 6 percent are foster children, and 2 percent are adopted.[10] Although no official data are available on step-parent families, surveys show that they make up around 10 percent of all families.[11] Data on assisted reproduction with donor gametes are very difficult to obtain since absolute numbers are too low to be considered statistically relevant. Estimates surmise that around 400 to 500 children conceived with donor eggs are born in Germany every year[12] despite egg donation being prohibited.[13] Sperm donation, which is permitted, leads to the birth of about 1,000 to 1,200 children per year.[14] In 2018, over 90,000 children lived with foster families, which is about 0.7 percent of all minor children.[15] Only 2 percent of these children are adopted by their foster parents, but most of them do not return to their original parents, leading to long-term foster care.[16]

Legal Recognition of Parents

When thinking about the position of social parents under German law, it is important to understand how the law recognizes parental rights to analyze the way social parents fit into this framework. In particular, the distinction between two different levels has to be taken into account: parenthood as a legal status and parental responsibility. Additionally, the law protects contact rights without granting any of the more extensive rights and obligations typically associated with parental figures.

The Status of a Legal Parent: Parenthood

The legal status of parenthood is a permanent and highly formalized bond between parent and child that lasts for a lifetime.[17] This status is created to ensure a very stable connection and leads to a variety of legal consequences such as parental responsibility, name, maintenance, nationality, and inheritance rights. Since the status is permanent but the concrete situation of the child can change, the welfare of the child is considered only when creating the abstract rules allocating the status, but there is no room for the examination of the individual welfare of the child in question when applying these rules to particular cases.[18]

Usually, parenthood is assigned at the birth of the child and a child can have a maximum of two legal parents. The pathways to acquire parenthood at birth are modeled after the most likely genetic relationship even though a genetic bond is not an actual prerequisite to becoming a legal parent. The legal mother is always the woman who gives birth to the child (§ 1591 German Civil Code—BGB); her status is final and can end only through adoption. Although egg donation and surrogacy are prohibited under the Act for the Protection of Embryos (Embryonenschutzgesetz), this can be circumvented by going abroad. If German law is applicable, it is always the woman giving birth who becomes the legal mother, even if this person is not a genetic parent and/or is the surrogate.

The legal father is the mother's husband if she is married (§ 1592 no. 1 BGB). Alternatively, a man can, irrespective of a genetic bond, become the legal father of a child by recognition, that is, a formal declaration that he wants to become the (legal) father (§ 1592 no. 2 BGB). The recognition, however, is valid only if the mother consents to it. This can allow a social father to become the legal father as long as the child does not already have a legal father. Finally, the genetic father can acquire legal fatherhood by a court decision (§ 1592 no. 3 BGB), also against his will. Legal fatherhood can end through adoption and due to a challenge of paternity if there is no genetic bond between legal father and child. The right of the genetic father to challenge paternity is excluded if the current legal father has a "social family relationship" (*sozial-familiäre Beziehung*) with the child (§ 1600(3) BGB). This is the only term in the Civil Code that refers to a purely social role where a person actually takes care of a child and thus to a position somewhat similar to a social parent. It is also one of the very few instances where German law protects the social connection over the genetic one and the social role plays a role in determining fatherhood. Generally, taking over the social function of a parent to a child does not have any consequences for the status as a legal parent.

In principle, only legal parents have rights and obligations toward the child. However, benefits considered to fall under public law are less restrictive: parental leave—unlike maternity leave, which is linked to the biological process of birth and a right only of the person giving birth—is granted to legal parents as well as other full-time caregivers such as foster parents, stepparents, and even grandparents or siblings (§ 15(1) no. 1 BEEG)[19] for a maximum of three years with the state substituting the previous income up to a certain maximum for up to two years. The same goes for the monthly child benefit (§ 2(1) BKGG).[20] Similarly, for inheritance tax purposes, stepchildren of married or partnered parents benefit from the same exemptions as legal children (§ 15(1) no. 2 ErbStG).[21] The most relevant obligation of a legal parent is the payment of maintenance for the child, which falls on them regardless of whether they also have parental responsibility. Social parents are required to support only members of the same household under the principles of social law, but this obligation ceases automatically as soon as they no longer not live in the same household (§ 7(3), (3a) SGB II).[22] Additionally, under certain conditions, courts have found an implied contract between the adults responsible for the birth of the child even if one of them does not become a legal parent under which the child can claim maintenance.[23]

Parental Responsibility

The most important right and obligation of a legal parent is the exercise of parental responsibility, which ends when the child comes of age. Parental responsibility involves two different aspects: taking care of the financial assets and—more importantly—of the personal well-being of the child.[24] This includes the day-to-day care for the child, supporting education and development of the child, the right to determine the place of residence, medical care, and religious questions. Parents with joint parental responsibility must agree on all decisions regarding the child (§ 1627 BGB). If the parents cannot come to an agreement in case of a decision of considerable importance, they can apply for a court order assigning one of them the right to decide in this particular instant (§ 1628 BGB). Otherwise, this option is not available and the status quo remains unless the parents agree.

To acquire full parental responsibility, a person must be a legal parent. However, parental responsibility automatically follows legal parenthood only when mother and father are married. Otherwise, by law, only the mother has parental responsibility and the father must acquire it through a mutual declaration of both legal parents (§ 1626a BGB). If the mother does not consent, the father can apply for a court order granting him sole or joint parental responsibility if this is in the best interest of the child (§ 1671(2) BGB).

People other than the legal parents can obtain limited parental responsibility only for decisions in everyday matters that do not have a permanent effect on the child (so-called *kleines Sorgerecht*). The matters included in this authorization are determined on a case-by-case basis but usually involve acts implementing the more fundamental decisions: for example, they cannot decide which school the child attends, but they can pick them up, arrange private tutoring, and allow participation in extracurricular activities. Further, limited parental responsibility only supplements the right of the holder(s) of full parental responsibility, who retain their position and the last word.

Holders of full parental responsibility can lose this position against their will through a court decision if the welfare of the child is in danger (§ 1666 BGB) or in case of separation if sole parental responsibility is in the best interest of the child (§ 1671(1) BGB). Unlike in the case of parenthood as a status, the welfare of the child is assessed individually by looking at the concrete circumstances of the child at a certain point in time. Since the person(s) with parental responsibility are in charge of the day-to-day care of the child, it is imperative to take into account the individual situation and to recognize that changes may occur, for example, when one parent enters into a new relationship. If the welfare of the child is not in danger but a holder of parental responsibility still cannot take care of the child, a court can suspend parental responsibility temporarily (§ 1674 BGB).

Further, parents who have full parental responsibility can grant—even by implication—the authority to exercise their parental responsibility to others (*Sorgerechtsvollmacht*). The Civil Code does not contain provisions on this, but it has been accepted by the courts[25] even though the boundaries are still developing. The authorized person can be a social parent or any other caregiver who can then act for the legal parents. However, since only courts can transfer parental authority, the legal parents retain parental responsibility and ultimately remain responsible for ensuring the welfare of the child. This also means that they cannot irrevocably grant the authority to exercise parental authority to a third person but must remain able to revoke the authority at any time.[26] Therefore, granting the authority to exercise parental responsibility can help a social parent to gain certain rights concerning the child, but these rights remain at the mercy of the legal parents.

Contact

Finally, the law provides for a contact right, that is, the right to maintain personal relations with the child without any decision-making power or financial obligations,[27] independently of legal parenthood and parental responsibility. The kind of contact varies from regular weekend visits to occasional afternoons and depends on the individual circumstances of the case including factors such as previous relationship, age, wishes of the child, and contact commitments with others. Traditionally, this allowed legal fathers to keep up contact after a separation when the mother had sole parental responsibility. Today, usually both legal parents share parental responsibility even after a separation and the contact right has become more important in other cases: it is available to grandparents, siblings, and any person whom the child formed an attachment to (*enge Bezugsperson*) if this benefits the welfare of the child (§ 1685 BGB). A relevant attachment usually exists if a person acted as a caregiver in a common household for a significant time in the past. Thus, this provision can apply to social parents, for example, former stepparents or foster parents. A similar contact right exists for the genetic but not legal father who additionally can demand to be informed about important milestones of the child (§ 1686a BGB). The genetic father even has this contact right if he consented to an open stepchild adoption of the child by the same-sex partner of the mother.[28] However, there is no obligation to remain in contact with the child and the child does not have a corresponding contact right.[29] Thus, even though the best interest of the child is a criterion, this right is very much constructed from the adult's perspective.

Legal Recognition of Social Parents: Three Common Contexts

Same-Sex Couples

Currently, German law does not provide for a way for same-sex couples to obtain the status of legal parents together at birth because the rules are still modeled after genetic ties. Thus, it is likely that in these families at least one of the primary parental figures of a child remains a social parent at least temporarily. Although the Constitution protects equally same-sex and different-sex legal parents,[30] this protection extends only to people who already are legal parents. With a female same-sex couple, the woman who gives birth to the child becomes the legal mother. Since the provisions allocating fatherhood explicitly apply only to men, the second woman cannot become a second mother to the child at birth, even if both women are married.[31] This has been criticized and likely violates the Constitution because it discriminates against same-sex couples: a woman married to a woman cannot become the parent of a child born by her wife but a man in the same situation can, even if there is no genetic relation. This question was referred by two courts[32] to the Constitutional Court, which will decide soon. A reform proposal,[33] which would rectify the situation, has been under consideration since 2019. For male same-sex couples it is even more difficult because they need a surrogate mother, which is prohibited in Germany. However, if they enlist the services of a surrogate abroad and she is not married, one of the men can become the legal father of the child by recognition. Politically, it seems unlikely that the prohibition of surrogacy will change anytime soon, although a domestic regulation would be preferable to the current situation where couples go abroad and then return with the child creating legal uncertainty.[34] Yet, this also means that, at present, provisions on acquiring parenthood at birth for male same-sex couples have no area of application and are not considered separately of surrogacy. The only way for same-sex couples—male or female—to become legal parents of a child together is thus through adoption. Either they adopt a child together or one of them adopts the child of the other partner through stepchild adoption. Where limited parental responsibility and contact rights are concerned, there are no specific rules for same-sex couples, but they benefit from the same provisions as heterosexual couples.

Stepparents

Stepparents become a legal parent only if they adopt their new partner's child. Therefore, they generally do not have any rights or obligations toward the child. However, under certain restrictive conditions, stepparents can acquire limited parental responsibility (§ 1687b BGB). First, the legal parent and the stepparent have to be married or in a registered partnership. Additionally, the stepparent can acquire limited parental responsibility only if the legal parent was awarded sole parental responsibility. Since normally after a separation both legal parents share parental responsibility (cf. § 1671 BGB), this condition is often not met. Finally, limited parental responsibility of the stepparent depends on the right of the legal parent, which has three consequences: (1) the stepparent cannot decide without the legal parents' consent, (2) the legal parent can revoke the right at any time, and (3) in case of a divorce or the legal parents' death, the rights of the stepparent cease immediately. In a situation where a child has lived with their legal parent and stepparent and the legal parent dies, the child is most likely separated from the stepparent who is treated like any third person, except for a contact right under § 1685 BGB. The stepparent can petition the court to grant a provisional order to retain parental responsibility (*Verbleibensanordnung*, § 1682 BGB), but in the long term the child most likely will have to live with the other legal parent, who may not have had much contact with the child.

Nonparental Primary Caregivers

If parents are temporarily unable to care for the child, foster parents can assume the role of the primary caregiver. The rights and obligations of foster parents are regulated only fragmentarily. Foster parents can be either persons—usually but not necessarily—unknown to the child who take care of the child with formal permission by social services (§ 33, 44 (1) SGB VIII) or factual foster parents who will generally be relatives or family friends; both are treated equally under civil law as long as they act as parents full-time.[35] If a child lives with foster parents, either parental responsibility remains with the legal parents or a court revokes their rights because the welfare of the child is in danger. In the latter case, the court appoints a legal guardian, usually separately from the foster parents. However, a transfer of full parental responsibility to the foster parents is also possible when the legal parents consent (§ 1630 (3) BGB). If that is not the case, foster parents—in formal and informal situations—are assigned by law limited parental responsibility for everyday matters (§ 1688(1)(1) BGB) and a right to make decisions in emergency situations (§ 1629(1)(4) BGB). Additionally, foster parents manage all public benefits for the child (§ 1688(1)(2) BGB). The concept of the law explicitly sees the foster parents as representatives of the legal parents acting on their behalf rather than as a legal guardian of the child acting for the child (§ 1688(1)(1) BGB).

If legal parents keep parental responsibility, they can—at least in theory—decide to take back the child at any time. Should this happen, the foster parents retain only a contact right under § 1685 BGB. However, if the child had already been living with them for a significant amount of time, the foster parents can take steps to prevent this by obtaining a court order to establish that the child remains with them (*Verbleibensanordnung*, § 1632(4) BGB) but only for as long as there is a danger to the welfare of the child. Such a danger can also originate from a separation from the foster parents.[36] However, even a court order does not extend full parental responsibility to the foster parents but only perpetuates the situation of limited parental responsibility. To ensure a more stable environment for children in foster care, Parliament recently passed a reform proposal to amend § 1632(4) BGB and add the possibility of an order for unlimited duration if an improvement of the situation for the child with the legal parents is highly unlikely.[37]

Discussion

When looking at ways to improve the legal position of social parents—in the interest of both children and parents—it remains important to distinguish between parenthood, parental responsibility, and, to a lesser degree, contact. So far, changes were mainly limited to the area of parental responsibility and contact where the most common types of social parents, specifically stepparents and foster parents, acquired certain but narrow rights. The most pressing need for change concerns same-sex couples: even though same-sex marriage was introduced in 2017, the provisions attributing parenthood at birth have not been adjusted to this, often making same-sex parents social parents but not legal parents. However, such a reform would not solve all or even most problems of cases where social parents are concerned. While the bond between social parent and child can be formalized if the child has only one legal parent through a recognition (father) or stepchild adoption (mother/father), there is no such possibility if a child already has two legal parents. Often, social parents take care of children who already have two (legal) parents who want to remain their parents. Although it is not explicitly specified, it is generally assumed that a child can have a maximum of two legal parents with full parental responsibility.[38] Thus, the two-parent paradigm where the legal status forms a prerequisite for full parental responsibility substantially limits the possibilities to improve the situation of social parents by granting them more extensive rights.

Today, the two-parent paradigm is increasingly challenged, not only because of changing family forms but also because it is now possible for a child to have more than two genetic parents. Projecting forward, one could argue to abandon the two-parent paradigm, at least under certain conditions when the lived reality of a child includes more than two parental figures, either because the parents intended this situation (e.g., a lesbian couple with a known sperm donor who wants to play an active role) or because it developed later (e.g., after a separation and a new partnership of one or both parents). For example, a political project already considered the possibility of a stepchild adoption that preserves the ties to the genetic parents, but it was never implemented.[39]

In situations with more than two persons who are or could be in a parental role, the question of who is chosen as the two legal parents requires a difficult balancing of interests, which the legislator and courts struggle with. Especially the situation where a child has both a legal and a genetic father—both of whom would like to be the father of the child. Currently, the genetic father cannot challenge the paternity of the legal father if the latter has a social family relationship with the child (§ 1600(2) BGB). This is true even if the genetic father also has a social family relationship with the child.[40] This result seems questionable. Taking into consideration the individual case, for example based on an assessment of which father would be the better one and therefore in the best interest of the child, is not a solution either: it would require the court to make the permanent and (almost) unchangeable decision on the status of legal parenthood based on circumstances that are difficult to predict and likely to change.[41] Allowing more than two legal parents would enable courts and the legislator to avoid making this decision. From a normative perspective, there are two possibilities that come back to the two main parental positions: The more radical solution would allow multiple parents to obtain the full legal status of parenthood. On the other hand, it would be an option to separate parental responsibility from the legal status and grant full parental responsibility to more than two parents, which would follow and expand the changes already established for stepparents and foster parents in certain situations.

In both scenarios, it is important to include the perspective of constitutional law because of its binding effect on the legislator. The question of parental rights is discussed in connection with article 6 of the Constitution. Article 6(2) protects legal parents, which includes adoptive parents, and grants them a particularly strong position.[42] This article not only grants rights to the parents but also imposes on them the obligation to care for their child. Article 6(2) is based on the traditional concept of genetic parenthood and requires the legislator to generally align the allocation of parenthood with the genetic realities,[43] meaning that social parents are not afforded the same protection.[44] However, social parents fall under article 6(1), which more broadly protects the family in its lived reality and thus also the bond between social parent and child.[45] So far, the Constitutional Court has not yet had to decide on the issue of multiple parents as such, but in the situation of two men competing for fatherhood, the court specified in applying article 6(2) that there can be only two parents because otherwise it expects role conflicts and disputes, which can have a negative effect on the development of the child.[46] Effectively, the Constitutional Court therefore argues that multiple parents are not in the best interest of the child, even if this might not accurately reflect current psychological research.[47] This concern affects both multiple legal parents and multiple holders of full parental responsibility because the argument of the Court is relevant in both cases. So far, the decisions of the Constitutional Court allow the conclusion that it is skeptical toward allowing multiple parents, and while it might tolerate such a reform of the law of parenthood—an outcome that is politically unlikely at present—it currently seems rather farfetched to expect that the Constitutional Court might require the introduction of multiple parenthood from a constitutional perspective.

It is further necessary to consider the European Convention on Human Rights (ECHR), which is binding for Germany. Article 8 ECHR bases the protection of parents on a social bond and not on the legal or genetic position[48] and therefore is more open toward allowing multiple parents. The situation is similar to the protection under article 6(1) of the Constitution, but the ECHR does not contain a separate provision specifically on parents. However, even though the ECHR is binding, it grants the member states a margin of appreciation where the positions of the states differ.[49] Thus, while the ECHR is unlikely to prohibit a state to allow multiple parenthood, it also does not oblige a state to provide a position of legal parenthood as long as the social parent and the child are able to continue their lived relationship.[50] The member states are free to choose the way in which they achieve this goal, meaning that a right to personal contact—which the German legislator extended due to decisions by the ECtHR and the Constitutional Court[51]—fulfills this requirement.

If one could overcome reservations from a constitutional point of view, multiple legal parenthood would be the solution that really consequently follows the psychological concept of attachment. It would require a change not only of the law of parenthood but also of several other areas of family law and beyond. Therefore, it is certainly not impossible but does seem to make quick changes regarding multiple parenthood unlikely.

However, compared to the very rigid concept of legal parenthood, assigning parental responsibility is much more flexible already today. The welfare of the child is a suitable criterion to designate parental responsibility because necessary adjustments can be made in the future even though the importance of continuity in attachment figures always has to be considered. It is therefore much easier to grant parental responsibility to social parents by severing the connection between legal parenthood and parental responsibility[52] rather than allowing multiple legal parents. This is evident when looking at the current protection of social parents, which is achieved through granting limited parental responsibility. However, the problem remains that joint holders of full parental responsibility must come to an agreement regarding decisions for a child. Two solutions for this problem come to mind: reducing the need for a joint decision or considering the ability of the parents to reach an agreement as part of the welfare of the child when assigning parental responsibility to an additional parent, something that is already done in a similar way when deciding whether to deviate from the normal case of joint parental responsibility after a divorce.

NOTES

1 In 2018, 70 percent of all children lived with their married parents. Bundesministerium für Familie, Senioren, Frauen und Jugend, "Familienreport 2020" (2021), 40.

2 For data from 1996, see Bundesministerium für Familie, Senioren, Frauen und Jugend, "Familienreport 2017" (2018), 12.

3 Statistical data from the Federal Statistical Office, "Familien und Familienmitglieder mit minderjährigen Kindern in der Familie nach Lebensform und Gebietsstand" (2021), www.destatis.de/DE/Themen/Gesellschaft-Umwelt/Bevoelkerung/Haushalte-Familien/Tabellen/2-6-familien.html.

4 Familienreport 2020, 41.

5 Familienreport 2020, 47.

6 Familienreport 2017, 12.

7 Familienreport 2020, 51.

8 Familienreport 2020, 51.

9 Marina Rupp, "Gleichgeschlechtliche Lebenspartnerschaften und ihre Kinder," *Unsere Jugend* 7–8 (2013): 306–315, 307.

10 Rupp, "Gleichgeschlechtliche Lebenspartnerschaften," 306, 308.

11 Christine Entleitner-Phleps, *Zusammenzug und familiales Zusammenleben von Stieffamilien* (Wiesbaden: Springer, 2017), 15ff.; Rüdiger Peukert, *Familienformen im sozialen Wandel* (Wiesbaden: Springer, 2019), 334ff.

12 Peukert, *Familienformen im sozialen Wandel*, 353.

13 § 1(1) no. 1 Act for the Protection of Embryos (Embryonenschutzgesetz). Parents typically go abroad for the procedure and then return to Germany, where the child is born.

14 Peukert, *Familienformen im sozialen Wandel*, 352; Gesetzesbegründung zum Samenspenderregistergesetz, BR-Drucks. 785/16, 15.

15 Statistical data from the Federal Statistical Office, "2018 erstmals über 1 Million erzieherische Hilfen für junge Menschen" (2019), www.destatis.de/DE/Themen/Gesellschaft-Umwelt/Soziales/Kinderhilfe-Jugendhilfe/Tabellen/hilfen-erziehung-jungevolljaehrige.html;jsessionid=02DFF659DA719E876A19ECF4A38A9B9A.internet8732.

16 Peukert, *Familienformen im sozialen Wandel*, 345.

17 Joachim Gernhuber and Dagmar Coester-Waltjen, *Familienrecht* (Munich: Beck, 2020), § 1 para. 28; Karlheinz Muscheler, *Familienrecht* (Munich: Vahlen, 2017), para. 187.

18 Tobias Helms, "Abstammungsrecht und Kindeswohl," *Das Standesamt* (2014): 225–232.

19 Gesetz zum Elterngeld und zur Elternzeit (Bundeselterngeld- und Elternzeitgesetz—BEEG) (Law on parental pay and parental leave).

20 Bundeskindergeldgesetz (BKGG) (Law on child benefit).

21 Erbschaftsteuer- und Schenkungsteuergesetz (ErbStG) (Law on inheritance and gift tax).

22 Sozialgesetzbuch (SGB) Zweites Buch (II) (Social Law Book II).

23 BGH, May 3, 1995, XII ZR 29/94 (for a heterosexual couple); OLG Brandenburg, October 26, 2020, 9 UF 178/20 (for a female same-sex couple). Such a contract under which a third person (the child) has a claim is called a contract for the benefit of third parties and is provided for under § 328 BGB.

24 See, e.g., Gernhuber and Coester-Waltjen, *Familienrecht*, § 59 and § 60; Dieter Schwab, *Familienrecht* (Munich: Beck, 2020), § 66 and § 72.

25 The Federal Court of Justice decided on this issue for the first time only in 2020. BGH, April 29, 2020, XII ZB 112/19. But lower courts had paved the way before, e.g., OLG Karlsruhe, April 13, 2015, 18 UF 181/14.

26 Anja Amendt-Traut, "Sorgerechtsvollmachten," *Zeitschrift für das gesamte Familienrecht* (2020): 805–813, 810.

27 Critical Dieter Schwab, "Rechte am Kind ohne Verantwortung? Zur Begründung von Umgangsbefugnissen Dritter," in *Zwischenbilanz—Festschrift für Dagmar Coester-Waltjen*, ed. Katharina Hilbig-Lugani et al. (Bielefeld: Gieseking, 2015), 223–233.

28 BGH, June 16, 2021, XII ZB 58/20.

29 Werner Dürbeck, in Staudinger BGB, 2019, § 1685 para. 9.

30 BVerfG, February 19, 2013, 1 BvL 1/11, 1 BvR 3247/09.

31 BGH, October 10, 2018, XII ZB 231/18.

32 OLG Celle, March 24, 2021, 21 UF 146/20; KG Berlin, March 24, 2021, 3 UF 1122/20.

33 Draft bill of the Ministry of Justice, Diskussionsteilentwurf des Bundesministeriums der Justiz und für Verbraucherschutz zum Enwurf eines Gesetzes zur Reform des Abstammungsrechts (2019), www.bmjv.de/SharedDocs/Gesetzgebungsverfahren/DE/Reform_Abstammungsrecht.html?nn=6704238.

34 For an overview on surrogacy in Germany, see Anatol Dutta, "Surrogacy in Germany," in *Eastern and Western Perspectives on Surrogacy*, ed. Jens Scherpe, Claire Fenton-Glynn, and Terry Kaan (Cambridge: Intersentia, 2019), 35–47.

35 Gernhuber and Coester-Waltjen, *Familienrecht*, § 68 para. 19.

36 BVerfG, March 31, 2010, 1 BvR 2910/09.

37 Gesetz zur Stärkung von Kindern und Jugendlichen (KJSG) (Law in support of strengthening children and youth).

38 The only exception occurs when an adult is adopted, where the ties to the original family are not severed but the adoptee gains an additional set of parents (§ 1770(2) BGB).

39 See Tobias Helms, "Wie viele Eltern verträgt ein Kind? Mehrelternfamilien aus rechtlicher Sicht," in *Moderne Familienformen*, ed. Katharina Hilbig-Lugani and Peter M. Huber (Berlin: De Gruyter, 2019), 125–128, 126.

40 BGH, November 15, 2017, XII ZB 389/16.

41 Bettina Heiderhoff, "Was kann, was darf, was will der Staat?," in *Regelungsaufgabe Vaterstellung: Was kann, was darf, was will der Staat?*, ed. Anne Röthel and Bettina Heiderhoff (Frankfurt am Main: Metzner, 2014), 9–18, 17.

42 Anne Sanders, *Mehrelternschaft* (Tübingen: Mohr Siebeck, 2018), 172.
43 BVerfG, April 9, 2003, 1 BvR 1493/96.
44 BVerfG, February 19, 2013, 1 BvL 1/11, 1 BvR 3247/09.
45 BVerfG, February 19, 2013, 1 BvL 1/11, 1 BvR 3247/09.
46 BVerfG, April 9, 2003, 1 BvR 1493/96.
47 For the psychological background, see chapter 1.
48 ECtHR, June 13, 1979, no. 6833/74 (*Marckx v. Belgien*).
49 Walter Pintens, "Familienrecht und Rechtsvergleichung in der Rechtsprechung des Europäischen Gerichtshofes für Menschenrechte," *Zeitschrift für das gesamte Familienrecht* (2016): 341–351, 346f.
50 In the context of surrogacy, ECtHR, May 18, 2021, no. 71552/17 (*Valdís Fjölnisdóttir and others v. Iceland*).
51 Alexandra Altrogge, in BeckOGK BGB, 15.2.2021, § 1685 para. 2ff. and § 1686a para. 2ff.
52 See, e.g., the situation in England, chapter 8.

10

Social Parenthood in Greece

ELENI ZERVOGIANNI

The regulation of parent-child relationships in Greece still revolves around the principle that a child can have no more than two parents of different sex. Yet the increase of blended families and the rising social acceptance of same-sex partnerships, coupled with the broad availability of medically assisted reproduction techniques, make it increasingly common that persons other than the child's legal parents assume parental responsibilities. The law in Greece largely does not recognize the relationship between a social parent and a child, although in 2021 a new law (Law 4800/2021 that amended the Civil Code) provided some protection, establishing a right of contact between a social parent and a child. Drawing upon the findings of psychological studies that the preservation and strengthening of the bonds between children and their social parents is in the children's best interest, this chapter addresses the legal issues and challenges that arise in such settings, explaining the protection that Greek law does—and, more typically, does not—offer.

Demographic Data

Greece follows the general European trend of a decreasing marriage rate and increasing divorce rate.[1] Nevertheless, Greek society is still rather traditional. Only 11 percent of the children are born to unmarried parents.[2] Same-sex partners cannot marry, but since December 2015 they have been able to enter a registered partnership.[3] Each year since then approximately 200 to 250 such partnerships have been registered,[4] a number that is rather small considering that the Greek population is around 10 million.

No statistics are available for de facto situations, such as partners who neither marry nor register as cohabitants, or blended families. However, from the increase in the divorce rate, the fact that in three-quarters of divorces there are children involved, and the fact that more than 10 percent of the persons who get married have been previously divorced,[5] it can be inferred that the number of blended families is steadily increasing. Almost 92 percent of children live in households with two adults, whether the children's legal or social parents,[6] 7.5 percent live in one-parent households, and 0.5 percent live in other arrangements, such as foster care.[7] Children living in a one- or no-parent household seem to be slightly more likely to be living in relative poverty.[8] Given the homogeneity of the Greek population, race is not a relevant factor in these statistics.

Finally, regarding medically assisted reproduction, the only available data are unofficial. More than 4,500 children are born each year from medically assisted reproduction,[9] which corresponds to 5 percent of the total number of births, and the proportion of successful procedures in which donated gametes were used exceeds 10 percent.[10] There are no reliable estimates about the number of children born through surrogacy and then staying in Greece, but it would seem that there are fewer than one hundred such cases per year.[11]

Legal Recognition of Parents

Greece is a unitary state. The main provisions of Greek family law, including those on legal parenthood and parental responsibilities, are included in the fourth book of the Greek Civil Code (GrCC) of 1940 (arts. 1346–1694), which has been substantially amended by newer legislation. Moreover, special laws regulate particular issues, such as Law 4356/2015, which regulates a "cohabitation agreement" as a form of registered partnership between persons of different or the same sex, and Law 4538/2018, which regulates adoption and foster care and complements the relevant provisions of the GrCC. Within this regulatory framework, there exist a few scattered rules on social parenthood. However, a preliminary step to assess the legal position of "social parents" is to distinguish social parenthood from legal parenthood.

As a general rule, a child cannot have more than two legal parents, who have to be of different sexes.[12] This is based on the rules establishing legal parenthood and the overall regulation of the parent-child relations.

Traditionally, the basis for the establishment of legal parenthood has been biology. The woman who gives birth to the child is considered to be the child's legal mother (art. 1463 GrCC), and her husband or (different-sex) registered partner is presumed to be the legal father, unless his paternity is challenged on the basis that he is not the biological father of the child (arts. 1465 and 1467 GrCC and art. 9 of Law 4356/2018). If the child's mother neither is married nor has entered a registered (different-sex) partnership, paternal descent can be established only by means of acknowledgment by the father. This acknowledgment may be either voluntary, provided that the mother also consents to it (art. 1475 GrCC), or (if voluntary acknowledgment fails) judicial, in which case paternity is established by means of a court ruling. In both cases the establishment of fatherhood is based on biology: the court ruling on the acknowledgment is contingent upon proof of the biological connection between the father and the child (art. 1479 GrCC), while voluntary acknowledgment can also be challenged if it does not reflect the biological truth (art. 1477 GrCC).

The enactment of the regulatory framework on medically assisted reproduction in 2002 (Law 3089/2002, which amended the GrCC) amended the traditional rules on parental descent, shifting the focus from biology to socioemotional bonds, as the will of a person to have a child prevails over biology. Thus, there is no room for the contestation of paternity if the husband or registered partner of the mother consented to medically assisted reproduction with donated gametes (1471 para. 2 GrCC). Furthermore, even if the donor's gametes are known and the child has only one legal parent, there is no room for the establishment of legal parenthood against the will of the donor or against the will of the mother (arts. 1460 and art. 1479 para. 2 GrCC). Moreover, in the case of gestational surrogacy, which is thoroughly regulated (art. 1458 GrCC), if the conditions of the law are met, maternal descent is established at birth with the woman who wished to have the child and not with the surrogate (art. 1464 GrCC). The latter's relation to the child is not recognized legally in any respect. Legal parenthood through adoption is also based on the will of the parties, provided that the adoption is in the best interest of the child (art. 1542 GrCC). Greek law permits only the full adoption of minors, which leads to the complete disruption of the child's bonds with the biological family (art. 1561 GrCC).

Medically assisted reproduction is accessible to couples of different sexes, married or not, as well as single women (art. 1456 GrCC).[13] Moreover, individuals may adopt, but joint adoption or second-parent adoption is possible only for married couples (art. 1545 GrCC). Thus, same-sex partners, irrespective of whether they have entered a registered partnership, have access to both adoption and medically assisted reproduction only individually, not as a couple.

The establishment of legal parenthood has consequences for the name and citizenship of the child, support obligations, and succession rights. Moreover, legal parents are holders of the right and obligation of parental care (γονική μέριμνα), which comprises the "personal care" of the minor, the administration of the child's property, and the child's legal representation (art. 1510 GrCC). "Personal care" includes the child's upbringing, education, supervision, and determination of place of residence (art. 1518 GrCC). As a rule, both parents, married or not, automatically have the right to exercise parental care, and they must do so jointly and in the best interest of the child (art. 1510 and (new) art. 1515 GrCC).[14] If they cannot reach a common decision, they can apply to the court, which then decides the issue (art. 1512 GrCC). The court may assign the sole exercise of parental care to one of the parents if joint exercise of parental care is no longer a workable option or if the other parent does not act in the best interest of the child (art. 1514 GrCC. See also art. 1532 GrCC). Legal parents exercise parental care in person, meaning that in principle they may not convey it to others, while third persons who assume parental responsibilities against the will of either parent are considered to interfere with this parent's right.[15] Finally, the legal parent who does not reside with the child has the right to contact (art. 1520 GrCC), which is seen as a distinct right, independent of parental care. The right to contact guarantees the preservation of a relationship between the parent and the child through regular communication and visits, including the stay of the child at the home of the parent with whom the child does not reside. After its recent amendment in 2021, the new article 1520 explicitly stipulates that the contact should be as extensive as possible, and it is presumed to amount to one-third of the total time of the child, unless it is in the interest of the child to restrict contact.[16]

The following analysis shows that, except for foster care, which is comprehensively regulated as an institution complementary to parental care, within this framework there is little room for the legal recognition of social parenthood.

Legal Recognition of Social Parents: Three Common Contexts

Same-Sex Couples

For same-sex couples, the legal recognition of social parenthood is critically important because there is no possibility for both partners to become legal parents of the child. As discussed below, there is some debate about this issue, but no legislative measures have been adopted. Thus, in same-sex families and different-sex stepfamilies alike, the law does not grant to the legal parent's partner any parental rights, irrespective of whether the latter lives in a formalized relationship with the legal parent. It is legally irrelevant that the child lives in the same household with the partner of the legal parent. The legal parent may not assign to another person extensive tasks pertaining to the care of the child. Moreover, if the child has two legal parents, who will necessarily be of different sex, and both parents exercise parental care jointly but the child lives with only one parent, it may be an infringement on the right of parental care of the nonresidential parent if the partner of the residential parent exercises parental responsibilities as well.[17] In short, the legal status of the partner of the legal parent is similar to that of a babysitter:[18] the partner is not entitled to make any decision, even in everyday matters. Thus, if the child needs medical treatment, the social parent is not entitled to consent to the treatment, even in cases of emergency.[19]

The main protection for social parents in case their relationship with the legal parent ends is the new article 1520 paragraph 2 sentence 2 GrCC, as amended in 2021: "The parents do not have the right to obstruct the contact of the child with third persons, who have developed a social-emotional bond of family nature with the child, if contact serves the best interests of the child." This new provision clearly draws upon the relevant case law of the European Court of Human Rights (ECtHR).[20] Undoubtedly the contact right of the social parent is significantly more limited as compared to the contact right of legal parents. It is granted only if it is definitively proven that it serves the best interests of the child—it is not enough to prove that it does not harm the child. It is up to the court to decide the specifics regarding the contact of the social parent on a case-by-case basis. This provision is so new there are not yet decisions applying it.

Beyond these limited rights, social parents do not have significant rights. If the legal parent dies or is not in a position to exercise parental care, for example, the social parent is not entitled to care for the child (art. 1602 GrCC), although, in the absence of another legal parent, a court might appoint the social parent as a guardian for the child (art. 1592 GrCC).[21]

Beyond these, if the same-sex partners have entered into a registered partnership, further consequences may stem from the legal bonds of affinity between the legal parent's partner and the child (art. 1462 GrCC), even if the partner does not act like a parent. The partner of the legal parent and the child are relatives by affinity of the first degree in a direct line. This constitutes an impediment to marry or to conclude registered partnership (art. 1357 GrCC, art. 2 of Law 4356/2015). More importantly, in case of tortious death of the partner of the legal parent or of the child, the surviving one may be considered a "member of the family" and claim compensation for the nonpecuniary damage suffered because of this death (art. 932 GrCC), provided that there has been an actual loving bond between them. In addition, having a relation by affinity, even if it stems from a same-sex partnership,[22] makes the adoption of an adult possible (art. 1579 GrCC). In this way, once the child reaches majority, legal parenthood can be established between the adult son or daughter and the social parent, without disrupting the relations of the adoptee and the (initial) legal parents (arts. 1584–1585 GrCC). This form of multiparentality, which is the only one explicitly regulated in Greek law, has a significant impact on rights of succession and maintenance.

Stepparents

The relation between the stepparent and the child is governed by the same rules as same-sex couples. Two additional rules of the GrCC may apply if the legal parent and the stepparent marry (which is legally possible if they are of different sex), neither of which refers to parental responsibilities. First, if the child is born to unmarried parents and the child's mother marries, the mother's new husband—the stepparent—may, according to article 1506 GrCC, give his name to the child if both the mother and the child consent.[23] Second, if the stepparent paid maintenance to the child despite no legal obligation to do so, the stepparent may reclaim the money from the legal parent under the conditions of article 1490 paragraph 2 number 5 GrCC.[24] Finally, if the legal parent and stepparent are married, and there is only one legal parent, legal parenthood may be established between the stepparent and the child by means of second-parent adoption (Art 1545 GrCC).

Nonparental Primary Caregivers

A child may be placed in foster care either by court decision or contractually, if the sole legal parent or both legal parents,[25] acting in the best interests of the child, conclude a relevant agreement with the foster parent (art. 1655 GrCC, arts. 10 and 11 of Law 4538/2018). Foster parents, who act as representatives of the legal parents, are entrusted with the daily care of the child and the handling of emergencies and are thus also entitled to consent to the medical treatment of the child in urgent cases (arts. 1655 and 1659 GrCC).[26] They do not bear the costs of maintenance of the child and may be granted an allowance by the state (art. 12 of Law 4538/2018), while further social benefits of legal parents may extend to them as well.[27] During foster care, the child's legal relationship with their legal parents remains, in principle, unaltered. The fundamental decisions regarding the child rest by the parents.[28] The foster parents have the right to be heard before any decision of the parents regarding the child (art. 1659 GrCC), but they do not have the right to act against their will if this has been explicitly stated (art. 1658 GrCC), with a possible exception if their act best serves the interest of the child.[29] In all cases, foster parents are controlled by social services (art. 1665 GrCC, art. 13 of Law 4538/2018). By means of court decision, the foster parents may be entrusted with further parental responsibilities, if the child is well integrated in the foster family and the child's bonds with the legal parents have weakened (art. 1660 GrCC) or if the legal parents are considered unfit (art. 1532 GrCC).

When foster care relies solely on a contractual arrangement between the legal parents and the foster parents, the former can recall it anytime (art. 1662 GrCC). If the child has been placed in foster care by means of a court decision, the legal parents (or the guardian) may apply to the court for its termination, which can then terminate foster care if the circumstances that led to the initial judgment no longer exist (art. 1662 GrCC) and this serves the best interest of the child (art. 1664 GrCC). After the termination of the placement, the law grants foster parents the right to contact if this is in the best interest of the child (new art. 1520 para. 2).

Before 2018 and the enactment of Law 4538/2018, if a child lived with a person other than a legal parent, a foster care agreement could be inferred from that living arrangement. With the passage of Law 4538/2018, informal arrangements are not considered valid and instead are treated under the doctrine of *negotiorum gestio* (arts. 730ff. GrCC).[30] It is also possible to treat informal foster care agreements as a "de facto contractual relation." Under this doctrine, the person caring for the child and the legal parents are understood to have a de facto contract, which governs until one party declares it invalid—a declaration that does not have retrospective effects.[31] Invalidating the de facto foster care agreement would not affect any contracts the foster parents concluded, as representatives of the legal parents, with third parties while taking care of the everyday affairs of the child.[32]

Discussion

Legal versus Social Parenthood

The Greek legislature has been reluctant to grant parental responsibilities to persons other than legal parents, even if another person is playing a large role in raising the child. This approach evidently aims at the protection of the legal family. The same rationale runs through family law provisions. For example, the only permissible adoption of minors is full adoption, which completely disrupts the relationship between the child and the birth parents. Similarly, family law does not confer any legal recognition to the relationship between a surrogate and the child she gave birth to.

In its absoluteness, this rather traditional view seems to ignore modern social reality, where relations within a family become increasingly complex. When a same-sex couple decides to raise a child together but the law recognizes only one person as a legal parent, there is no protection for the relationship between the child and the other person—the social parent. Similarly, in same-sex and different-sex stepfamilies alike, the "third" person is already in the family and it could be in the interest of the child, and quite possibly of everyone else involved, to legally recognize this reality. The approach of family relations on the basis of a functional criterion, drawn upon real situations, rather than a formal criterion, such as legal parenthood, is a clear trend in the case law of the ECtHR.[33] Thus not only social parenthood,[34] but even prospective social parenthood,[35] can be seen as a protected form of "family life" according to article 8 of the European Convention on Human Rights.

Social Parenthood: The Current State of the Debate

To date, discussions of the recognition of parental responsibilities for social parents pertain to scenarios where the child has only one legal parent. During the discussions that preceded the enactment of Law 4356/2015 on registered partnership, the Greek ombudsman submitted a proposal:[36] if one of the (same- or different-sex) partners is the sole holder of the right of parental care, the court may assign parental responsibilities to the other partner, so that they both exercise them jointly. Moreover, according to the same proposal, if the only legal parent or holder of parental care dies or is no longer able to exercise parental care, the court may assign the partner as guardian. This proposal gained support by a party of the opposition and was discussed in Parliament, but in the end it was not adopted. It nevertheless triggered a debate on the topic and has been favorably discussed in the literature.[37] The Report of the Committee that has been assigned the drafting of the National Strategy for the Equality of LGBTQI+ also stressed the importance of adopting a regulation to this effect because this legal protection is critical until same-sex parenthood is recognized.[38]

Challenges and Outlook

The first question when dealing with the regulation of de facto family relations is whether there is room for the expansion of legal parenthood. The practical significance of this solution goes well beyond the allocation of parental responsibilities because legal parents and children have the obligation to maintain each other and are also granted succession rights. Of course, such a development would presuppose that the legislator abandons the principle that a child cannot have more than two parents of different sex. As other countries increasingly recognize the claim for same-sex couples to parent a child together as legal parents, it is likely only a matter of time before Greece adopts a relevant regulation. Indeed, the 2021 Report of the Committee on the National Strategy for the Equality of LGBTQI+ persons discussed the expansion of marriage to same-sex couples, which, on the basis of antidiscrimination concerns, would necessarily bring about adjustment of the rules on the establishment of legal parenthood, but the report did not formulate a concrete proposal.[39] Accepting that a child may have more than two legal parents is definitively a further step and a much thornier one. Opening up the floor for this debate in Greece, before the recognition of same-sex parenthood, seems premature.

If, or to the extent that, the discussion on the recognition of legal parenthood for social parents is off the table, it is crucial to come up with a regime that grants social parents some parental responsibilities. An idea worth examining is whether the rules on foster care could serve as a pattern for the regulation of social parenthood in the context of same-sex and blended families. What is of particular interest in this respect is the case of contractual foster care. Indeed, in spite of the nontransferability of the right of parental care, the Greek legislature explicitly recognizes the possibility of legal parents assigning by means of a contract the everyday care of the child to a foster parent. If it is possible to assign the everyday care of the child in its totality to a foster parent, why not recognize the possibility to assign it to the partner of the legal parent with whom the child resides as well?

The situation appears simpler in cases where the child has only one legal parent, but it is more complicated if the child has two legal parents who hold parental rights, even if just one of them exercises these rights. The decision on the assignment of some responsibilities to the social parent would have to be a joint decision of the legal parents.[40] If one of the legal parents does not agree, the other parent can bring the case before the court (art. 1512), which will decide the issues on the basis of the best interests of the child. Given that the aim of such a possible future regulation would be to cover de facto situations, it would be essential that the conclusion of the contract can be inferred by the behavior of the parties involved. Otherwise, a great part of cases of social parenthood would remain unresolved. Once this contract is concluded, the relations of the parties could be regulated along the same lines as in foster care. In this sense, the social parent could not act against the expressed will of the legal parent(s), and in case of disagreement between the social parent and the legal parent(s), the opinion of the latter shall prevail. This would be necessary to guarantee the functionality of the solution.

A thornier issue is the recognition of rights of social parents, other than the right to contact, after the dissolution of the relation between the legal parent and the social parent or, generally, after the termination of the contract in any way. There seems to exist a consensus that if the child had only one legal parent and this parent dies, in principle the social parent should be appointed guardian by the court and also take care of the child until a guardian is appointed.[41] The legislature could and should proceed further than that. Article 1601 GrCC on foster care could serve as a source of inspiration for the main lines along which a solution could be sought.

More concretely, according to the law currently in force, if the child has two legal parents, one of whom dies or is no longer in a position to exercise parental responsibilities, the other legal parent automatically assumes the sole parental care of the child.[42] However, if a social parent, usually the partner of the deceased legal parent, had been living in the same household with the child and was actively involved in raising the child by means of a contractual arrangement, as described above, it could be claimed that even if the child has another legal parent, the social parent should have the possibility to proceed before the court and claim the assignment of parental care, in full or in part, if this best serves the interest of the child. This could be the case especially if the social parent has had a long-lasting relationship with the child and the bonds of the child with the other legal parent with whom the child had not been residing have weakened overtime. Resting upon the assumption that the best interests of the child should prevail over biology, a similar rule could also apply, even exceptionally, in cases of separation of the legal and social parent. The adoption of such a regulatory scheme, though, should be further coupled with amendments of further provisions, especially regarding the obligation to maintain the child.

In sum, Greek law provides very limited recognition for social parents. This is largely because Greek law is based on the paradigmatic case of two different-sex legal parents who are married and are raising a child together. There is some recognition for people who act like parents but do not fit this paradigm—such as the 2021 law allowing a right of contact between a social parent and a child—but generally the recognition is limited. As this chapter concludes, the adoption of future legislative steps, possibly on the pattern of the regulation of foster care, is necessary, but still unrealized.

NOTES

1 OECD Family Database, "The Structure of Families" (SF3.1), www.oecd.org/els/family/database.htm.
2 OECD Family Database (SF2.4), www.oecd.org.
3 Law 4356/2015.
4 Hellenic Statistical Authority, press releases for the years 2016–2019 on natural movement of population data, www.statistics.gr.
5 OECD Family Database, table SF3.2.B. and chart SF3.1.D, respectively, www.oecd.org.
6 OECD Family Database, SF1.2, www.oecd.org.
7 OECD Family Database, SF1.2, www.oecd.org.
8 OECD Family Database, table SF1.3.B, www.oecd.org.
9 See the presentation of statistics gathered by the National Authority of Assisted Reproduction from Assisted Reproduction Units for the year 2015, available at http://eaiya.gov.gr/παρουσιαση-στατιστικων-δεδομενων-τω/.
10 National Authority of Assisted Reproduction from Assisted Reproduction Units for the year 2015.
11 Cf. Pantelis Ravdas, "Surrogate Motherhood in Greece: Statistical Data Derived from Court Decision," *Bioethica* 3, no. 2 (2017): 40–58, https://ejournals.epublishing.ekt.gr/index.php/bioethica.
12 Art. 5 para. 2 of Law 4491/2017 on gender identity introduces an exception to this rule. According to this provision, the correction of the sex of one of the parents does not have any effect on the parent-child relationship.
13 The issue is vividly debated when it comes to single men (who could also have a child using a surrogate). See in English, Eleni Zervogianni, "Greece," in *Eastern and Western Perspectives on Surrogacy*, ed. Jens M. Scherpe, Claire Fenton-Glynn, and Terry Kaan (Cambridge: Intersentia, 2019), 147, 156, with further references.
14 The joint exercise of parental care of children born out of wedlock has been recently introduced by Law 4800/2021. An exception to the joint exercise of parental care is provided when legal parenthood has been established by court decision against the will of the father.

15 E. Kounougeri-Manoledaki, *Family Law II* (in Greek), 7th ed. (Athens: Sakkoulas, 2018), 273–274; A. Georgiades, *Family Law* (in Greek), 2nd ed. (Athens: Sakkoulas, 2017), § 30 no. 3, 4.

16 For the amendment, see art. 13 of Law 4800/2021.

17 V. Peraki, "Possibilities of Exercise of Parental Care of Children of Same-Sex Partners" (in Greek), *Efarmoges Astikou Dikaiou* (2020): 567, 571–572 with further references.

18 Peraki, "Possibilities of Exercise," 573.

19 See art. 12 para. 2 of Law 3418/2015. In extremely urgent cases, the doctor may act without any consent to prevent an imminent danger to the life of the child.

20 *Nazarenko v. Russia* (2015) (challenge of paternity/contact); *Fatkhutdinov v. Russia* (2020) (challenge of paternity/contact); and *V.D. and Others v. Russia* (2019) (foster parent contact).

21 If another legal parent exists, they automatically assume the sole exercise of parental care. Exceptionally this does not hold if legal fatherhood has been established by court decision against the will of the father (art. 1515 para. 2).

22 Peraki, "Possibilities of Exercise," 571.

23 This provision existed already in the initial version of the Civil Code of 1940 (in art. 1531) and evidently aimed to "keep up the appearances."

24 It could be supported that this provision applies by analogy also when the (same-sex or different-sex) registered partner of the legal parent grants maintenance to the child.

25 This holds also in cases where one of the parents has the sole exercise of parental care because the issue pertains to the so-called core of parental care. See G.-A. Georgiadis, *Foster Care for Minors* (in Greek) (Athens: Sakkoulas, 2018), no. 297 with further references; cf. new art. 1519 GrCC.

26 See K. Fountedaki, *Short Commentary on the Civil Code*, ed. A. Georgiades, 9 (in Greek) (Athens: Sakkoulas, 2010), arts. 1656–1659 no. 4; Georgiadis, *Foster Care for Minors*, no. 421.

27 See, e.g., Nikolopoulos, Expert opinion, *Efarmoges Astikou Dikaiou* (2021), 128ff.

28 See in detail Georgiadis, *Foster Care for Minors*, no. 354ff.

29 See Georgiades, *Family Law*, § 45 no. 26.

30 Fountedaki, *Short Commentary on the Civil Code*, art. 1655, no. 14; Georgiadis, *Foster Care for Minors*, no. 333. See also note 21 above.

31 See, among others, M. Stathopoulos, *General Part of the Law of Obligations*, 5th ed. (Athens: Sakkoulas, 2018), § 14 nos. 58 and 62.

32 Cf. Georgiadis, *Foster Care for Minors*, no. 335, reaching the same result on a different legal basis.

33 M.-A. Kostopoulou, *ECHR and Establishment of Legal Parenthood* (in Greek) (Athens: Nomiki Vibliothiki, 2021), 19–20.

34 See Georgiadis, *Foster Care for Minors*, no. 297; cf. new art. 1519 GrCC.

35 *Anayo v. Germany* (2010); *Schneider v. Germany* (2011).

36 Proposal of December 7, 2015, www.synigoros.gr/?i=equality.el.files.437553.

37 Peraki, "Possibilities of Exercise," 576.

38 See the report of the Committee, titled "Ethniki Stratigiki gia tin Isotita ton LOATKI+" (in Greek) (2021), https://primeminister.gr/wp-content/uploads/2021/06/ethniki_statigiki_gia_thn_isothta_ton_loatki.pdf, 47. The Committee was set up by decision of the prime minister on March 17, 2021, and submitted its report on June 29, 2021.

39 Report, 46.

40 See Georgiades, *Family Law*, § 45 no. 26.

41 See the previous subsection, "Social Parenthood: The Current State of the Debate."

42 See the earlier subsection on stepparents.

11

Social Parenthood in the Netherlands

MACHTELD VONK AND WENDY SCHRAMA

There is a growing diversity of family forms in the Netherlands, ranging from married different-sex and same-sex couples to informal cohabiting couples, stepfamilies, families through sperm and/or egg donation, and families through surrogacy. In recent decades much attention has been paid to the law regulating parent-child relationships. There has been a strong focus on equal rights for families with same-sex parents and intentional multiparent families in the aftermath of full marriage equality in 2001.[1] Greater attention has also been directed to the position of unmarried fathers, but less so for stepfamilies. The Government Committee on the Reassessment of Parenthood[2] published an influential report in 2016, which has since led to further research and the drafting of a number of proposals to amend the current law on parent-child relationships, described in this chapter. At present, it seems the legislature has opted for a one-size-fits-all approach to the various kinds of social parents that will be discussed in this chapter. We will come back to the question of whether that is a good idea in the discussion.

Demographic Data

There are no recent demographic data from the same source on all the different family types in the Netherlands, but information from different sources and different years may give the reader some idea of Dutch family demographics. In 2020, the Netherlands counted some 8.0 million households,[3] of which 2.6 million were households with one or more children living at home (in almost 1.9 million of these households the youngest child living at home was under eighteen and in the other 0.7 million households the youngest child was eighteen or older). Of these households, 60 percent consisted of married adults with one or more children, some 18 percent of unmarried adults with one or more children, and some 22 percent of one adult (usually a mother) with one or more children.[4] Research with data from 2017 on complex families shows that 19 percent of minor children have experienced parental divorce, parental repartnering, the addition of stepsiblings to their family, and/or the birth of half siblings.[5] In 2020, 1,114 same-sex couples entered into a marriage, and 770 same-sex couples entered into a registered partnership.[6] In 2018, 70 children were born into a female same-sex relationship and three to a male same-sex couple.[7] We have as yet no data on children born through surrogacy or on children born through egg and/or sperm donation. There are, however, data on the number of fertility treatments with donated sperm (865), eggs (18), or embryos (21) carried out in Dutch hospitals/clinics in 2020.[8] That same year, 23,039 children lived in a foster family, ranging in duration from a couple of weeks to a couple of years.[9]

Legal Recognition of Parents

Legal rules governing parent-child relationships are laid down in the Dutch Civil Code (Burgerlijk Wetboek) in Book I, which deals with the law of persons and family law. This is a national law, originally dating from 1970 but since then often and thoroughly amended. The last big change dates from 2014 when the position of lesbian coparents was considerably improved. In addition to the Civil Code, article 8 of the European Convention on Human Rights (ECHR) has gained much influence on national family law, in particular regarding parentage and contact.[10] This is in part the result of the fact that Dutch courts can set aside Dutch family law on the basis of article 8 of the ECHR when judging matters relating to *family life* and *private life*. Typical for the relationship between parents and children is the mandatory nature of the law. Only in the manner prescribed by law can rights be obtained, and there is little room for individual choice by families.

The three distinct aspects of parent-child relationships in the Civil Code are parental status (parentage), parental responsibility, and contact. Originally, the idea underlying the Civil Code was that married different-sex couples would be the child's legal parents exercising parental responsibility by taking care of their children. Parental status, parental responsibility, and contact are vested in the same persons in this scenario. The law on parents and children served to reinforce moral values that heterosexual marriage outranked all other types of families. The law discriminated against children born outside marriage. Gradually, with changes in society, the law changed as well. Informal families and families with same-sex parents are common now, and the law has been amended to include them. Equality has been the driving force for change.[11]

As a rule, parentage is a lifelong bond that comes into being if the conditions of the Civil Code are met. Legal certainty about parental status is traditionally of great importance, also in light of the division of responsibilities between state and family. Social benefits, tax law benefits, and the position in inheritance law are based on legal status as parent or child.[12] Traditionally, biological ties have been the basis for awarding the status of legal parentage and parental responsibility. The ties are often presumed to exist, for instance for fathers in marriage or fathers in informal couples when recognizing a child. There is no DNA testing or other evidence required (see below for further discussion of these issues). In the past decades, social (nonbiological) parentage has increasingly been recognized as well, in particular for co-mothers in female same-sex-parent families who can acquire parental status through the law on parentage since 2014.[13] However, there is still an important difference between genetic and nongenetic legal parents. Legal parentage of a genetic parent can be severed only through adoption, whereas the legal parentage ties of a nongenetic parent can be dissolved by the court upon application by the child. Both the birth mother and the legal nonbiological parent have limited options for severing the legal ties between the nongenetic parent and the child. These options are constrained by lapse of time on the one hand and knowledge about or consent to the use of genetic material from another person or sexual intercourse with another person on the other hand.[14]

Parental responsibility is generally awarded to legal parents, but social parents can have parental responsibility as well, even when they do not have the legal status of a parent. Parental responsibility entails the right and duty to take care of the child and to raise the child. It includes a right to decision making about important issues such as schooling, place of residence, medical care, and daily activities. Parental responsibility can be held by one parent or caregiver or by two parents or caregivers jointly, and it ends automatically when the child reaches the age of eighteen.

Contact is mostly of importance for families who do not or no longer share the same household with their parents. Legal parents have a duty and a right to contact with their child, regardless of whether they exercise parental responsibility.[15] Contact does not come with decision-making rights, but a legal parent with parental responsibility needs to inform and consult the other legal parent without parental responsibility on important issues in relation to the child.[16]

If an adult is not a legal parent and has no parental responsibility but has a close personal relationship with the child, that person might be able to maintain contact with the child after they no longer live in the same home. This right is determined by the extent of the relationship between the adult and the child.[17] The question of when a relationship between a person and a child merits the making of a contact order by the court is for a large part determined by jurisprudence from the European Court of Human Rights on the basis of article 8 of the ECHR.[18] Elements that may play a role are the existence of genetic tie (biological parent who is not a legal parent) and the role in the child's life (foster parent, stepparent, de facto social parent). Whether the court will subsequently make a contact order is subject to the child's best interests.

The obligation to support a child is mainly, but not exclusively, based on legal parentage. All legal parents are under a duty to support their children, but also stepparents in a formalized relationship with a parent and social parents with parental responsibility have this duty.[19]

In conclusion, Dutch family law is based on the principle that a child can have (only) two legal parents. That said, there is room for two adults with parental status and two adults (not necessarily the same ones) who can exercise parental responsibility. Contact is not limited by a specific number of adults but depends on the status as a legal parent and/or the factual relationship with the child.

Legal Recognition of Social Parents: Three Common Contexts

An influential report was published in 2016 with regard to the recognition of social parenthood: it paid attention to the recognition of social parenthood in multiparent families, in stepparent families, and in foster families. These proposals and the current view of the legislator on whether or not to transform these proposals into law will be discussed in the various sections below. Currently, recognition of social parents is based mainly in article 8 of the ECHR and may, for instance, lead to a right to contact after separation of child and social parent if this is in the child's best interest. Furthermore, the law contains a general obligation for anyone who looks after a child to take care of the child and their well-being and to promote their development.[20]

Same-Sex Couples

As of 2014, female same-sex couples can both become legal parents automatically on the birth of a child in their relationship or through recognition by the co-mother before or after the birth of the child, depending on their relationship status and their choice of sperm donor. All birth mothers automatically have the full package of rights: they are the legal mother of the child, with parental responsibility.[21] The second parent's position largely depends on the type of relationship with the birth mother. Male second parents who are married or have a registered partnership with the birth mother will automatically become the child's second legal parent and will have joint parental responsibility with the birth mother.[22] For female second parents who are in a marriage or registered partnership with the birth mother, there is an extra requirement for automatic legal parenthood for the co-mother. After the birth of the child, a declaration has to be submitted to the civil registrar indicating that the child was conceived with sperm of a donor whose identity is not known to the birthmother.[23] The idea behind this choice is that when the mothers opt for a donor who is known to them, the three persons involved may wish to make other choices, for instance opting for making the donor a legal parent by recognition. The Government Committee recommended the introduction of legislation that would delete the requirement to submit a declaration about the status of the donor, but as of yet no legislative action has been taken in this regard.

Second parents in informal families (not married or registered partners) need to recognize the birthmother's child to obtain the legal status of parent and need to apply for joint parental responsibility with the birthmother.[24] This applies to both male and female second parents.

Recognition may take place even before the child's birth. It requires the birth mother's consent.[25] In case the birthmother refuses to consent to the recognition, the intended male or female second parent can apply to the court for consent to recognize the child.[26] Here biology starts to play a role because there are different legal rules that the court must apply when judging such a request depending on whether or not the applicant is a biological parent.[27] Such an application by a biological father will generally be awarded because it is regarded to be in the child's interest to have a legal parental tie with a biological parent. Such a request will be denied only if it seriously interferes with the relationship between mother and child or if it would put the development of the child at risk. If the applicant is not a biological parent, they will have to show they were the birthmother's life companion at the time that they consented to an act that can have resulted in the conception of the child (such as artificial insemination with donor sperm). The court has to assess whether recognition in such a situation would be in the child's best interests. There is hardly any case law on such requests by female second parents. On the other hand, if the intended mother has second thoughts and does not wish to become a legal parent, the birth mother or child may ask the court to declare that the intended mother is the child's legal mother.[28] After recognition, both mothers have the same rights and duties with regard to the child. The couple can register joint parental responsibility, there is a child support duty, and in other areas of law the co-mother and the child have exactly the same rights and duties as all legal parents and children.

Before the introduction of legal parentage for co-mothers, adoption was the only option for same-sex partners. Adoption is still an option, and some female same-sex couples specifically choose adoption because it is more likely to be recognized abroad than same-sex parenthood by operation of law. Male same-sex couples can also become legal parents but will always have to resort to adoption to sever the legal ties with the birthmother. The court has to determine whether the adoption is in the best interest of the child and whether the other conditions set out in the Civil Code are met.[29]

The current topic of debate in the Netherlands concerns the legal status (or lack thereof) of intentional multiparent families. Since Dutch law limits the number of legal parents and holders of parental responsibility to two, though these need not be vested in these same persons, it is not possible to grant equal parental rights and duties to all caregivers in these families. Depending on the factual situation, some rights can be divided over at most three persons. For instance, in a married or informal couple of two women, the birthmother will always be the legal mother vested with parental responsibility. The co-mother could obtain parental responsibilities jointly with the birthmother, while the donor becomes a legal parent through recognition with the birth mother's consent. Empirical research shows that not many co-mothers opt for this possibility: most co-mothers are legal parents with parental responsibility.[30] Furthermore, if there is *(intended) family life* between the donor and the child, there is a contact right, regardless of parental status.[31]

The Government Committee proposed to introduce full parental rights and duties for up to four intentional parents, but the legislature recently proposed a very watered-down version of partial parental responsibilities for up to two additional social parents. Despite the fact that the legislature has not chosen to introduce legal multiparenthood at this time, it is nonetheless interesting to take a brief look at the proposal by the Government Committee. Under the proposal, intentional multiparent families would be able to draw up a contract before the conception of the child containing agreements on a number of issues with regard to the child and their parenting that they can submit to the court for approval. The court would approve the agreement unless it did not contain all the necessary elements or it was clearly not in the child's best interest. If the agreement was approved by the court, a pregnancy could be brought about and all intended parents (with a maximum of four) would become legal parents with full parental responsibility at the birth of the child.[32]

After much discussion, the legislature drafted a much less far-reaching version to accommodate multiparent families. In the new draft, the parents in a multiparent family who do not have the status of legal parent can acquire partial parental responsibility (*deelgezag*). For intentional multiparent families, it would be possible to acquire partial parental responsibility without court intervention. Other multiparent families will need to acquire judicial approval. In both cases agreement between the holders of full parental responsibilities and the intended holders of partial parental responsibilities is required. Partial parental responsibility would include the right to make decisions in the context of the child's daily care and the right to be consulted about more substantial decisions such as schooling and medical treatment. However, if the holders of full parental responsibility and the holders of partial parental responsibility do not agree on these issues, the holders of full parental responsibility will decide. This is obviously a far cry from the equality for multiparent families proposed by the Government Committee. This draft bill has not yet been finalized into an actual bill that would be introduced in Parliament.

Stepparents

After divorce or separation and repartnering of one of the legal parents, the legal position of the stepparent depends on their relationship with the legal parent. Regardless of whether the stepparent is in a formal relationship with the legal parent or not, there are hardly any rights and duties for formal or informal stepparents. If the legal parent and the stepparent are married or in a registered partnership, the stepparent will be under a duty to financially maintain stepchildren under the age of twenty-one who are part of the stepfamily.[33] If the stepparent informally lives together with one of the parents, there is no duty to maintain informal stepchildren. Whether or not a stepparent can acquire legal status with regard to a stepchild depends on whether the stepchild already has two legal parents and whether both legal parents have acquired parental responsibility. Children born during a marriage or registered partnership will, as a rule, have two legal parents (the exception being those children born in a female same-sex marriage or registered partnership who were conceived with sperm from a known donor and were not subsequently recognized by the co-mother or the donor). Children born outside of marriage will automatically have a mother and may acquire a second parent through recognition. If the legal parents were married (or in a registered partnership) at the moment of the child's birth, they will both have parental responsibility, which continues after the divorce. Since two persons is the maximum number for parental responsibility, it will not be possible for the stepparent to acquire parental responsibility for the stepchild (leaving aside some rare exceptions).

If the legal parents were not married (or in a registered partnership), it is possible that only the mother has parental responsibility. In that case, there would be room for one person to obtain parental responsibility, but this is generally quite complicated for the stepparent because of the strict conditions that have to be met and checked by the family court.[34] In theory, there is an option for a stepparent to become a legal parent through adoption, but this rarely succeeds if the child already has two legal parents.[35] This is, generally speaking, an option only if the other legal parent has no parental responsibility and agrees with the adoption. If the relationship of the legal parent and the stepparent ends, the legal position of the stepparent is equally poor. At best, there might be a right to apply for a contact arrangement, but whether the court will determine a contact arrangement is dependent on the child's best interests.[36]

As described in the section on same-sex parents, the Government Committee proposed to amend the law to make parental responsibility for up to four holders possible if all parties involved agree. This would give stepparents who have a substantial caring role for their stepchildren a legal position during the relationship with the parent but also in the event of separation. The legislature decided to introduce a less far-reaching form of parental responsibility for the surplus caregivers—partial parental responsibility as described above.

Nonparental Primary Caregivers

There are different legal regimes under which a child can be placed in a foster family—on a voluntary basis by the child's parents or by means of a child protection order. In the case of a voluntary foster care arrangement in which parents place their child with another caregiver (be it a family member or someone unrelated to the child), this alternative caregiver is not attributed with any form of legal parenthood or legal parental responsibility. The caregiver, however, has an obligation similar to that of a person with parental responsibility to care for the child, regardless of the length of the placement.[37]

In case of formal foster care in the context of a child protection measure, whether or not the foster parents will receive any parental rights depends on the measure in place. Children may be placed with a foster family under a supervision order in combination with an out-of-home placement order.[38] In that case, parental responsibility remains with the parents, unless the court decides that certain elements of this responsibility will be vested in the youth care agency.[39] The foster parents will have the same obligations with regard to the child's care and upbringing as the parents with parental responsibility.[40] However, they can make few decisions without the consent of the parents and/or the consent of the youth care agency. Foster parents can make some daily care decisions for the child, but more far-reaching decisions and especially those that require the signature of a person with parental responsibilities (such as opening a bank account and decisions about medical care) cannot be made by the foster parents. They will need the consent of the parents or the youth care agency.

Once the child has been living with an alternative caregiver for more than a year (be it voluntarily or under a child protection measure), the parents or the youth care agency need the consent of the court to change the child's place of residence if the alternative caregiver does not agree with this.[41] The court will base its decision on the child's best interest.[42] Furthermore, the child may develop *family life* with the alternative caregiver, which may lead to a right to contact between child and alternative caregiver once the child returns to the parents or is moved to another family.[43] Whether or not a contact order will be made by the court depends on the best interests of the child.[44]

Once it is clear that the original parents cannot resume the care for the child, their parental responsibility may be terminated by the court. The court can attribute either the youth care agency or the foster parents with guardianship.[45] If the youth care agency is attributed with guardianship, nothing much changes for the foster parents, except for the fact that the consent of the parents is no longer required for decisions about the child's upbringing. If the foster parents, instead of the youth care agency, are attributed with guardianship, they are attributed with full responsibility for the child's upbringing and the role of the youth care agency is finished. Once the foster parents have guardianship over the child, this guardianship can be terminated only by the court.[46] Adoption is not a logical step in Dutch child protection practice and rarely occurs, even though it is possible under the law.[47] Adoption is most likely to take place if a child has been abandoned at birth or if the child no longer has parents or family.

The Government Committee suggested the introduction of a new form of adoption in Dutch law, which could benefit long-term foster children and the foster parents in particular. This form of adoption, so-called simple adoption, would leave legal parental ties with the original parents intact while at the same time creating legal parental ties with the foster parents, thus introducing a form of multiparenthood through adoption.[48] The legislature decided not to follow-up on this proposal for the time being. The option of partial parental responsibility, as was discussed above, is deemed to be a suitable solution for long-term foster parents. However, since the holders of partial parental responsibility will have no decision-making powers, it would not solve most of the problems experienced by foster parents.

Discussion

The question as to what status should be attached to caring for a child is a complex one. The question has been addressed to some extent by the Government Committee that proposed the introduction of multiparenthood and multiparent parental responsibility.[49] However, the Dutch government will—as a first step—introduce only a rather small change with a new type of "partial" parental responsibility for a maximum of two additional caregivers. We predict that the call for legal recognition of some types of new family forms will eventually result in the introduction of more far-reaching options to include additional social parents on a more equal basis.

However, we think it is essential to fundamentally rethink parentage law, not on a step-by-step basis as has been the case in the past decades. Reacting to social changes on a case-by-case basis results in a quite complicated and sometimes inconsistent system. We would advocate rethinking family law: who is a parent, what rights and duties go with parental status, and for what reasons. Not all types of parents may need to have all rights and duties. A fundamental study involving other disciplines, such as legal theory and philosophy and social science, needs to be included for such a redesign.

Caring may involve the need for decision-making power, but also the fact of caring for a child itself may give birth to a desire to be recognized as a (social) parent. The question is whether both the practical need for status (where there is no other person with decision-making power as an extreme example) and the emotional need for status (a third parent caring for a child on equal terms with the two legal parents who feels like "a back seat driver" because despite the fact that caring and decision making are shared in practice, they have no legal status, or later in life the child itself) are valid reasons for attributing some legal status. We think they are. Being a parent/caregiver and child and being recognized as such, is after all part of these person's identity and *family life* (ECHR) that needs to be protected by the state.[50] The question is of course what form this recognition should take. Should all social parents discussed in this chapter receive the same form of legal recognition, or should we distinguish between various forms of care? Should meaning be attached to a preconception intention to parent, and if so what meaning? What is the role of the procreational responsibility of the social parent?[51] Should the preconception intention to parent lead to full multiparenthood or to a division of rights and duties among the parents? And if so, on what grounds—biology, genetics, giving birth, consent, actual care?

Important to take into account when answering these questions is first of all the international framework regarding children and their caregivers/parents that can be derived from ECHR and Convention on the Rights of the Child, which requires us to make the best interests of the child the central element in this decision-making process. However, these interests are not the only ones to be taken into account. We think parents' rights should also be included in the weighing of interests. The question is how a legal (civil law) system could best regulate this. One extreme would be to make an individual assessment in each specific case; the other extreme would be to have rules that embody the best interest of the child, which means there is little room for a court to individually balance the interests in each case. Currently our legal system is based on the second model; we should reflect on whether there should be more room for individual assessments in specific cases.

How many legal parents a child can have is closely related to the issue of what rights and duties legal parents have. When the law would allow for various types of parental status with sets of different rights and duties, the number could perhaps be higher than in the scenario where this is not the case. In our mind, the number of legal parents should be limited, but to what number is debatable. We are of the opinion that adults who are in a position where they have procreational responsibility not only should have a right to be recognized as a parent with at least some parental status but also should—in the best interest of the child—be held accountable for having exercised this procreational responsibility. It should, however, be the prerogative of the parties (the child and the other legal parents), and not of the state, to decide whether or not to apply to a court for determination of parentage of an unwilling parent.

NOTES

1 W. M. Schrama, "Marriage and Alternative Status Relationships in the Netherlands," in *Routledge Handbook of Family Law and Policy*, ed. J. Eekelaar and R. George (Oxon: Routledge, 2020), 14–25.

2 Staatscommissie Herijking Ouderschap (Government Committee on the Reassessment of Parenthood), *Kind en ouders in de 21ste eeuw* (Child and parents in the 21st century) (December 7, 2016). For an English summary of the report, see www.government.nl/documents/reports/2016/12/07/child-and-parent-in-the-21ste-century.

3 Centraal Bureau voor de Statistiek, "Huishoudens nu" (2021), www.cbs.nl/nl-nl/visualisaties/dashboard-bevolking/woonsituatie/huishoudens-nu.

4 Nederlands Jeugdinstituut, Cijfers over gezinnen (July 29, 2021), www.nji.nl/nl/Databank/Cijfers-over-Jeugd-en-Opvoeding/Cijfers-per-onderwerp/Cijfers-per-onderwerp-Gezinnen#ch334972.

5 Ruben de Graaf, "Kinderen in complexe gezinsverbanden" (Centraal Bureau voor de Statistiek, October 2, 2020), www.cbs.nl/nl-nl/longread/statistische-trends/2020/kinderen-in-complexe-gezinsverbanden.

6 Centraal Bureau voor de Statistiek, "Trouwen" (2020), www.cbs.nl/nl-nl/visualisaties/dashboard-bevolking/levensloop/trouwen.

7 Centraal Bureau voor de Statistiek, "Kinderen van paren van gelijk geslacht 1990–2018" (October 31, 2019), www.cbs.nl/nl-nl/maatwerk/2019/44/kinderen-van-paren-van-gelijk-geslacht-1990-2018.

8 Ministerie van Volksgezondheid, Welzijn en Sport, Jaarverslag 2020 Stichting donorgegevens kunstmatige bevruchting, www.rijksoverheid.nl/documenten/rapporten/2021/05/31/jaarverslag-2020-sdkb.

9 Pleegzorg Nederland, Factsheet Pleegzorg 2020 (June 2021), www.jeugdzorgnederland.nl/wp-content/uploads/2021/06/Factsheet-pleegzorg-2020-DEF.pdf.

10 S. Wortmann, "Doorwerking van fundamentele rechten in het Nederlands familierecht," in *De invloed van fundamentele rechten op het materiële recht*, ed. J. Gerards and C. Sieburgh (Kluwer: Den Haag, 2013), 215–236.

11 M. Vonk, "Een huis voor alle kinderen. De juridische verankering van intentionele meeroudergezinnen in het afstammingsrecht" (Nederlands Juristenblad, 2013), 2244–2249.

12 Although in many acts foster children and stepchildren are also included.

13 Wet Lesbisch ouderschap van 25 November 2013, Stb. 2013/480, https://zoek.officielebekendmakingen.nl/stb-2013-480.html.

14 Art. 1:200–1:202 DCC (father); art. 1:202a–1:202 DCC (co-mother) and art. 1:204–1:205 DCC (recognition by either father or mother).
15 Art. 1:377a DCC.
16 Art. 1:377b DCC.
17 Art. 1:377a DCC.
18 For a recent discussion of the Court's jurisprudence, see C. Fenton-Glynn, *Children and the European Court of Human Rights* (Oxford: Oxford University Press, 2021), chap. 8, "Family Formation and Parenthood."
19 Arts. 1:392–395 DCC and art. 1:253w DCC.
20 Art. 1:248 and 1:247 sub 2 DCC.
21 Art. 1:198 sub 1 under a DCC and art. 1:253b DCC.
22 Art. 1:198 sub 1 under a DCC.
23 Art. 1:198 sub 1 under b DCC.
24 Arts. 1:204 and 1:252 DCC.
25 Art. 1:204 sub 1 under c DCC.
26 Art. 1:204 sub 4 DCC.
27 Art. 1:204 sub 3 or 4 DCC.
28 Art. 1:207 under 1 DCC.
29 Art. 1:227–228 DCC.
30 M. Antokolskaia, W. M. Schrama, et al., *Meeroudergezag: een oplossing voor kinderen met meer dan twee ouders?* WODC 2014, sec. 1.3.2, https://repository.wodc.nl/handle/20.500.12832/2062.
31 Art. 1:377a DCC.
32 See, for instance, I. Boone, "Co-parenting before Conception: The Low Countries' Approach to Intentional Multi-parent Families," *Family & Law*, February 2018, www.bjutijdschriften.nl/tijdschrift/fenr/2018/02/FENR-D-18-001; and N. Cammu, "Legal Multiparenthood in Context: Experiences of Parents in Light of the Dutch Proposed Family Law Reforms," *Family & Law*, July 2019, www.bjutijdschriften.nl/tijdschrift/fenr/2019/07/FENR-D-18-00009.
33 Art. 1:392 (1) under c jo 395 Dutch Civil Code. Only so long as the parent and the stepparent are married/registered partners. After a divorce there is no such duty any longer.
34 Art. 1:253t Dutch Civil Code.
35 Arts. 1:227–228 Dutch Civil Code.
36 See, for instance, Court of Appeal Den Bosch, July 9, 2020, ECLI:NL:GHSHE:2020:2086, http://deeplink.rechtspraak.nl/uitspraak?id=ECLI:NL:GHSHE:2020:2086, where the court qualifies the relationship between the former stepfather and the child as a close personal relationship but denies contact in the interest of the child.
37 Arts. 1:248 and 1:247 sub 2 DCC.
38 Art. 1:255 DCC and art. 1:265b DCC.
39 Art. 1:265e DCC. This concerns, among others, a decision with regard to registration at a school and consent to medical treatment.

40 Art. 1:248 DCC.

41 Art. 1:253s sub 1 and 2 DCC.

42 Art. 1:253s sub 1 and 2 DCC.

43 For an overview of the influence of the European Convention of Human Rights on parenthood, see Fenton-Glynn, *Children and the European Court of Human Rights*, chap. 8, "Family Formation and Parenthood"; A. Margaria, *The Construction of Fatherhood: The Jurisprudence of the European Court of Human Rights* (Cambridge: Cambridge University Press, 2019); and also C. Mol, "Non-traditional Family Forms & the International Dimension of Family Life: A Report on the ERA Seminar Recent Case Law of the European Court of Human Rights in Family Law Matters," *Family & Law*, June 2016, www.bjutijdschriften.nl/tijdschrift/fenr/2016/06/FENR-D-16-00006.

44 Art. 1:377a DCC.

45 Art. 1:295 DCC.

46 Art. 1:327 DCC.

47 Art. 1:227–1:230 DCC.

48 M. J. Vonk and G. C. A. M. Ruitenberg, "We Need to Talk to Martha; or, The Desirability of Introducing Simple Adoption as an Option for Long-Term Foster Children in the Netherlands," *Family & Law*, June 2021, www.bjutijdschriften.nl/tijdschrift/fenr/2021/02/FENR-D-21-00005.

49 M. Vonk, "Zijn alle gezinnen gelijk? Een nadere analyse van de voorstellen van de Staatscommissie Herijking Ouderschap over de juridische verankering van het meerouderschap," *Ars Aequi*, October 2017, 790–795.

50 See, for instance, S. Bou-Sfia on identity rights and family law, "De betekenis van identiteitsrechten voor kinderen in het Nederlandse Familierecht, Een onderzoek naar de artikelen 8 IVRK en [illegible] EVRM" (PhD diss., Utrecht, 2021), https://dspace.library.uu.nl/handle/1874/406106.

51 M. J. Vonk, "Towards a New Concept of Parenthood: Procreational Responsibility," in *European Challenges in Contemporary Family Law*, ed. K. Boele-Woelki and T. Sverdrup (Cambridge: Intersentia, 2008), https://scholarlypublications.universiteitleiden.nl/handle/1887/29280.

12

Social Parenthood in Russia

OLGA KHAZOVA

Due to transformations in family relations, being a legal parent today does not necessarily mean being a genetic parent, and social parentage may create family ties as well. Moreover, social parenthood is on the rise, and increasing attention is being paid to this social phenomenon. The growth of social parenthood can be mostly explained by two separate, though sometimes overlapping, developments: first, a rise in divorce rates and remarriages is increasing the number of families where at least one of the adults is not genetically related to the child; second, advancements in biomedical science and assisted reproduction technologies are creating families where parents are not necessarily genetically related to their children.

Russia is also seeing these changes. The past few decades have clearly shown an increasing variety of types of families in Russia and different family conditions in which children are born and raised. As a result, families are becoming more complex and diverse.[1] At the same time, as will be shown in this chapter, social parenthood is almost completely outside of any legal regulation, and the discrepancy between the social reality and the law is increasingly becoming a problem. Recent cases by the European Court of Human Rights may, however, lay the groundwork for at least some reform.

Demographic Data

Analysis of the social parenthood phenomenon and attempts to develop a possible legal framework are complicated by the absence of data. Russia does not keep official statistics on different family forms, particularly on the number of women raising minor children without husbands or partners.[2] Similarly, there are no statistical data—from official sources or demographers—on the prevalence of same-sex relationships or the number of children raised by same-sex couples. As a leading Russian demographer has stated, "The domestic information space for discussions [about social parenthood] is poorly structured in terms of categorical certainty, extremely limited in terms of scientific knowledge, and is often littered with speculation and unverified statistical data."[3]

There are some data about children born to unmarried parents. The demographers who study families have found that nonmarital births have become a widespread phenomenon across all social strata.[4] In 2016, the proportion of children born to unmarried parents among all births constituted 21.1 percent.[5] There are, however, many misconceptions about this phenomenon, and among the most common is the conflation of nonmarital birth rates with single motherhood.[6] Today's birth rate outside of marriage is largely formed not by single mothers but by cohabiting couples (de facto "married") who, for some reason, did not register their marriage.[7] Therefore, in this regard, the notion of "single motherhood" is misleading because the data on the number of women who are considered to be "single mothers" under the law do not reflect the real situation;[8] "single mothers" may be living with a partner or a husband who may not be a biological father of the child they are raising together, provided he did not formally acknowledge (his paternity) or adopt the child.

Despite the absence of official statistics, there are some data—particularly based on the high divorce rate[9] and significant number of remarriages[10]—that indirectly demonstrate that social parenthood is widespread. As one of the most prominent Russian demographers and sociologists has noted, in recent years about 30 percent of marriages in Russia, for both men and women, have been remarriages, and many families based on remarriage do not have common children at all.[11] Therefore, if one adds to this the unregistered marital unions, it is reasonable to assume that a significant number of children are being raised by persons who have neither blood nor legal relations with the child. As noted above, however, there are no data about social parenthood in families headed by same-sex couples.

As to children who, for whatever reason, do not live with their parents and are placed into custody or guardianship, approximately 55 percent are placed with unrelated individuals and approximately 45 percent with family members.[12]

With regard to assisted reproduction, the available data indicate that there were 709 surrogate mother pregnancies that ended at term in 2018.[13] There are, however, no figures available on the exact number of children born through assisted reproduction that are donor conceived or, in other words, not related to at least one of their parents.

Legal Recognition of Parents

Parent-child relations are regulated by the Family Code 1995 (FC), the main federal law, which covers all of the Russian Federation.[14] Under the Russian Federation Constitution 1993 (as amended in 2020), subjects are vested with the right to enact family laws within their competence ("regional laws"),[15] so long as they are in conformity with the provisions of the FC. In practice, however, there is little space left for regional legislation because the FC covers the overwhelming majority of family law issues. The FC and other legal acts must not contradict the Russian Constitution.

The Russian legal system is a civil law system, belonging to the legal family of continental law. It is not based on judge-made law, but the highly authoritative views of the Supreme Court and its guiding instructions, nevertheless, are mandatory for the courts.

Before moving to a more detailed discussion of legal parenthood, two basic points should be noted from the outset. First, for a child born within marriage, there is a legal presumption of paternity for the husband of the child's mother. For a child born outside of marriage, paternity can be established either voluntarily through acknowledgment or by a court decision. In either scenario, paternity can be contested if it is proved that the legal father is not the biological father. Exceptions in this regard are stipulated in the case of a child being conceived through assisted reproduction technologies. Second, Russia does not recognize civil partnerships or unions between any couple (same sex or different sex); similarly, Russia does not recognize same-sex marriages.

Legal Parenthood

From a legal point of view, it is irrelevant to the parent-child relationship whether the child's parents live together, are divorced, or have never been married, provided the child's filiation has been properly established. In this respect, the end of relations between the child's parents does not lead, under normal scenarios, to any substantial change in legal relations of each of the parents toward their common child.

In Russia, a child may not have more than two parents. Further, although it is not directly stated in the FC, it is clear from different legal provisions related to the rules of birth registration that the parents are of different sexes. If a child has been born to unmarried parents and paternity has not been established, the child is registered in the civil status registry as having only one legal parent—the mother. In such a case, the "father" line is left blank.[16] In the rare case when a single parent is the father, he is registered as a legal father and the "mother" line is left blank.

In the case of adoption, Russian law provides that adoptive parents replace the birth parents both legally and socially. This means that legal bonds between a child and the birth parents are terminated and analogous legal bonds between an adopted child and adoptive parents are created.[17]

Legal Parentage in Case of Assisted Reproduction

Assisted reproduction, including surrogacy, is considered a medical treatment; therefore, those who get access to respective treatment are supposed to have fertility problems. As to surrogacy, the law names only couples[18] and single women who have fertility problems, but not single men. At the same time, under the Ministry of Health regulation, a single woman is permitted to have access to artificial insemination with a donor's sperm where she does not have "a sexual partner."[19] Oocyte and sperm donation, if necessary, is possible, although certain restrictions apply in cases of surrogacy, and using the surrogate's eggs is prohibited; gamete donation can be either anonymous or non-anonymous,[20] but donors do not acquire any rights toward children conceived with their genetic material.[21]

A married couple who consents to the use of artificial fertilization or embryo implantation is registered in the birth registry as the legal parents of a child born as a result of these methods (FC, arts. 51(4) and 52(3)). A single woman can gain access to fertility treatment on equal bases, and the rules on her registration as a legal mother are similar to those that apply to the registry of birth of a child conceived naturally.

The situation with a single man is much more complicated and controversial, although he too may have fertility problems. There are no provisions in the law that specifically concern single men who have no fertility problems and no female partner. Technically, in the context of assisted reproduction, for a single man parenthood can occur only through surrogate motherhood, and this is exactly where most of the controversies lie. As the result of existing inconsistencies in the law, surrogate motherhood is hardly available for single men, and they face serious problems when trying to register the birth of a child born through surrogacy.[22]

Under the law, the woman who gives birth to a child is considered the child's mother. Therefore, when a surrogate gives birth, the intended parents may be registered as the child's parents only with the consent of the surrogate. In other words, a surrogate has the right to keep the child if she wants.

If a surrogate gives her consent to the registration of the intended parents as the legal parents in the birth registry book and on the child's birth certificate, the birth registration procedure is essentially the same as a child conceived naturally. From the moment of registration, the surrogate is considered a legal stranger to the child and does not have any legal right to contact with the child. If a surrogate decides to keep the child and does not consent to the intended parents' registration as the child's legal parents, she can be registered as the child's legal mother in the birth registry. If she is married, her husband is registered as the child's father. After a child's birth has been officially registered, parent-child relations are considered to be finalized.

Thus, provided there is no dispute over the child's origin, no court judgment is required to finalize parental rights with regard to a child conceived through assisted reproduction, including a child born by a surrogate. Adoption cannot be used to establish legal parentage with regard to children born though assisted reproduction.

Parental Rights and Duties

Neither parental custody nor parental responsibility exists in Russian legal doctrine and legislation, and a parent with whom a child resides is not considered as a "custodial parent." Instead, under the law, parents have equal rights and duties toward their children, even if they do not live together (FC art. 61). This means that both are legal representatives of their common child; they each have the right and the duty to take care of their children and to raise them, and this formally does not depend, as already noted, on their marital status.[23] They both bear responsibility for maintaining, nurturing, and developing their children, and they are both obliged to take care of the children's health and their physical, mental, spiritual, and moral development. Particularly, as stated in the FC, a nonresident parent has the right to communicate with the child, participate in the child's upbringing, and decide on the child's education. The resident parent shall not prevent the child from communicating with the other parent, unless such communication is detrimental to the child's physical and mental health or moral development (FC art. 66), although the reality is, regrettably, often different. When a judge considers a divorce case, if there is a dispute over a child, the judge makes a decision on the child's place of residence and payment of child support.

Parents have a preferential right, superior to that of all other persons, to nurture their children (FC art. 63(1)). They also have the right to demand the return of their child from any person withholding the child without lawful authority (FC art. 68(1)). In cases of a dispute, the parents can apply to a court to protect parental rights. All else equal, such a child-related dispute should be resolved in favor of the parents.[24] Depending on the facts and taking into account the opinion of the child, the court may, however, refuse to satisfy the parents' claim if it concludes that returning the child to the parents is not in the child's interests (FC art. 68(1)). Such an intrusion into parental rights is considered an extreme measure, justified by extraordinary circumstances, the best interests of the child being paramount. From a legal point of view, this will lead to termination of parental rights or their restriction.

Legal Recognition of Social Parents: Three Common Contexts

Despite the widespread nature of social parenthood in Russia, it is almost completely outside any legal regulation.

Same-Sex Couples

As noted in the previous part, same-sex family relationships are not legally recognized in any way. If a child's parent is in a relationship with a same-sex partner, the partner does not acquire any rights or responsibilities toward the child. From a legal point of view, the partner is a stranger to the child, and such a situation is similar to the one related to the stepparents or de facto caregivers, as will be explained in more detail below. This exclusion of the same-sex partner is true even if the legal parent and the partner decided to conceive and raise a child together. The only person with rights and obligations is the legal parent.

Stepparents

Russian law does not recognize any legal relationship between a child and a stepparent. The only exception concerns the duty of an adult child. In very limited circumstances,[25] an adult child must provide maintenance for a stepparent (FC art. 97).

Therefore, after a divorce or separation, if one of the parents enters a relationship with another person and the new spouse or a new partner assumes full parental responsibility for the child and treats the child as their own, a question arises about that person's legal status toward that child. Under Russian law, such a person is considered a legal stranger toward the child and cannot claim any rights, including a right to contact, irrespective of how much time, energy, and love such a person gives the child and how emotionally close such a person and the child are or have been.

Nonparental Primary Caregivers

In regard to informal care by a relative, friend, or community member, if the child's parents are temporarily unable to care for a child—for example, due to work abroad, a business trip, or health issues—and decide to place the child with a relative or a friend without any formal arrangements, this does not affect, from a legal point of view, parental rights and does not confer any rights or duties on the person who takes care of the child. Although such a person may act as the child's primary caregiver, the child's parents keep all their parental rights and remain legally responsible for the child.

With regard to de facto caregivers (informal care), the law contains a rule similar to the one on the stepparents' right to claim maintenance, in very limited circumstances, from an adult child whom they brought up (FC art. 96). This rule does not concern foster parents and guardians.

Formal Placement of a Child with a Custodian or Guardian, or with a Foster Parent

When children are left without parental care, custody or guardianship is established for the purposes of the child's maintenance, upbringing, and education as well as for the protection of their rights and interests (FC arts. 121(1), 145(1–4)).[26] Custody is established for children under the age of fourteen; guardianship is established over children from fourteen to eighteen years of age. When making a decision on placement of a child under custody or guardianship, the child's opinion is taken into account. The appointment of a custodian to a child who has reached the age of ten years is carried out with the child's consent. For ease and to avoid confusion, this chapter uses the term "guardianship" to refer to both custody and guardianship.

A child is placed under guardianship of the child protection authority in two situations. First, when parents fail to fulfil their parental duties and a child is neglected and needs to be protected, the child protection authority intervenes, and under a court order, the child is placed under its guardianship. Second, the child's parents may jointly approach the child protection authority for the appointment of a guardian for their child for a certain period of time when they will not be able, for justifiable reasons, to perform their parental duties, identifying a specific person whom they want to serve as guardian. From the moment of formal appointment, the guardian acquires all the rights and duties related to the child's upbringing, education, and legal representation. From that moment on, the parents of the child, unless otherwise stated in the federal legislation, lose their rights and duties toward their child (FC art. 148^1 (2)). The guardian, who legally replaces the parents, has the right to demand, on the basis of a court order, the return of the child who is under guardianship from any person who holds the child without lawful authority, including the child's parents or other relatives or adoptive parents. The guardian does not have the right to prevent the child from communicating with the child's parents and other relatives, except in cases where such communication is not in the interests of the child (FC art. 148^1 (4–5)).

Placing a child with a foster family exercised under the control of the child protection authority is regulated by the same legal rules that concern guardianship, and foster parents exercise the rights and duties of a guardian in relation to the foster child or children (FC art. 153(2)).

When defining the legal position of the foster parent with whom a child had been residing for a certain period of time, if the parents decide to terminate the foster family placement of their child, it is necessary to differentiate between two different scenarios similar to those noted above. When a child was placed with a foster family by the child protection authority as a child protection measure, a thorough investigation of the biological parents' family is required. If it is established that the parents' behavior has improved, the parental rights could be restored or restrictions lifted and the child could be safely returned to the family. Under the second scenario, the parents who asked for temporary placement of their child still keep their preferential right, superior to that of all other people, to nurture their children. Therefore, provided there are no grounds that would justify the refusal to return a child to the legal parents from the foster parent, the child will be returned to the family and the foster parents will lose their guardianship over that child.

Foster Parent versus Biological Parent: ECtHR Case

The case of *V.D. and Others v. Russia*, considered by the European Court of Human Rights, is an example of a dispute between a foster parent (the first applicant) and the child's legal parent.[27] In this case, the former foster parent, while claiming violation of article 8 of the European Convention on Human Rights, argued that she had been taking care of a seriously disabled boy during the first nine years of his life; during that period, she had been acting as his legal guardian and remained the only significant adult in his life (para. 72). However, a Russian court terminated the foster parent's guardianship over the child, and the boy's biological parents resumed full parental authority over him. The European Court noted that a child's interests dictated that the child's ties with their family be maintained, except in cases where the family had proved particularly unfit. It follows, the Court continued, that family ties may be severed only in very exceptional circumstances and that everything must be done to preserve personal relations and, if and when appropriate, to "rebuild" the family. The Court further noted that it was true that the boy's parents acquiesced to the appointment of the foster parent as the child's guardian. At the same time, as pointed out by the Government, the legal parents never formally renounced their parental authority over their son; neither were they restricted in nor deprived of that authority (para. 117). In the light of the foregoing, the European Court concluded that the decision to terminate the foster parent's guardianship over the boy and to return him to his legal parents corresponded to his best interests, was taken within the authorities' margin of appreciation, and was based on "relevant and sufficient" reasons. The interference with the foster parent's family life was thus "necessary in a democratic society."

At the same time, the European Court did recognize the importance of protecting the relationship between the former foster parent and the child. The former foster parent claimed that the refusal by domestic authorities to allow her contact with the boy was a violation of article 8 of the European Convention. On this count, the European Court found that the complete and automatic exclusion of the former foster parent from the child's life was "a result of the inflexibility of the domestic legal provisions—in particular, the denial of contact rights without giving proper consideration to the child's best interests," and the Court thus concluded that this exclusion amounted to "a failure to respect the [foster parent's] family life" (para. 128).

Discussion

In Russia, as has been shown in the previous part of this chapter, social parenthood is almost completely outside of any legal regulation, and the discrepancy between the social reality and the law is increasingly becoming a problem. This is illustrated by three cases against Russia in the European Court of Human Rights. The judgments of that Court have provoked a response by the Russian Supreme Court and discussions of social parenthood among legal scholars. Although, so far, no serious proposals to amend existing legislation have been made, there is a hope that the European Court judgments will trigger a legislative response.

Two cases concern almost identical situations: when a child's father and a husband of the child's mother turned out to be not a genetic father. In the case *Nazarenko v. Russia*, the mother challenged the father's paternity, and it was established in the court proceedings that he was not the child's biological father.[28] The Russian courts accepted that he had raised and cared for the child over a period of five years, but the courts abrogated his parental status and he became a legal stranger to that child. The father thus lost all parental rights with respect to the child, including the right to maintain contact with her. His name was removed from the child's birth certificate, and the child's family name had to be changed.

The father challenged this determination in the European Court of Human Rights. The Court noted that as a result of the inflexibility of Russian law concerning contact rights—which grants contact rights only to a limited set of people—a person who, like the applicant, was not related to the child but who had taken care of the child for a long period and formed a close personal bond with the child could not obtain contact rights in any circumstances, irrespective of the child's best interest. In the Court's opinion, a person who had brought up a child for some time as his own should not be completely excluded from the child's life after it was revealed that he was not the biological father, unless there were relevant reasons relating to the child's best interests for such exclusion. By denying the applicant the right to maintain contact with his daughter without any examination of the question of whether such contact would have been in child's best interest, Russia had failed to comply with its obligation under article 8 of the European Convention on Human Rights to respect the applicant's family life (paras. 66, 68). The judgment was unanimous.

In what seems to be a clear response to the *Nazarenko* case, the Plenum of the Russian Supreme Court, in its Decree of 2017,[29] noted the possibility of preserving the parental status of a man who turns out to not be the biological father of the child if otherwise the child is left without a legal father at all. The Plenum explained that if a mother contests paternity but the court does not find that a different man is the biological father, and the person registered as the father of the child would like to keep his legal paternity despite not being biologically related to the child, the courts may dismiss, in exceptional cases, a claim to challenge the paternity. When making such a decision, the court should proceed from the best interests of the child. When prioritizing the child's rights and interests, the court should also take into account the specific circumstances of the case, including the length of the relationship between the child and the person registered as the father, the child's sustained emotional attachment to that person, and the person's intention to continue to raise that child and to care for the child as his own child.

In *Fatkhutdinov v. Russia*, with almost identical principal facts to the *Nazarenko* case, the European Court also unanimously found a violation of article 8 of the European Convention on Human Rights.[30] Finally, in the case *V.D. and Others v. Russia*, briefly discussed in the previous part, the facts were different, though comparable. A former foster mother had been raising a boy for nine years, seeking to maintain contacts with the child.

These three cases have provoked some discussion of social parenthood among specialists and proposals to make amendments to the FC. It was suggested that the law should stipulate the right of the child to communicate with a person who is not genetically related to the child but who lives together with the child in the same household or was previously in the family whose relationships with the child ended for reasons beyond that person's control, except where communication with that person is contrary to the interests of the child. In such a case, a mirror rule should provide for the right of the other person to maintain contact with the child.

These provisions would cover not only situations that have been the subject of examination by the European Court in the cases referred to above but also cases where a child lives together with a stepparent. As described above, under current law stepparents are considered as legal strangers toward the children they are raising and with whom they may have close emotional bonds. Similar consideration exists with regard to the spouse of a guardian of a minor child; the spouse has no rights with regard to the child either. However, due to the current generally negative attitude to the same-sex unions, more time will be needed for this recognition to be extended to the same-sex partner of a legal parent who is acting like a parent.

One of the main counterarguments is that maintaining the child's relationship with the social parent may negatively impact the existing family relations. For instance, in the case of a strong parental resistance to the child's contacts with the social parent, the question arises whether the child can properly appreciate and accept, even taking into account the child's evolving capacities, all the nuances of family relations and the risk of disruption to family life by such interference.

No doubt, this is a complicated and very sensitive area of personal relationships. No matter how valid and well-founded the concerns may be, they fail to fully take into consideration the spread of the social parenthood phenomenon and the importance for the child to keep contact with a person who used to play a significant part in the child's life and who is still dear to the child. Taking into account the importance of loving and responsive relations developed during childhood, allowing such relationships to continue can play an important positive role in the child's future development.

NOTES

1 See A. G. Vishnevskyi, ed., "Russian Population 2007," Fifteenth Annual Demographic Report (2009), 136, www.hse.ru/data/2010/02/19/1232112962/people-2007.pdf.

2 S. Zakharov, "Single Motherhood in Russia: Single Motherhood—Flurry of Interest," *Demoskop Weekly*, no. 553–554 (May 1–19, 2013), www.demoscope.ru. The number of children living with a single father after their parents' divorce is still statistically insignificant.

3 Zakharov, "Single Motherhood in Russia."

4 Vishnevskyi, "Russian Population 2007," 131.

5 See "Russia: Preliminary Demographic Results of 2017 (Part I)," *Demoskop Weekly*, no. 759–760 (February 12–25, 2018), www.demoscope.ru.

6 See Zakharov, "Single Motherhood in Russia."

7 See Vishnevskyi, "Russian Population 2007," 131.

8 Technically, there is no legal definition of a "single mother" in the law. A woman who gave birth to a child outside legal marriage and where paternity has not been established is conventionally called a "single mother"; she is entitled to some additional allowances and certain protections under the labor legislation.

9 Between 2009 and 2019, the divorce rate varied between 4.9 and 4.0. See https://rosstat.gov.ru.

10 See S. V. Zakharov, ed., "Russian Population 2015," Twenty Third Annual Demographic Report (2017), chap. 2, www.demoscope.ru.

11 A. Sinelnikov, "Marital and Reproductive Behavior as a Barrier to a Demographic Explosion" (paper, Institute of Demography, Moscow, November 9–10, 2021).

12 According to statistics from the Ministry of Education (Minprosvet) in 2020 (103-РИК_РФ_2020).

13 V. S. Korsak, A. A. Smirova, and O. V. Shurygina, "Materials of the Russian Association for Human Reproduction: Report for 2018," *Russian Journal for Human Reproduction* 2 (2021): 8.

14 Among other relevant federal laws, the Federal Law on the Acts of Legal Status 1997 and the Federal Law on Protection of Citizens' Health 2011 should be named.

15 Currently, the Russian Federation consists of eighty-five subjects (political subdivisions), conventionally called "regions."

16 In order not to leave the "father" line blank, the law permits a false entry about the father's name to be made "under the mother's instructions" on the child's birth certificate and in the birth registry book.

17 The law permits the maintenance of legal ties between an adopted child and the relatives of the deceased natural mother or father.

18 There is a discrepancy between the Federal Law on Protection of Citizens' Health 2011 and the Family Code, as the latter names married couples, and not cohabitees, for the purpose of surrogacy (FC art. 51(4)).

19 See RF Ministry of Health Order of July 31, 2020, no. 803н, "On the Order of the Use of Assisted Reproductive Technologies, Contraindications and Restrictions," pt. IV.

20 RF Ministry of Health Order of July 31, 2020, no. 803н, pt. IV.

21 See the Decree of the Plenum of the RF Supreme Court, "On the Application of the Law by the Courts in Cases Relating to the Determination of the Origin of Children," no. 16, May 16, 2017, para. 32.

22 For more details, see O. Khazova, "Surrogacy in Russia," in *Eastern and Western Perspectives on Surrogacy*, ed. Jens M. Scherpe, C. Fenton-Glynn, and T. Kaan (Cambridge: Intersentia, 2019), 281–306, 297–300.

23 Provided their parental rights were not restricted by a court judgment or they were not deprived of parental rights.

24 O. N. Nizamieva, ed., *Commentary to the Family Code of the Russian Federation* (Moscow: Prospekt, 2011), 238–239.

25 In a very limited number of situations where stepparents are unable to work and are in need, they cannot receive assistance from their own children or spouse/former spouse, and the stepchildren themselves are able to work and have sufficient means to provide such maintenance.

26 The placement of a child under custody or guardianship is regulated, apart from the FC, also by the Civil Code, the Federal Law on Guardianship and Custody, and other RF regulatory legal acts.

27 *V.D. and Others v. Russia*, ECtHR (appl. no 72931/10), judgment April 9, 2019.

28 *Nazarenko v. Russia*, ECtHR (appl. no. 39438/13), judgment July 16, 2015.

29 Decree of the Plenum of the RF Supreme Court no. 16, May 16, 2017, para. 29.

30 *Fatkhutdinov v. Russia*, ECtHR (appl. no 36335/18), judgment September 29, 2020.

13

Social Parenthood in Sweden

EVA RYRSTEDT

Most children in Sweden live with both their legal parents.[1] However, a rising number of children live in blended families or in new types of families, due to societal developments as well as increases in assisted reproduction. Swedish legislation lags behind this development, and thus in many regards there is a lack of legislation to safeguard the relationship between different types of parents and children. In particular, Swedish law does not yet recognize—with one minor exception—social parenthood.[2] Thus, even if a person acts like a parent and has a close bond with a child, there is very limited legal protection of that relationship, for either the social parent or the child. In this chapter, I address some demographic data first and then address the legal recognition of both legal and social parents—or, rather, the lack of it—concerning social parents. According to Swedish law, social parents (apart from foster parents who have legal custody, which is much the same as parental responsibility) have no independent rights in relation to the child. Finally, I address normative issues and discuss the need for new legislation.

Demographic Data

The population of Sweden is just over 10 million.[3] The starting point for the demographics of interest in this chapter is the approximately 2.17 million children under the age of eighteen who live in about 1.2 million families.[4]

In Sweden, as in many other countries, there is a multitude of types of families, and while some are accepted by society, others are not. The oldest and most accepted form is the nuclear family, consisting of a man and a woman married to each other and their common children. The concept is nowadays also used for an unmarried cohabiting couple with common children, both biological and adopted.[5] Another established form is the family who takes in a foster child. Almost 70 percent of all families are nuclear families.[6] Furthermore, while almost 75 percent of all children under the age of eighteen live with both parents, only about 59 percent of all children live in families with both parents and only full siblings.[7] In families with foreign-born parents, the number is somewhat lower. The number rises slightly when at least one of the parents has a postsecondary education.[8]

Non-nuclear families in Sweden are referred to as “star” families.[9] The concept is negatively defined, as *not* being a nuclear family. The “star” family thus does not have a firm definition. I use the term “family” in this chapter to refer to two or more persons (adults and children) who live in a relationship formed with the intent of a commitment to support and love.[10] The relationship must thus be long-lasting.[11] Statistics Sweden, a government agency, defines a family as the individuals in a relationship, such as parents, children, spouses, and cohabitees, who live and are registered[12] in the same dwelling.[13]

With the acceptance of divorce, families in which there is a single adult have become more common. Approximately 19 percent of children live in a family where the adult is single.[14] The figure is marginally higher for children with foreign-born parents. However, it is notable that while 13 percent of children in Sweden live with a single mother, the figure for children with parents born abroad is 19 percent.[15] Blended families are somewhat common: 6.3 percent of children under the age of eighteen live in blended families,[16] while about 8.6 percent of families are blended.[17] These families may consist of legal parents—different or same sex—in relation to a common biological or adopted child, or of stepparents, stepchildren, stepsiblings, or half siblings.

There are also situations where two couples—often same-sex couples—have a child together. Such a child might live alternately with both families or live with one of the families and see the other set of parents at certain times. These two couples may also live together and as such form one family with the child. Also—and more common in cases with two immigrant parents—a family may consist of more than two adults, or an adult may belong to several families through having multiple partners. Another type of family is what in Sweden is referred to as a “living apart together” family—with the adults maintaining a relationship but not sharing a home. While this is more common when the children are older, it is not unusual in families with young children.

Legal Recognition of Parents

All national legislation in Sweden is decided by Parliament, including the incorporation of articles 1 to 42 of the Convention on the Rights of the Child and the European Convention on Human Rights.[18] In addition, there are EU regulations, which are legally binding. There are also other lower-level provisions, decided by other authorities. Thus, the relationship between parents and children is regulated primarily by national law.

The gender-neutral Cohabitees' Act (Sambolag 2003:376) may apply when two persons live together permanently, as a couple with a joint household.[19] In addition, marriage has been gender neutral in Sweden since the Marriage Code of 1987 (Äktenskapsbalk 1987:230) was changed in 2009.[20]

Legal parenthood is one of the most important features of Swedish family law and is the basis for many rules on the relationship between parent and child. Legal parents are registered as parents in the national registration and serve as the basis for legal issues like custody (which is quite similar to parental responsibility), residence, and access or contact. Only two persons can be legal parents. This is regulated in the Children and Parents' Code (Föräldrabalk 1949:381).

Legal Parenthood

A person is deemed the legal parent through giving birth to the child,[21] and their spouse—male or female—is presumed to be the legal parent of the child.[22] Apart from becoming a parent through giving birth or being married to the person giving birth, parenthood can be acknowledged through a person confirming to the Social Welfare Board that they are the genetic parent through contributing with sperm. The Social Welfare Board is a municipal board responsible for social services and regulated in the Social Services Law (Socialtjänstlag 2001:453). The confirmation must be approved by the Social Welfare Board and by the person having given birth. The person having given birth can be substituted by a specially appointed legal custodian or a temporary legal custodian. The Social Welfare Board can approve the confirmation only if it is assumed to be correct.[23] Parenthood can also be decided through a court decision.[24]

Increasing numbers of people are receiving help to conceive a child through forms of assisted reproduction, where giving birth and consenting to insemination and in vitro fertilization may constitute parenthood.[25] Couples, regardless of sexual orientation, have access to this treatment, as do single people. However, because Sweden does not permit surrogacy, couples or single people—including male same-sex couples and single men—who are unable to conceive themselves, are precluded in practice from forming families through assisted reproduction.[26] As a result, the law treats different types of families and constellations of fatherhood and motherhood differently.

If a child is conceived through sperm donation, performed according to the Law on Genetic Integrity (Lag 2006:351 om genetisk integritet m.m.) and with the consent of the intended parent, the sperm donor will normally be excluded as the father.[27] However, the child may eventually—when mature enough—find out about the biological parenthood through requesting the hospital special records.[28] Corresponding legislation exists regarding egg donation.[29] As a result, the same applies to a double donation.

If the insemination is done privately, without those involved following the procedure according to the law on genetic integrity, the sperm donor may be deemed a parent. If the intended couple is married, the question may never arise due to the presumed parenthood of the person who is married to the person giving birth.[30]

The outcome for a couple or a single person who goes abroad to seek help to have children through surrogacy differs depending on the constellation of the intended parents. If a person's sperm is used, they will be deemed the legal parent[31] under Swedish law.[32] However, a person whose egg has been used will have to adopt the child to become the legal parent, in the same way as if a donor egg had been used.[33] The same applies to two persons having sperm undergoing surrogacy; the one supplying the sperm is deemed to be a parent, the other is not. This may, of course, lead to difficulties for the intended parents on their return to Sweden and also a great deal of uncertainty as to whether or not they will both be recognized as the legal parents.[34] In many cases, adoption will be the only way to achieve parenthood, for either one or both of the parents. An adoption will always be assessed with the best interests of the child in mind.[35] Such an assessment may not always have the result the intended parents have planned.

Parenthood can thus also be established through adoption.[36] In Sweden, this is normally conducted as a closed adoption, where the adopted child is seen in all regards as belonging to the new family.[37] However, the adoption will be registered in the Swedish Population Register according to the Population Registration Act (Folkbokföringslag 1991:481), and even though such notations are classified,[38] the child will, when mature enough, be able to find out about the adoption.[39]

Giving birth is thus an assured way to be regarded as a parent, as is, generally, being the genetic and biological contributor of sperm. The only way to revoke legal parenthood due to giving birth is to give the child up for adoption. The legal parenthood constituted through being married to the person giving birth may, however, be revoked,[40] as may an acknowledgment[41] and under specific circumstances an order of parenthood, in cases where someone is found not to be the genetic or biological contributor of sperm.[42] This can be done by either the legal father or the child starting legal proceedings.[43] Thus, someone who might want to be acknowledged as a legal parent cannot start proceedings and can be prohibited from being acknowledged as a legal parent. That said, it is also possible for someone representing the child to start proceedings. The person wanting to overturn the fatherhood may thus try to have a "good man"[44] appointed for the child.[45]

As long as two adults are accepted as legal parents, they will have the same fundamental rights in relation to the child. However, certain adjustments may need to be made if they do not live together. There are times when joint legal custody, joint residency, and even access or contact is not appropriate.[46]

Legal Custody or Parental Responsibility

Legal custody in Sweden is quite similar to the concept of parental responsibility, but there are some differences, and I thus use the concept of legal custody in the following.

Normally the legal parent(s) have legal custody of a child under the age of eighteen. However, the court may entrust one or two specially appointed legal custodians with the legal custody. One example of such a situation is when the court transfers legal custody from legal parents to foster parents, or to parents in private placement, as I explain further in the "Nonparental Primary Caregivers" section.[47] Another situation when a legal custodian is needed is when a child comes to Sweden as an unaccompanied refugee child.[48] A person may be appointed temporary legal custody when it is urgent. That doesn't normally encompass the physical part of the legal custody.[49]

Legal custody encompasses a responsibility for the child's personal circumstances and is to make sure that the child's needs of care, security, and good upbringing are met. Children are to be treated with respect regarding their person and individuality and must not be subject to corporal punishment or other offensive treatment. The legal custodian is also responsible for the child being supervised in accordance with their age, development, and other circumstances and is to see to that the child is satisfactorily provided for and educated. In order to hinder the child from causing damage, the legal custodian has to ensure the child is supervised or that other suitable measures are taken.[50] The legal custodian is also normally the legal guardian and is as such responsible for the child's economic circumstances.[51]

Joint legal custody is the most common form of custody among legal parents, even when they do not live together. Sole legal custody is also an option; it is awarded primarily in the case of parents who do not live together and are unable to cooperate.[52] Residency often alternates between parents having joint legal custody.[53] The child may also live with one parent and have access to or contact with the other.[54]

Legal Recognition of Social Parents: Three Common Contexts

Apart from foster parents and private placements, which will be addressed later in this chapter, or specially appointed legal custodians including temporary ones, a nonlegal parent cannot be a legal custodian or have the right to reside with the child (residency). It is also not possible for a child to have more than two legal parents. If a nonlegal parent wants to have access or contact with the child, it is primarily an issue for the legal custodian. They have an obligation to fulfill the child's need of access or contact with a person close to the child. However, if the legal custodian(s) do not act upon this responsibility, the only way for someone who is not a legal parent to acquire access to or contact with the child is to turn to the Social Welfare Board, which may or may not start proceedings in order for the court to decide on access or contact. The Board's decision is based primarily on the child's need for access to or contact with their grandparents as well as to other adults particularly close to the child.[55] It is stressed in the preparatory works (the underlying documents to the law, e.g., a bill or a report) that it can be other relatives, foster parents, a stepparent, half siblings, or children in a same-sex relationship. It is thus the Social Welfare Board that decides whether or not to start proceedings. The criterion for starting such proceedings is if a parent is opposed to the child seeing those with whom the child has previously had close and good contact. Also, it is required that it would be detrimental to the child if that contact ended. However, the Social Welfare Board primarily needs to try to get the parents to agree to the contact. To battle over a child is often seen as detrimental to the child. It is presumed that the Social Welfare Board is better equipped to determine whether or not the benefits of contact outweigh the negative effect of a court case. It is emphasized in the preparatory works that it is possible for the Social Welfare Board to not start proceedings often enough. The Social Welfare Board has a clear responsibility for children not unnecessarily losing contact with persons close to them, when it would be in the best interest of the children to have such contact. This is of special importance since these persons cannot start proceedings themselves.[56] It is thus not surprising that even if there are no official data, this is a tool that is not used very often.[57]

This means that a social parent does not have any independent rights in relation to the child, either during the relationship with the parent or after the relationship has ended, regardless of whether the couple are or have been married or are or have been cohabitants. However, the social parent may be obligated to pay maintenance for a child living with the couple, for which child the other parent—thus the legal one—is the legal custodian, during the time the social parent is married to or has a child together with the legal parent. In such a case, the social parent must top up the child support the other legal parent is paying. This obligation ends, however, if the couple divorces or separates.[58]

A number of difficulties arise when only one of the adults in a relationship is the legal parent of the child. These often occur in cases of assisted reproduction and may be the case both in different-sex and same-sex relationships and regardless of whether the couple is married or cohabits. It occurs when the child has been conceived without the parties having adhered to the rules in the Children and Parents' Code and the Law on Genetic Integrity. The nonlegal parent then does not have any right to adopt the child born into the family (which is seen as a stepchild), without the consent of the legal parent being the legal custodian. The nonlegal parent will subsequently not be able to share that responsibility. This regulation poses the greatest problems if the couple divorces or separates because a social parent does not have an independent right to start proceedings to have access to or contact with the child. They must turn to the Social Welfare Board, if the legal custodian does not allow access or contact, as explained above.[59] It also means the social parent can no longer be a party in a stepchild adoption since the couple is no longer married or cohabitating.[60] The situation might be less complicated if the legal parent passes away since the social parent, in the absence of any legal parent who can object, might apply to adopt the child. However, an adoption will always be assessed with the best interests of the child in mind.[61]

Same-Sex Couples

As described above, if a child is born to a married couple, both parents are presumed to be legal parents, regardless of whether they are different sex or same sex, even though the presumption can be rebutted. But because Sweden does not recognize surrogacy, only a same-sex couple where someone is able to give birth benefits from the marital presumption. For same-sex couples without that possibility, the person who has contributed their sperm will be deemed a parent, while the second person would need to adopt the child. For all same-sex couples, if the adults are not married, the nongenetic parent is not automatically a legal parent as a result of the cohabiting relationship. Instead, they need to take an affirmative step to become a legal parent, such as adoption or acknowledgment under the condition that the assisted reproduction has taken place in accordance with the regulation in the Children and Parents' Code and the Law on Genetic Integrity.[62] If the partner does not take steps to become a legal parent, they will be only a social parent. Such a parent is not able to share the legal custody or have any other independent rights. However, that parent may, in the case of assisted reproduction conducted according to the Children and Parents' Code and the Law on Genetic Integrity, also later invoke their consent and be deemed a parent to the child.

Another situation that arises for same-sex couples is when two couples agree to have children together. (Although these families can occur with different-sex couples, they are more common with same-sex couples.) Let us say that a male same-sex couple agrees to have four children together with a female same-sex couple. The biological parents will be the legal parents. Let us further say that the children live alternately with both families. The couples have the children crosswise, so each of the four children has a biological connection to one of the men and one of the women, and to their half siblings. The children also, of course, have important bonds with their social parents and their stepsiblings. This setup will probably work as long as the two families are intact, even though the social parents will not have any independent rights during that time, regardless of whether they are married or cohabiting. If the couples' relationships end, neither the children nor the social parents will have any independent rights regarding a continued legal, social, or economic relationship. They will not even have a standing regarding access or contact, as explained above. The same is true for the half siblings' and stepsiblings' mutual need for access or contact.

Stepparents

Another very common example of social parenthood is blended families where the couple already has children from a previous relationship when they marry or move in together. The stepparent and stepchild may form very close bonds with each other, as may the stepsiblings. The stepparent is not, however, able to share the legal custody or have any other independent rights, regardless of whether the couple are married or cohabiting. That will probably be fine as long as the relationship is intact. If the couple's relationship ends, neither the children nor the social parents will have any independent rights regarding a continued legal, social, or economic relationship. They will not even have standing regarding access or contact, as explained above. In this kind of relationship, there appears to be a strong need for the children to have a relationship with their former stepparent(s), but many times also with their siblings, whether biological half siblings or stepsiblings.

Nonparental Primary Caregivers

The regulation concerning foster families, foster parents, and foster children is found mainly in the Social Services Act (Socialtjänstlag 2001:453). The regulation governing involuntary placements is also found in the Care of Young Persons Special Provisions Act (Lag 1990:52 med särskilda bestämmelser om vård av unga). The foster care regulation can also be applied when someone such as a relative cares for the child. However, such a placement may also be made through what is called a private placement.[63] In general, the legal parents will at first retain legal custody (with some restrictions regarding involuntary cases).[64] However, after at the longest a two-year placement in one foster family and thereafter yearly, the Social Services Board must consider whether there are reasons to apply for a transfer of legal custody.[65] If so, the Social Welfare Board then instigates the proceedings, as it does for private placements.[66] Furthermore, the Children and Parents' Code regulates when such a transfer from the legal parents to the foster parents, or to parents in a private placement, should be made to enable the child to stay with their new family.[67]

Sweden does not often allow adoption by foster parents or private placements unless the biological parents agree, so this is a middle way to ascertain that children in long-term placements can stay in the family they know when that is in the best interests of the children. This is thus a very important way to safeguard the relation between the child and the new family.

Discussion

Currently, Swedish law limits children to a total of two legal parents. In many situations, however, children might benefit from having legally recognized relationships with more than two adults. This is, however, an issue I need to consider from two different angles. I first address the question of parenthood based on biological facts and then address social parenthood. The examples on parenthood based on biological facts demonstrate the principle that a child can have only two parents, which also informs the general lack of recognition for social parents. Whichever form of parenthood we discuss, I advocate that acknowledging a certain type of parenthood need not entail the same rights and obligations for all.

Biological and Genetic Parenthood

Although Swedish parentage rules are rooted in a biological or sometimes a genetic view of parenthood, there are a number of practices that demonstrate that this is not always the case. As for social parents, these types of parents are often excluded from acting as parents. For example, the institution of closed adoption shows the persistence of the image of the family as one or two adults with children. This rather limited image of a family is also apparent when we look at how a third person is denied the right to be a legal parent in a situation where there are already two parents. This might be the case where a married couple has had a child but a third person appears to be a biological or genetic parent.

A corresponding situation might also arise in a case where someone has donated gametes or served as a surrogate mother but later regrets their choice to the extent that it means that they do not have any access to or contact with the child.

The most important question is thus what reasons lie behind the regulation that leads to such a loss for the child. The history of nuclear families is important here. Furthermore, the sense that parents' rights are more important than children's rights is prominent in the legislation, even though we talk about the best interests of the child. However, every individual has a right to an identity,[68] and perhaps it is time to understand that a child has a right to know about their biological and genetic parents and siblings. This can be easily achieved in countries like Sweden through information given to the child at an early age as well as ascertaining biological parenthood through DNA analysis.

Social Parenthood

The other angle from which we need to approach the issue of parenthood concerns social parents and social siblings. According to Swedish law, social parents (apart from foster parents who have legal custody or other specially appointed legal custodians) have no independent rights in relation to the child. Once more, it is interesting to establish that a child might eventually lose access or contact not only to important adults but also to different types of siblings with whom they may have lived their entire life. Naturally, the situation also implies that the child does not have any rights in relation to the social parent.

When discussing whether several persons may be recognized as legal parents, it might instead suffice to recognize someone as a social parent as long as such a parenthood can form the basis for residency, access, or contact. For example, if a legal parent and a stepparent split up, a recognition of the former stepparent as a social parent with rights to, for example, access would facilitate an ongoing relationship between the stepparent and the stepchild. It is often in the best interests of the child to have a relationship with both adults and siblings who have played a large role in their lives, but perhaps less important that these adults have the status of legal parent or be legal custodians able to make decisions on the children's behalf. Such a significant change could however be justified where the adult has acted like a true parent for a very long time. An example could be a same-sex couple, where one of the parents has remained a social parent and where there has never been more than one legal parent.

Changes in Legislation and the Best Interests of the Child

In changing the regulations, we need to use the concept of the best interests of the child and children's wishes as the starting point. Thus, the question is whether the concept of the best interests of the child is always in concordance with what the child wishes. Perhaps it is not, at least not regarding young children. However, in this context, where the aim is to add a relationship with someone close to the child, the child must have the final word. In my view, this also goes for young children who express a view or a sentiment, not least because of exactly that. If the child is young, the child perhaps has not formed the close bonds that would justify a social parent having an important role in the child's future. Imposing access or contact between a child and an adult, or between children, against a child's "true" wishes can never be productive. The regulation regarding the social parent and the child thus needs to be built on the principle of voluntariness. In a corresponding way, it cannot be in the best interests of the child to have a relationship with an adult who is negative toward such a relationship. Sweden does not even force an unwilling legal parent to have a relationship with the child.

Finding out what a child wants, however, can be difficult, regardless of the age of the child, especially if the child has been affected by views that the legal parent holds. It is thus important to develop methods that evaluate the child's "true" wishes. It may be normal for a legal parent whose relationship with the social parent has ended not to want to be forced to have that person in their life any longer. Nevertheless, as this relationship is most often in the best interests of the child, it is a matter in which the legal parent should not have a final say.

Why, then, is a change—based on the best interests of the child—so difficult to introduce? Well, change often occurs through medical, technical, or social evolution. New phenomena, such as "star" families, are often resisted by parts of society and sometimes take a long time to be accepted and subsequently to become part of the legal framework. Family law is surprisingly deep-rooted in people's perception of how a family is formed and is thus steeped in tradition.[69] However, it might be possible to regulate the consequences of a societal development like star families; they entail the determination of relationships between adults and children, where no legal parenthood exists. They may also concern other legal effects, as well as economic effects, after a relationship ends. The consequences may also concern social insurance regulation, such as financial support to families with children. We should safeguard relationships in all types of families. I firmly believe it is important to apply the bases of need and closeness to children's relationships, rather than to stick to the norm of the nuclear family.

NOTES

1 "Family Type for Children and Young People Living at Home 0–21 Years by Region, Sex, Age and Family Type. Year 2014–2021," Statistics Database (November 13, 2020), www.statistikdatabasen.scb.se/pxweb/sv/ssd/START__LE__LE0102__LE0102B/LE0102T18N/. See also "Full Siblings, Half-Siblings and Step-Siblings among Children and Young People Living at Home 0–21 Years by Sex, Age and Family Type. Year 2014–2021," Statistics Database (November 13, 2020), www.statistikdatabasen.scb.se/pxweb/sv/ssd/START__LE__LE0102__LE0102C/LE0102T22/. SCB is the abbreviation for Statistics Sweden.

2 However, there is now a committee directive (En föräldraskapsrättslig lagstiftning för alla, Dir. 2020:132) founding the work of an investigation into, e.g., the rights and obligations of social parents, and a report SOU 2022:38.

3 "The Population of Sweden," Statistics Database (March 26, 2021), www.scb.se/hitta-statistik/sverige-i-siffror/manniskorna-i-sverige/sveriges-befolkning/, and "Population by Region, Marital Status, Age and Sex. Year 1968–2021," Statistics Database, March 26, 2021, www.statistikdatabasen.scb.se/pxweb/sv/ssd/START__BE__BE0101__BE0101A/BefolkningNy/. With a sincere thank you to law student Erik Rosenberg, who has helped me with the statistics.

4 "Family Type for Children and Young People Living at Home 0–21 Years"; "Families with Children and Young Persons Aged 0–21 Living at Home by Region, Age of Children, Type of Family and Number of Children. Year 2014–2021," Statistics Database (November 13, 2020), www.statistikdatabasen.scb.se/pxweb/sv/ssd/START__LE__LE0102__LE0102J/LE0102T19N/. For a slightly higher number of children, see "Children and Young People 0–21 Years with Swedish and Foreign Background by Region, Gender and Age. Year 2002–2021," Statistics Database (November 13, 2020), www.statistikdatabasen.scb.se/pxweb/sv/ssd/START__LE__LE0102__LE0102A/LE0102T16N/.

5 "Nuclear Family," *National Encyclopedia*, March 26, 2021, www.ne.se/uppslagsverk/encyklopedi/l%C3%A5ng/k%C3%A4rnfamilj.

6 "Families with Children and Young People Living at Home 0–21 Years by Region, Children's Age, Family Type and Number of Children in the Family. Year 2014–2021," Statistics Database (March 26, 2021), www.statistikdatabasen.scb.se/pxweb/sv/ssd/START__LE__LE0102__LE0102J/LE0102T19N/?rxid=f45f90b6-7345-4877-ba25-9b43e6c6e299.

7 "Family Type for Children and Young People Living at Home 0–21 Years"; see also "Full Siblings, Half-Siblings and Step-Siblings."

8 "Three Out of Four Children Live with Both Their Parents," Statistics Database (March 26, 2021), www.scb.se/hitta-statistik/statistik-efter-amne/levnadsforhallanden/levnadsforhallanden/barn-och-familjestatistik/pong/statistiknyhet/barn--och-familjestatistik/. In Sweden, the concept of "a foreign background" is used and defined as oneself or both of one's parents being born outside of Sweden.

9 "Ingrid skapade stjärnfamiljen," RFSU, February 24, 2011, www.rfsu.se. See also Erik Mägi and Lina-Lea Zimmerman, "Stjärnfamiljejuridik: Svensk familjelagstiftning ur ett normkritiskt perspektiv," *Polen* (2015): 18. See further Språktidningen, https://spraktidningen.se.

10 This is a very old concept whose meaning builds on the culture in which it exists. It has to do with production and consumption of food, reproduction and socialization, common control of property, and loyalty toward others. "Family," *National Encyclopedia*, www.ne.se/uppslagsverk/encyklopedi/l%C3%A5ng/familj.

11 Compare, e.g., with the Cohabitees' Act.

12 The main rule is that all individuals are registered in a dwelling at an address in Sweden, according to Folkbokföringslag (1991:481) (Population Registration Act) .

13 "Background Facts—Population and Welfare Statistics 2017:1 Development of Statistics Sweden's Statistics on Children and Their Families," Statistics Sweden (2017), www.scb.se/contentassets/ddfcaaff5e2f4f7ba4fb7c09a4655808/le0102_2015i16_br_be96br1701.pdf.

14 With significantly more single mothers than single fathers. "Family Type for Children and Young People Living at Home 0–21 Years."

15 "Olika levnadsvillkor för barn med svensk och utländsk bakgrund," SCB, June 29, 2017, www.scb.se/hitta-statistik/statistik-efter-amne/levnadsforhallanden/levnadsforhallanden/barn-och-familjestatistik/pong/statistiknyhet/barn--och-familjestatistik-2016/.

16 "Different Living Conditions for Children with Swedish and Foreign Backgrounds," Statistics Database (March 26, 2021), www.statistikdatabasen.scb.se/pxweb/sv/ssd/START__LE__LE0102__LE0102B/LE0102T18N/, regarding the year 2019.

17 "Families with Children and Young People Living at Home 0–21 Years."

18 Lagen (2018:1197) om Förenta nationernas konvention om barnets rättigheter. Lag (1994:1219) om den europeiska konventionen angående skydd för de mänskliga rättigheterna och de grundläggande friheterna and chap. 2, sec. 19 of the Constitution of Sweden.

19 Sec. 1 of the Cohabitees' Act. However, legislation on cohabitation has encompassed homosexual cohabitees since 1988 according to the law on homosexual cohabitees (Lag (1987:813) om homosexuella sambor).

20 Lag (2009:253) om ändring i äktenskapsbalken.

21 Chap. 1, secs. 10 and 11 Children and Parents' Code and through the act of giving birth itself—mater semper certa est.

22 Chap. 1, secs. 1, 2, 9, and 11a (in force January 1, 2022) Children and Parents' Code. See further Prop. 2020/21:176, Modernare regler för bekräftelse av föräldraskap, faderskapsundersökningar och för att åstadkomma könsneutral föräldraskapspresumtion.

23 Chap. 1, secs. 3, 4, 13, and 14, Children and Parents' Code.

24 Chap. 1, sec. 3, Children and Parents' Code.

25 Chap. 1, secs. 8 and 9, Children and Parents' Code.

26 Chaps. 6 and 7, Act on Genetic Integrity (Lag (2006:351) om genetisk integritet m.m.).
27 Chap. 1, sec. 5, para. 2 Children and Parents' Code.
28 Chap. 6, sec. 5 and chap. 7, sec. 7 Act on Genetic Integrity.
29 Chap. 1, secs. 1, 7, and 8 Children and Parents' Code.
30 Chap. 1, secs. 1 and 11a Children and Parents' Code.
31 Chap. 1, sec. 5 Children and Parents' Code.
32 Court decisions from other countries may or may not, due to international private law, be acknowledged in Sweden.
33 Due to the Mater semper certa est principle.
34 However, in Sweden a report with suggestions on a new regulation on foreign parenthood and adoption in certain cases recently was received, SOU 2021:56, Nya regler om utländska föräldraskap och adoption i vissa fall, and a bill, Prop. 2021/22:188, and now changes in the law.
35 Chap. 4, sec. 1 Children and Parents' Code.
36 Chap. 4 Children and Parents' Code.
37 Chap. 4, sec. 21 Children and Parents' Code.
38 Chap. 22, sec. 1 Public Access to Information and Secrecy Act (Offentlighets- och sekretesslag 2009:400).
39 "The Population Registration Activities and Related Activities," Skatteverket (May 15, 2020), www4.skatteverket.se/rattsligvagledning/edition/2018.4/329108.html.
40 Chap. 1, sec. 2 and chap. 3, secs. 1 and 2 Children and Parents' Code.
41 Chap. 1, sec. 4, para. 2 Children and Parents' Code.
42 Chap. 58, sec. 1 Code of Judicial Procedure (Rättegångsbalk 1942:740).
43 Chap. 3, secs. 1 and 2 Children and Parents' Code.
44 A "good man" can represent the child in a series of situations; see, e.g., chap. 11 Children and Parents' Code.
45 See further Anna Singer Karnov under 1:1 and 3:2 and 3:5 FB and Lexino Eva Ryrstedt under 1:1 and 3:5 FB.
46 Chap. 6, secs. 14a and 15 Children and Parents' Code.
47 Chap. 6, secs. 2 and 8 Children and Parents' Code.
48 See further Prop. 2020/21:150 Ett stärkt barnrättsperspektiv i vårdnadstvister, 95. See also, e.g., Vårdnadshavare, www.socialstyrelsen.se, October 2021.
49 Chap. 6, sec. 2 Children and Parents' Code. See further Prop. 2020/21:150, 85.
50 See chap. 6, secs. 1 and 2 Children and Parents' Code.
51 Chap. 10, secs. 2 and 3 Children and Parents' Code.
52 Chap. 6, secs. 2–5 Children and Parents' Code.
53 Chap. 6, sec. 14a Children and Parents' Code. Today about 30 percent of all children with parents who do not live together live with both parents alternately. "Nearly Three Out of Ten Children Live Alternately," Statistics Database (May 8, 2021), www.scb.se/hitta-statistik/statistik-efter-amne/levnadsforhallanden/levnadsforhallanden/undersokningarna-av-levnadsforhallanden-ulf-silc/pong/statistiknyhet/barns-boende-2016-2017/.

54 Chap. 6, sec. 15 Children and Parents' Code.

55 Chap. 6, sec. 15, para. 3 and sec. 15a Children and Parents' Code. See also Prop 2005/06:99, Nya vårdnadsregler, 90.

56 Prop. 2005/06:99, 56 and 90.

57 However, there is now a committee directive, En föräldraskapsrättslig lagstiftning för alla, Dir. 2020:132, founding the work of an investigation into, e.g., the rights and obligations of social parents.

58 Chap. 7, sec. 5 Children and Parents' Code.

59 Chap. 6, sec. 15a Children and Parents' Code.

60 Chap. 4, sec. 6 Children and Parents' Code.

61 Chap. 4, sec. 1 Children and Parents' Code.

62 Chap. 1, secs. 1, 2, 7, 8, 9, 9a, 11a, 11b, and 11c. See further Prop. 2020/21:176, Modernare regler för bekräftelse av föräldraskap, faderskapsundersökningar och för att åstadkomma könsneutral föräldraskapspresumtion, 25 and 78.

63 Chap. 6, secs. 5 and 6 Social Services Act.

64 Sec. 11, paras. 4 and 5 Care of Young Persons (Special Provisions) Act.

65 Chap. 6, sec. 8b, Social Services Act, sec. 13c Care of Young Persons (Special Provisions) Act, and chap. 6, sec. 8, Children and Parents' Code. See further prop. 2020/21:35, Regelbundna överväganden av vårdnadsöverflyttning och särskilda lämplighetskrav för offentliga biträden, with further references, and Prop. 2021/22:178.

66 Chap. 6, sec. 8, Children and Parents' Code.

67 Chap. 6, sec. 8, Children and Parents' Code.

68 See, e.g., the UN Convention on the Rights of the Child, arts. 7 and 8.

69 Cf. Eva Ryrstedt, *Bodelning och bostad, ekonomisk självständighet och bostad* (Lund, 1998), 393; and Ryrstedt, "Normative Patterns in the Context of Divorce in Sweden," in *Normative Patterns and Legal Developments within the Social Dimension of the EU*, ed. Ann Numhauser-Henning and Mia Rönnmar (Oxford: Oxford University Press, 2013), 253–266.

Conclusion

The Future of Social Parenthood

CLARE HUNTINGTON, COURTNEY G. JOSLIN, AND CHRISTIANE VON BARY

Compelling psychological and sociological arguments support the legal recognition of social parents. Psychologically, a person who acts like a parent is a parent, especially from a child's perspective. Without legal recognition, this bond—and the child's well-being more generally—is at risk. Sociologically, social parenthood is widespread. Children are growing up in families with same-sex parents, stepparents, and nonparental primary caregivers, many of whom lack legal recognition under traditional rules governing parenthood. Given these realities, the question is not whether social parents exist and whether they are important to children but rather how the legal system will respond to these aspects of modern family life.

Almost all countries surveyed in the book recognize social parents, but the countries take different approaches. In a few countries, like Canada and the United States, social parents can attain the status of a full legal parent. By contrast, the other countries generally do not treat social parents as legal parents, but almost all provide some means for protecting the relationship between a child and a social parent. Of the nine countries covered in this book, eight allow a social parent and child to maintain contact, and the ninth country, Russia, is beginning to open the door to such recognition.

Deciding to recognize social parents is only the beginning of the discussion. Countries must consider a host of issues, including, for example, whether social parents should stand in parity with legal parents or whether they should be treated as holding some different, lesser position; whether the relationship, where recognized, should accord only rights or also result in the imposition of responsibilities; whether the legal relationship should be fluid or permanent; whether all social parents must be treated identically; whether the law should limit a child to a maximum of two parents, including social parents; whether the test for recognizing social parents should assess the relationship from the perspective of the child, the adult, or both; and how the legal treatment of social parents in the jurisdiction furthers or impedes principles of equal protection across a variety of axes, including gender, sexual orientation, and marital status. Fully addressing these issues would take another book, but we use this final chapter to begin the conversation. We first briefly summarize the similarities and differences among the countries' approaches. Then we explore a few of the complex issues implicated by social parenthood.

A Range of Approaches

The approach to regulating social parenthood is typically shaped by how social parents fit—and do not fit—into the existing framework regulating parent-child relationships. As we describe below, the nine countries surveyed in this book grant social parents different levels of recognition, but most countries use similar criteria to determine which adults qualify as social parents.

Fitting Social Parents into Existing Forms of Legal Recognition

As countries decide how to treat social parents, they usually map their approach onto existing forms of legal recognition. As explained in the introduction, most of the nine countries have more than one form of legal protection for relationships between a child and an adult parental figure. The most comprehensive parent-child relationship is legal parenthood—a formal legal status that can be changed only in specific adjudicatory proceedings and which determines issues beyond family law, such as citizenship and inheritance. In some parts of the United States and Canada, social parents can be awarded the status of a legal parent, but most countries surveyed here grant social parents something less than legal parenthood.

Whether countries extend legal parenthood to social parents is shaped, at least in some jurisdictions, by the country's approach to another emerging issue—whether legal parenthood is limited to a total of two adults per child. In Mexico and all of the European countries surveyed in the book, legal parenthood is limited to two adults. Thus, if the child already has two legal parents, a social parent cannot be recognized as a legal parent. By contrast, in some parts of the United States and Canada, it is possible for a child to have more than two legal parents, making it easier to add a social parent as a legal parent.

Rather than treating social parents as legal parents, many countries recognize social parents through the robust but not as comprehensive relationship often called "parental responsibility." In this form of legal recognition, a person—who may, but in some countries need not, be a legal parent—can be accorded the authority to make decisions for the child and provide day-to-day care for the child; this person also has corresponding obligations. In some countries, including England, each holder of parental responsibility can in principle make decisions for the child without consulting the other holder(s) of parental responsibility. By contrast, in other countries, such as Germany, an agreement between the holders of parental responsibility is usually necessary. Depending on the country, it is possible for a child to have two legal parents and a third adult who has parental responsibility. Thus, even in some countries that limit the total number of legal parents to two, more than two people can have some parental rights or obligations.

Finally, in addition to or instead of parental responsibility, some countries protect a right of contact between the social parent and the child. Typically, this is a limited right—granting only physical time with the child, not decision-making authority—but it does enable the social parent and the child to maintain a relationship. Separate contact rights exist, for example, in Germany, the Netherlands, and Sweden. Greece strongly emphasizes the different-sex marital family, but it too has moved in the direction of recognizing social parents through contact rights, adopting a contact-right provision in 2021.

Countries that recognize a right of contact have different rules about who can assert the right. In some countries, only the adult has the right to seek contact, but in other countries, the child can exercise this right as well. In still other jurisdictions, including Sweden, neither the adult nor the child has standing to initiate a proceeding seeking an order of contact; instead, an administrative agency must start the relevant proceedings, if it considers contact important for the welfare of the child.

Almost all surveyed countries recognize social parents through one or more of these existing forms, but a minority of jurisdictions provide no protection for social parents. In such jurisdictions, only legal parents have rights and obligations regarding the child. This was true in Greece until the 2021 legislative reform. And it is still the law in Russia, although as the chapter on that country explains, this may be changing in response to recent litigation before the European Court of Human Rights.

Another point of departure is the severability of the types of legal recognition. In some countries, the different levels of legal recognition are severable.[1] In these countries, a person can be a legal parent but lack parental responsibility, and parental responsibility can be held by someone other than a legal parent. This is true, for example, in England, where a person can have parental responsibility even if they are not a legal parent. By contrast, in other countries, including Greece and Russia, legal parenthood and parental responsibility are not severable. In these countries, only legal parents can exercise parental responsibility.

In other countries, like Germany, for example, the difference between legal parenthood and parental responsibility is recognized conceptually, but separating both rights is possible only in very limited circumstances when the welfare of the child is in danger. Germany does, however, recognize a more limited form of parental responsibility that can be accorded to a nonlegal parent. This limited form of parental responsibility covers only everyday matters and can be exercised only by mutual agreement with the legal parents.

Overall, the chapters demonstrate a trend in favor of permitting these different levels of recognition to be severed. This is especially pronounced in England and can be seen in more limited ways in the Netherlands and Canada. This severability is especially important for social parents because if they cannot be recognized as legal parents, severability of these forms of protection offers a mechanism for protecting the relationship with the child, whether it is through an order of parental responsibility or a right of contact. Severability also allows for a greater flexibility in cases where more than two adults are involved but only two legal parents are possible, as is the case under the majority of national laws.

Relevant Factors for Recognizing Social Parents

Even though the nine countries grant social parents different levels of recognition, most countries use similar criteria to determine which adults qualify as a social parent. The starting point is understanding that social parents frequently (although not always) lack marital and genetic connections to the child. Thus, often their connection to the child falls outside these common bases for establishing parental rights.[2]

To identify social parents, a key factor in most countries is whether the person *acts* like a parent. This functional, fact-specific inquiry examines the child's ongoing relationship with the adult, focusing on the lived reality of the relationship, the day-to-day role of the social parent, and the nature of the bond with the child. Depending on the country, this attachment between the adult and the child determines the form of legal recognition. In parts of the United States and Canada, proof of an attachment can lead to legal parenthood. In England, attachment can lead to parental responsibility. And in other countries, such as Germany, attachment leads only to a contact right, absent other factors. Of the countries surveyed in the book, only Russia extends no protection to persons functioning as parents who lack a marital or genetic connection to the child, although, as noted above, a ruling from the European Court of Human Rights might lead to a legislative change soon.[3]

Beyond a functional inquiry, some countries also consider marital ties. In the past, most countries did not treat a same-sex partner as a legal parent, unless the same-sex partner adopted the child. Due to growing acceptance of same-sex relationships and same-sex parenting, however, in most countries that permit same-sex marriage, the marital presumption is now typically extended to any person who is married to, or otherwise in a legally recognized relationship with, the parent giving birth to the child. This is true, for example, in Canada, England, the Netherlands, Sweden, and the United States. In these countries, the same-sex spouse, or in some countries the legally recognized partner, of the legal parent is considered a full legal parent of a child born during the marriage. But not all surveyed countries follow this trend. In Germany and Greece, the marital presumption does not apply to same-sex relationships (marriage and registered partnership, respectively), and thus the same-sex spouse or legally recognized partner is not automatically a legal parent and instead is in a more vulnerable legal position than the person who gave birth. Marital status can also be relevant to the establishment of parental responsibility. For example, in Germany, stepparents can obtain limited parental responsibility only when the stepparent is married to the legal parent.

Considerations for a Framework Governing Social Parenthood

Deciding to recognize social parents is only the beginning of the conversation for policy makers and courts. Countries considering how to recognize social parents must grapple with a range of issues that flow from the initial decision. In this section, we highlight two sets of questions that illustrate the complexity—and imperative—of recognizing social parents.

Balancing Equality and Heterogeneity

As detailed in this book, social parents are a heterogeneous group. Some social parents intended to bring the child into the world; other social parents came into the child's life years after the birth. Some social parents act as coparents with legal parents; other social parents care for children in the absence of legal parents. Some social parents receive payment from the state to care for the child; other social parents care for children informally, without remuneration from the state. This heterogeneity leads to two interrelated questions: whether to treat social parents as full legal parents or give them some rights and responsibilities that fall short of legal parenthood, and whether to treat all social parents the same.

As this book demonstrates, parity between social parents and legal parents is especially warranted for same-sex partners who form a planned family through assisted reproduction. These social parents typically assume a full parental role and do so throughout the entirety of the child's life. Too often, however, they are not recognized accordingly. As the chapter on same-sex parents in Italy describes, same-sex partners in that country are often treated like second-class parents, needing authorization from the legal parent for simple parenting tasks like taking the child to the doctor for a check-up. This unequal status can create strain within the family, making the social parent more vulnerable legally and sending a message to the child that the parents are not equal. The failure to treat parents similarly can also perpetuate discrimination against the family, which may impede the family's ability to care for their child.

In light of these concerns and as noted above, many countries surveyed in this book have concluded that the parental recognition of married spouses should not depend on the sexual orientation of the adults. In these countries—Canada, England, the Netherlands, Sweden, and the United States—spouses, regardless of gender, are recognized as legal parents. Other countries do not treat same-sex spouses as legal parents, but they do grant some parental rights and responsibilities to them. Germany falls into this category. In addition, with regard to families intentionally created through assisted reproduction, some countries have determined that legal recognition should not depend on whether the parties are married.

Some countries that do not recognize same-sex partners as full legal parents justify this treatment by noting that the partner is not the child's genetic parent. Other jurisdictions, including parts of the United States, have expressly rejected rules that elevate genetic connection over other bases for assigning legal parentage. These jurisdictions have reached this conclusion in part because a rule that elevates genetics over all other factors necessarily discriminates against same-sex couples and their children, since same-sex partners generally cannot both be the child's genetic parents.

Treating same-sex spouses as full legal parents can promote equality within same-sex families. But for other groups of social parents, recognition that falls short of legal parenthood may better fit the needs and interests of adults and children alike. For example, at least some stepparents and nonparental primary caregivers play a lesser, albeit still important, role in the child's life. In such situations, the relationship should be protected but perhaps not given the full status of legal parenthood. Additionally, in both contexts, legal parents are often still playing a role in the child's life, and the child and the social parent may not want to displace the legal parent. In the cases of nonparental primary caregivers in Appalachia, for example, most children still have legal parents, even though these parents are temporarily unable to care for the child. As that chapter describes, often the nonparental primary caregiver, the child, and the legal parent do not want the social parent to replace the legal parent; instead, the goal of legal recognition is to help the family function more smoothly.

In sum, failing to treat the social parent as a legal parent can raise equality concerns for some families, but for others, treating the social parent as a legal parent can interfere with the interests of the child and legal parent. In light of these differences, heterogeneous rules for the heterogeneous population of social parents may make good sense, but this approach poses its own set of challenges. For example, it raises the challenging question of which social parents should be treated as legal parents and which ones should be accorded more limited parental rights and, possibly, responsibilities. Further, if the inquiry is largely a functional, case-by-base adjudication, it will be difficult for a person to know their legal status at a particular point in time. And as the chapter on same-sex parents in Italy highlights, having caretakers within a single family with different statuses can strain family dynamics. There is no easy answer to these competing concerns, but a country grappling with social parenthood at least needs to be aware of the trade-offs between a one-size-fits-all approach to social parenthood and a tailored-to-diversity approach.

As a purely predictive matter, jurisdictions with multiple forms of parental recognition—legal parenthood, parental responsibility, and a right of contact—may be less likely to treat social parents (or at least all of them) as legal parents and instead may be more likely to accord the individual some parental rights or obligations. By contrast, jurisdictions that treat parenthood as an all-or-nothing proposition—adults are either parents with full rights and responsibilities, or legal strangers with no rights and no responsibilities—may be more likely to treat social parents as legal parents. Some U.S. states fall into this category. These differences are not inevitable: a jurisdiction that has legal parenthood, parental authority, and a right of contact *could* treat a social parent as a legal parent, but when there is the possibility of varying degrees of recognition, countries seem to take advantage of this tailoring option. Finally, if the jurisdiction does not recognize more than two legal parents, then it is more likely that a social parent will be recognized with something less than that of a legal parent. To do otherwise would raise questions about the impact on existing parent-child relationships. But in jurisdictions, such as parts of Canada and the United States, that allow multiple parents, treating the social parent as a legal parent need not displace existing parent-child relationships that are also important to the child.

The Role of Human Rights and Children's Rights in Social Parenthood

A second issue is determining how much weight to give to the rights of the child when assessing the rights and responsibilities of a social parent. As noted above, all the countries surveyed in this book that recognize social parents employ a functional inquiry that examines the day-to-day role of the person and the nature of that person's bond with the child. In this way, the countries consider the child's *perspective*. The question, however, is whether the child's *rights* are centered in the analysis.

In Europe, article 8 of the European Convention on Human Rights expressly protects a right to family life. This is a right of both children and adults. In several decisions, the European Court of Human Rights relied on this provision to find a right of contact between a child and a person other than a legal parent.[4] This right of contact extends to relationships between a foster parent and a child, at least where the child has lived with the foster parent for a significant period.[5] This approach to social parenthood rests on the lived reality of family life. In so doing, it de-emphasizes the formality of the arrangement and elevates the importance of the creation of familial ties through a shared life.

In the United States, courts also consider the child's relationship with the social parent and whether the child would be negatively impacted if the child's relationship with the social parent is not protected.[6] In this way, this body of law challenges the often-held perception that the U.S. law places less weight on the child's perspective. That said, U.S. courts usually do not rely expressly on the *rights* of children when adjudicating these issues and instead incorporate a consideration of children's interests when determining whether an adult should be accorded rights.

In addition, because of U.S. constitutional law, which strongly protects the rights of existing legal parents and treats foster parents as contracting parties with the state, U.S. jurisdictions tend to exclude foster parents from protection under functional parent doctrines. Even if a child has lived with a foster parent for years, the rules governing foster care generally do not protect the relationship between a child and foster parent, regardless of its potential importance to the child. The exclusion of foster parents is especially notable because the functional parent doctrines, which recognize other kinds of social parents, center a child's perspective.

There is no right answer to the question of how much to prioritize the child's perspective and whether to do so through an interests-based or rights-based framework. As with almost all matters, the social and legal context will affect a country's decision. In the United States, for example, both historical discrimination and ongoing structural inequalities mean that Black and Native American children are far more likely than other children to be removed from the care of their parents and placed in foster care, making it especially important to protect the bonds between legal parents and children. In Europe, with its more robust protection of human rights, including children's rights, emphasizing the child's perspective sits more easily in the system of legal regulation.

In short, balancing the needs of all the interested parties—the child, the parents of origin, the social parents—presents complicated and complex questions. The approaches surveyed here provide several models from which policy makers can choose.

Conclusion

Around the world, adults are acting as parents, even if they often lack a marital, biological, or adoptive tie to a child. Almost all the countries surveyed in this book have adapted to this reality by developing and applying doctrines that recognize and protect the relationship between these social parents and their children. The brief discussion in this chapter only begins to address the issues in any system recognizing social parents. We hope this book's curated, comparative descriptions of different legal approaches spark a fruitful debate and help policy makers consider options for addressing social parenthood. We are interested to see what the future will bring, as families continue to change and the law continues to adapt.

NOTES

1 The text addresses severability as distinct from legal guardianship, which is a separate concept.

2 All countries surveyed in this book apply the marital presumption, treating the spouse of the person who gives birth as a legal parent of the child, but countries vary on whether a same-sex spouse is entitled to this presumption. In some countries, such as Germany and England, marriage is also relevant for establishing the lesser form of parental rights—parental responsibility. In England, for example, parental responsibility is acquired separately from legal parenthood and the person married to the mother automatically has parental responsibility. By contrast, a person who is not married to or in some other legally recognized relationship with the mother has to go through a different route to acquire parental responsibility. The relationship status of the adults does not, however, seem to be a relevant factor for contact rights. Genetic connection is the other salient factor in granting legal recognition. All of the surveyed countries provide that proof of genetic connection is a means of establishing parental rights, even if a genetic tie is not always necessary and sometimes not sufficient. In recent decades, this factor has become especially important with regard to nonmarital children.

3 Article 8 of the European Convention on Human Rights protects a child's right to family life, and the European Court of Human Rights has affirmed this right in several decisions. See, e.g., the following decisions by the ECtHR concerning the contact right of the genetic but not legal father—*Fatkhutdinov v. Russia*, no. 36335/18 (September 29, 2020); *Nazarenko v. Russia*, no. 39438/13 (July 16, 2015)—and of foster parents—*V.D. and others v. Russia*, no. 72931/10 (April 9, 2019)—also discussed in the chapter on Russia.

4 See, e.g., the following decisions by the ECtHR concerning the contact right of the genetic but not legal father: *Fatkhutdinov v. Russia*, no. 36335/18 (September 29, 2020); *Nazarenko v. Russia*, no. 39438/13 (July 16, 2015); *Anayo v. Germany*, no. 20578/07 (December 21, 2010); *Gorgülü v. Germany*, no. 74969/01 (May 26, 2004).

5 *V.D. and others v. Russia*, no. 72931/10 (April 9, 2019).

6 See, e.g., *Brooke S.B. v. Elizabeth A.C.C.*, 61 N.E.3d 488, 499 (N.Y. 2016) ("A growing body of social science reveals the trauma children suffer as a result of separation from a primary attachment figure—such as a de facto parent—regardless of that figure's biological or adoptive ties to the children").

ACKNOWLEDGMENTS

By definition, a collected volume is a collaborative project. From the beginning, the editors and authors had meaningful and illuminating conversations about comparative work generally and social parenthood specifically. These enriched the book tremendously, and we are grateful for the time and effort each contributor put into this project.

Numerous other people played large roles in making this book possible. Nancy Dowd and Robin Lenhardt, the editors of NYU Press's series on Families, Law, and Society, provided encouragement and essential guidance. Clara Platter expertly shepherded the book through the writing and editing stages. Two anonymous reviewers offered constructive feedback on the proposal, and one anonymous reviewer provided truly exceptional comments on the full manuscript. Doug NeJaime played a foundational role in the early stages of the project as we debated the outlines of the undertaking. And Allison Scott dedicated two years of her law school career to this book. We thank all these individuals.

ABOUT THE EDITORS

An expert in the fields of family law and poverty law, Clare Huntington is the Joseph M. McLaughlin Professor of Law at Fordham Law School and serves as an Associate Reporter for the American Law Institute's Restatement of the Law, Children and the Law. She has worked as an Attorney Advisor in the Justice Department's Office of Legal Counsel and clerked on the U.S. Supreme Court. She earned her JD from Columbia Law School and her BA from Oberlin College.

Courtney G. Joslin is Martin Luther King Jr. Professor of Law at UC Davis School of Law. She is a leading expert in the areas of family and relationship recognition, with a particular focus on same-sex and unmarried couples. She served as the Reporter for the Uniform Parentage Act (2017), a product of the Uniform Law Commission, and is an elected member of the American Law Institute. She earned her JD from Harvard Law School and her BA from Brown University.

Christiane von Bary is a postdoc at the Institute for International Law, Ludwig Maximilians University of Munich. Her research mainly focuses on private international law as well as family and succession law, especially from a comparative perspective. She has worked on a variety of topics in family law, with a particular focus on parenthood and surrogacy. She obtained her PhD in 2017 from the University of Passau, with her dissertation on "Choice-of-Court and Arbitration Agreements in International Succession Law." She has spent time abroad as a visiting researcher at the University of Berne, Switzerland, and the University of Cambridge, UK.

ABOUT THE CONTRIBUTORS

MARION ADAMISTE is a Research Professional at the Center for Research on Youth, Families and Social Responses (JEFAR), Université Laval.

KRISTINA BRANT is Assistant Professor of Rural Sociology at Pennsylvania State University.

ABBIE E. GOLDBERG is Professor of Clinical Psychology at Clark University.

CORINNA SABRINA GUERZONI is Assistant Professor at Alma Mater Studiorum, University of Bologna.

CLAIRE HOUSTON is Assistant Professor at Western Law School.

OLGA KHAZOVA is Leading Legal Scholar at the Private Law Research Centre named after S. S. Alekseev and Professor at the Moscow School of Social and Economic Sciences.

DOUGLAS NEJAIME is Anne Urowsky Professor of Law at Yale Law School.

EVA RYRSTEDT is Professor of Private Law at Lund University.

MARIE-CHRISTINE SAINT-JACQUES is Professor at the School of Social Work and Criminology, Université Laval.

JENS M. SCHERPE is Professor of Comparative Law at Aalborg University and Emeritus Fellow at Gonville and Caius College, University of Cambridge.

Wendy Schrama is Professor of Family Law and Comparative Law at Utrecht University.

Sofía Treviño Fernández is a doctoral candidate and Research Fellow at Yale Law School.

Machteld Vonk is Professor of International and European Family Law at Radboud University, Nijmegen.

Eleni Zervogianni is Assistant Professor of Civil Law at Aristotle University of Thessaloniki.

INDEX